PRAISE FOR *DRUNK TANK PINK*

"The best science book I've read all year... a really provocative look at how much our behavior is contextually determined."
Malcolm Gladwell, author of *David and Goliath*

"One of the best... clearly written and easy to understand."
Scotsman

"Reading Adam Alter's book will change the way you look at our world. Seemingly banal things will begin to mean more than you ever realized."
Dan Ariely, author of *Predictably Irrational*

"A fantastic introduction to the wealth of weird and wonderful psychology research out there."
BBC Focus

"Adam Alter has collected the most wonderfully strange and surprising nuggets of recent psychological research in one book. I guarantee you'll want to share the incredible anecdotes in *Drunk Tank Pink* with friends."
Joshua Foer, author of *Moonwalking with Einstein*

"Solid, down-to-earth insights into why we think, feel and act the way we do."
Kirkus

"*Drunk Tank Pink* is a smart and delightful introduction to some of psychology's most curious phenomena and most colorful characters."
Daniel Gilbert, author of *Stumbling on Happiness*

DRUNK
TANK
PINK

THE SUBCONSCIOUS

FORCES THAT SHAPE

HOW WE THINK, FEEL,

AND BEHAVE

ADAM ALTER

ONEWORLD

A Oneworld Book
First published in Great Britain and the Commonwealth
by Oneworld Publications 2013

First published in the United States of America by the Penguin Group

This paperback edition published in 2014
Reprinted in 2014 and 2015

ISBN 978-1-78074-583-1
Ebook ISBN 978-1-78074-265-6

Printed and bound by CPI Group (UK) Ltd, Croydon, CR0 4YY

Oneworld Publications
10 Bloomsbury Street
London WC1B 3SR
England

For Mum, Dad, Dean and Sara

CONTENTS

Part Three

THE WORLD *AROUND* US

PROLOGUE

The academic journal *Orthomolecular Psychiatry* began its final issue of 1979 with a classic paper that kindled the imaginations of prison wardens, sports coaches, and exasperated parents alike. The paper's author, Professor Alexander Schauss, described a simple experiment featuring 153 healthy young men, a researcher, two large pieces of coloured cardboard, and a well-lit lab. One by one the men filed into the room to participate in an unusual test of strength. The experiment began when the men stared at one of the pieces of cardboard. For half the men the cardboard was deep blue in colour, while for the remaining half it was bright pink. After a full minute had passed, the researcher asked the men to raise their arms in front of their bodies, while he applied just enough downward pressure to force their arms back down to their sides. While the men recovered their strength, the researcher jotted a few brief notes before repeating the experiment, first asking the men to stare at the other piece of cardboard and then repeating the strength test.

The results were strikingly consistent. All but two of the men were dramatically weaker after staring at the pink cardboard, barely resisting the researcher's application of downward force. In contrast, the blue cardboard left their strength intact, regardless of whether it came before the first or second strength test. The colour pink appeared to leave the men temporarily depleted.

To prove the effect wasn't a fluke, Schauss conducted a second experiment. This time he used a more accurate measure of strength, asking the thirty-eight male participants to squeeze a measurement device known as a dynamometer. Without fail, one after another, all thirty-eight men squeezed the device more weakly after staring at the pink cardboard.

Schauss began describing the miraculous tranquillizing power of bright pink in public lectures across the United States. At one appearance, filmed for TV, a muscle-bound Mr California performed several effortless biceps curls but struggled to perform a single curl after staring at the pink cardboard. Given the colour's power, Schauss suggested that prison warders should consider detaining rowdy prisoners in pink cells, and two commanding officers at the US Naval Correctional Center in Seattle, Washington, repainted one of their holding cells bright pink. For seven months, Chief Warrant Officer Gene Baker and facility commander Captain Ron Miller watched as newly arrived inmates entered the pink cell angry and agitated but emerged calmer fifteen minutes later. New prisoners are traditionally aggressive, but the officers reported not a single violent incident during the seven-month trial period.

Admirers honoured the enterprising officers by calling the colour Baker-Miller Pink, and other facilities around the country painted special holding cells the same bubblegum hue. At a detention centre in San Jose, California some of the younger inmates were so weakened by the pink cell that their exposure had to be limited to just a few minutes a day. When smaller local jails began putting violent drunks into pink holding cells, the colour was unofficially christened Drunk Tank Pink.

In the early 1980s, Drunk Tank Pink became a minor popular-culture sensation. Schauss discovered that frazzled psychiatrists, dentists, doctors, teachers, and parents were painting their walls bright pink. Housing estates painted their interiors pink and reported a sharp decline in violent behaviour, and bus companies quashed vandalism by installing bright pink seats. When United Way charity workers wore pink uniforms, donors reportedly gave up to two or three times as much as they usually did. American football coaches at Colorado State and the University of Iowa painted their visitors' locker rooms pink in an attempt to pacify their opponents, until local athletics conferences decreed that the home and visitors' locker rooms had to be identical. Tex Schramm, long-standing coach of the Dallas Cowboys, called Schauss and asked whether his team should adopt the same strategy. Underdogs in the boxing ring began wearing pink trunks and sometimes even beat their heavily favoured opponents.

Drunk Tank Pink emerged as the unlikely solution to a host of difficult puzzles, from aggression and hyperactivity to anxiety and competitive strategy. The colour attracted a frenzy of academic interest late into the 1990s, and while some researchers found weaker evidence for the original effect, scattered demonstrations persisted. Schauss still calls Drunk Tank Pink a "non-drug anaesthetic", and he continues to field dozens of inquiries each year, more than three decades since Drunk Tank Pink's dramatic rise in popularity.

This book is an attempt to uncover the role of Drunk Tank Pink and dozens of other hidden forces as they shape how we think, feel, and behave. Some, like Drunk Tank Pink, emerge from nowhere to become pop-culture legends. Others, like sunshine and beautiful women, have long occupied a prominent place in folk wisdom, though folk wisdom often falls short when it tries to capture the complexities of human behaviour. And other forces still, like the names we give children and new business ventures, hide in plain sight, guiding our thoughts as we go about the business of everyday life unaware of their influence. Understanding these forces is more than a matter of idle curiosity, as some can be harnessed for the good while others are mitigated to prevent the bad. Some of them push us towards smarter decisions and happier outcomes, and others undermine our persistent quest for health and well-being. These forces (or *cues*, as psychologists call them) take many forms, arising from three different worlds: the mental world made up of small cues that burrow their way into our heads; the social world that connects us; and the wider physical world that surrounds us. Each of us is an ongoing product of the world *within* us, the world *between* us, and the world *around* us—and their hidden capacity to shape our every thought, feeling, and behaviour.

PART ONE

THE WORLD *WITHIN* US

1.

NAMES

The Birth of
Nominative Determinism

When Carl Jung, one of the most famous psychiatrists of the twentieth century, once wondered why he was so fixated on the concept of rebirth, the answer arrived in a flash of insight: his name meant "young", and from birth he had been preoccupied by the concepts of youth, ageing, and rebirth. Other renowned psychiatrists of the early twentieth century embarked on very different research programmes, but as Jung explained, "Herr Freud (whose name means Joy in German) champions the pleasure principle, Herr Adler (Eagle) the will to power, Herr Jung (Young) the idea of rebirth". As far as Jung was concerned, the names we're given at birth blaze a trail that our destinies tread for years to come.

Many years later, in 1994, a contributor to the Feedback column in the *New Scientist* magazine labelled the phenomenon *nominative determinism*, literally meaning "name-driven outcome". The writer noted that two urology experts, Drs A. J. Splatt and D. Weedon, had written a paper on the problem of painful urination in the *British Journal of*

Urology. Similar so-called aptronyms abound. The current Lord Chief Justice of England and Wales is Justice Igor Judge; his colleague Lord Justice Laws is a judge in the Court of Appeal. In the realm of athletic pursuits, Anna Smashnova was a professional Israeli tennis player, Layne Beachley is a seven-times world-champion surfer, Derek Kickett was an Australian Rules footballer, Stephen Rowbotham was an Olympic rower for Britain, and Usain Bolt is the fastest man in the world over the hundred-metre and two-hundred-metre distances. Some names herald less auspicious destinies: Christopher Coke is a notorious Jamaican drug dealer, and the rapper Black Rob was sentenced to seven years in prison for larceny. It's tempting to dismiss these anecdotes as scattered coincidences, but researchers have shown that our names take root deep within our mental worlds, drawing us magnetically towards the concepts they embody.

Indeed, names convey so much information that it's easy to forget that they don't have natural meanings as, say, numbers do. The number 10 will always have the same meaning regardless of whether you call it ten, *diez*, *dix*, or *dieci*, which is why scientists seeking extraterrestrial contact devise mathematical languages to communicate with alien life forms. A single pulse of noise will always signal one, or unity, whereas two pulses will always signal two. That universal property doesn't apply to names, which are language-bound. Jung's witty observation that Freud's name compelled him to "champion the pleasure principle" registers only if you know that Freud means "joy" in German. Names are powerful, then, only when they're associated with other, more meaningful concepts. Parents from certain cultures embrace this idea when naming their children. The Nigerian president Goodluck Jonathan grew into his name handsomely, and his wife, Patience, was named after a trait that first ladies sorely need as their husbands ascend the political ladder. According to one Nigerian proverb, "When a person is given a name, his gods accept it", which explains why exhausted parents sometimes name their children Dumaka (literally, "help me with hands") or Obiageli ("one who has come to eat"). The Mossi tribespeople of Burkina Faso have taken nominative determinism one step further, giving their children strikingly morbid names in a desperate bid to placate fate. Parents who have already lost more than one child (the Mossi infant mortality rate is tragically high) have been known to name their subsequent children Kida ("he is going to die"), Kunedi ("dead thing"), or Jinaku ("born to die").

Other parents do everything they can to protect their children from the tide of nominative determinism. In his native Russian tongue, Vyacheslav Voronin's name means "slave". As far as associations go, that's a significant cross to bear, so Voronin and his wife, Marina Frolova, decided to save their newborn son a similar indignity. Slight and sandy-haired, the boy was born in the summer of 2002 during a spate of terrible Russian floods. True to their promise, Vyacheslav and Marina chose a generic name designed to be devoid of meaning: BOHdVF260602. Although the name seems meaningless, BOHdVF260602 stands for "Biological Object Human descendant of the Voronins and Frolovas, born on June 26, 2002". For the sake of practicality, young BOHdVF260602 responds to the name Boch (roughly pronounced "Bawtch"). Vyacheslav claims that Boch's name "will make his life easier, so he won't interact with those idiots who think one's name defines his appearance. Every person who gets a traditional name is automatically linked to his historic background. This way, my son will be devoid of his father's legacy."

People name their children using all sorts of rules and approaches. Sometimes they borrow names from historical or literary heroes, sometimes they perpetuate ancestral naming traditions, and sometimes they just like how a name sounds or the fact that it reminds them of something appealing. In all cases, though, the otherwise meaningless name acquires meaning because it's associated with other concepts that are themselves meaningful. The power of association explains why Adolf, a common boy's name once associated with Swedish and Luxembourger kings, plummeted in popularity during and after World War Two. Meanwhile, the name Donald fell from favour when Donald Duck appeared in the 1930s, and parents stopped naming their sons Ebenezer in the 1840s when Charles Dickens's newly published book, *A Christmas Carol*, featured the miserly Ebenezer Scrooge. What makes Boch's name so unusual is that his parents went to great lengths to avoid choosing a name with even minimal associations. Though Vyacheslav was determined to spare Boch the teasing that he endured as a boy, it's hard to imagine Boch emerging from childhood without being teased about his name at least occasionally. The odds are stacked higher still, as the Russian birth registry has refused to record Boch's full name. According to Tatyana Baturina, a representative of the registry, "You can call your child a 'stool' or a 'table'. A child has a right to such a name. But one has to use common sense. Why should one suffer from the parents' choice? He will go to kindergarten, and then to school, and he will be mocked, all because of his name." It's not immediately clear that naming a boy "Stool" demonstrates more common sense than naming the boy "BOHdVF-260602", and he'd be unlikely to escape torment with either name.

Scattered anecdotes aside, do names really affect major life outcomes? Would Usain Bolt run more slowly with the name Usain Plod? Would urologists Splatt and Weedon have pursued different medical specialities with less "urological" names? These thought experiments are impossible to conduct in reality, so researchers have devised other clever techniques to answer the same question.

Names Influence Life Outcomes

Every name is associated with demographic baggage: information about the bearer's age, gender, ethnicity, and other basic personal features. Take the name Dorothy, for example. Imagine that you're about to open your front door to a stranger named Dorothy. What kind of person would you expect Dorothy to be? First, Dorothy is more likely to be an elderly lady than a young woman. Dorothy was the second most popular girl's name in the 1920s, and fourteen out of every hundred baby girls born during that decade were named Dorothy. That multitude of Dorothys is now approaching the age of ninety. In contrast, the name is almost non-existent among girls born during the twenty-first century. The reverse is true of the name Ava, which was almost non-existent before the twenty-first century but dominates the most recent US Census. Apart from age, names convey ethnic, national, and socio-economic information. Base rates suggest that Dorothy and Ava are almost certainly white, Fernanda is likely to be Hispanic, and Aaliyah is probably black. Luciennes and Adairs tend to be wealthy white children, and Angels and Mistys tend to be poorer white children. Likewise, Björn Svensson, Hiroto Suzuki, and Yosef Peretz are almost certainly males of Swedish, Japanese, and Israeli descent respectively. More narrowly, Waterlily and Tigerpaw sound like the offspring of ageing hippies, while Buddy Bear and Petal Blossom Rainbow sound like names that celebrities might choose for their children. (They are; those are the names of two of celebrity chef Jamie Oliver's four children.)

One reason why personal names are so important, then, is that they allow people to categorize us almost automatically. In their book *Freakonomics*, Steven Levitt and Stephen Dubner describe a strong relationship between a mother's education and the names she chooses for her children. White boys named Ricky and Bobby are less likely to have mothers who finished college than are white boys named Sander and Guillaume. Since education improves spelling, it comes as no surprise that white boys named Micheal and Tylor tend to have less well-educated mothers than do white boys named Michael and Tyler. Similar patterns emerge when you compare a child's name with family household income. White girls named Alexandra and Rachel tend to be wealthier than white girls named Amber and Kayla.

Of course, it's important to note that the relationships between income, education, and naming preferences are not causal—just because poorer children tend to have consistently different names from wealthier children doesn't mean that girls named Alexandra are financially better off *because* they've been named advantageously. A more likely alternative is that people from different socio-economic and educational backgrounds inhabit different cultural environments, which in turn shape their preferences for particular names. (Chapter 6 considers the relationship between culture and preferences more deeply.) For example, US residents who live in the southern states tend to be poorer than residents in the northern states, and, relative to Northerners, Southerners also tend to prefer the name Bobby. The marked cultural differences between Northerners and Southerners probably explain both their distinct naming preferences and the income gap that separates the two groups. The dark side of these relationships is that over time, people meet many more poor Bobbys than wealthy Bobbys, and many more wealthy Sanders than poor Sanders, so they start to form strong associations between the name and important life outcomes. Consequently, a seasoned recruiter who considers two job application folders—one submitted by Sander Smith and the other by Bobby Smith—will presume that Sander's parents are wealthier and better educated than Bobby's parents even before he opens the folders.

So, what would happen if you could turn back the clock and rename a child who was given a typically black name with a typically white name instead? Would the child's life be any different? Short of building a time machine, there's no way to test this conjecture in its purest form, but two economists have done the next best thing. They wondered whether two job applicants who were identical, except for the blackness or whiteness of their names, might inspire different responses from firms that advertised positions online. The researchers responded to five thousand job ads in Boston and Chicago and varied two features of the attached CVs: their quality (some were strong and others were weak), and the blackness or whiteness of the names (some were typically white names and others were typically black names). It's no surprise that the stronger CVs yielded more responses, but names also had a marked effect. Emilys, Annes, Brads, and Gregs fared better than Aishas, Kenyas, Darnells, and Jamals, even when their applications were identical on every important indicator of applicant strength. In fact, fictional applicants with white names received responses on 10 percent of their applications, whereas applicants with black names received responses on only 6.5 percent of their applications—a 50 percent difference. Put another way, on average white applicants only need to send out ten applications to get a single response, but black applicants need to send out fifteen for the same outcome. Also disturbing was the finding that a stronger application helped white applicants but did very little to improve the prospects of black applicants. Whereas employers rewarded stronger white applicants with 27 percent more responses than weaker white applicants, stronger black applicants received only 8 percent more responses than weaker black applicants (and 27 percent fewer even than *weak* white applicants). It's impossible to get a job without clearing the first hurdle, so these results bode ill for the state of racial bias in a society that some pundits describe as "post-racial".

If the damaging stereotypes that produced these disturbing results vanished, would names lose their power to shape important life outcomes? The Voronins must have believed so when they named their son BOHdVF260602, a name chosen because it was free of the usual demographic baggage. As it turns out, the Voronins were addressing only part of the issue. Our own names influence us even in the absence of other people. According to Belgian psychologist Jozef Nuttin's classic account, people feel a sense of ownership over their names. People tend to like what belongs to them, so Nuttin found that people preferred the letters that populated their names more than the letters that were absent from their names. In one study, Nuttin asked two thousand people who spoke one of twelve different languages to choose the six letters they liked most from their language's written alphabet—the letters they found most attractive without investing much thought in the process. Across the twelve languages, people circled their own name letters 50 percent more often than they circled name-absent letters. So, had Jozef Nuttin completed the study himself, he would have been 50 percent more likely to circle the letter Z than would have a fictitious Josef Nuttin, for whom Z would not have held a special personal meaning.

The magnetic attraction we feel towards our name letters contributes to a range of surprising outcomes. People donate to charities for all sorts of reasons: because they have a personal link to the cause, because it tugs at their heartstrings, and sometimes because they honestly believe the cause deserves their support. These rationales are easy to defend, but psychologists have shown that people tend to donate more often and more generously to causes that share their initials. The researchers examined Red Cross donation records following seven catastrophic Atlantic Ocean hurricanes that hit the United States between 1998 and 2005. There's no natural shorthand for referring to tropical storms, so the National Hurricane Center has labelled each tropical storm since the 1950s with a proper name. As you might expect based on the name-letter effect, people are drawn to hurricanes that share their initials. For example, people with K names donated 4 percent to all disasters before Katrina devastated New Orleans in 2005, but 10 percent of all Katrina donations came from K-named people, a 150 percent increase. You might be wondering whether people named Katrina, Kate, Katherine, Katie, or any other "Kat" names were responsible for the change. They weren't; the effect was just as strong when those people who shared more than just the first letter with Katrina were removed from the analysis. The same results were true for a range of hurricanes.

The positive association we have with our names explains most name-letter effects, but sometimes our initials also inspire thoughts and behaviours that arise through force of habit. One of the major differences between people with A surnames and people with Z surnames is where those names fall on default alphabetical lists. For better or worse, teach-

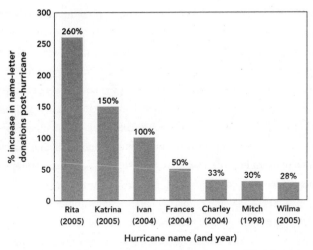

For each of the seven hurricanes examined, the proportion of Red Cross donations from people whose names shared the hurricane's initial increased immediately after the hurricane. For example, M-named people made up 30 percent more of the donor population during the two-month period after Mitch devastated Honduras and Nicaragua in 1998 than during the six-month period before the hurricane struck.

ers often call on students with A surnames before they call on students with B surnames, and so on through the alphabet till the Zahns, Zolas, and Zuckermans are called on last. Some teachers are sensitive to this issue, so they occasionally start at the bottom of the alphabet—but more often than not, they begin with A and end with Z. In a series of clever studies, two psychologists tested the idea that people whose family names were at the end of the alphabet might respond more quickly to scarce opportunities than their beginning-of-the-alphabet counterparts. Since people with N–Z names habitually wait behind people with A–M names, the researchers guessed that N-to-Zers might be chronically quicker to respond to limited opportunities because they so often have to wait their turn. That's exactly what they found when they offered a limited number of free basketball tickets to a group of graduate students.

The further down the alphabet the students' family names, the quicker they were to respond. In another study, the researchers found that PhD students with later-letter names were quicker to post their job-search materials online than were students with earlier-letter names. In fact, the students who posted their materials during the first three weeks had an average family-name letter of M (the twelfth letter), whereas students who posted their materials after the first three weeks had elapsed had an average family-name letter of G (the seventh letter). This *last-name effect*, as the researchers call it, illustrates just one more way that names subtly influence our lives.

Names, then, have the capacity to shape our outcomes because they're tied to important concepts that have real meaning. Sometimes they're associated with racial groups or socio-economic status, sometimes with charity appeals or being called on last at school. Some of those associations are positive and others are negative, and when you're a parent faced with a smorgasbord of choices, perhaps it's worth considering those associations when breaking the tie among several equally liked names.

Fairchild vs Pucinski: the Smoothly Fluent vs the Awkwardly Disfluent

When parents name their children, they're also faced with a second implied choice: a simple, smooth, common name or a complex but unique name. The choice isn't easy, because folk wisdom rewards both approaches. No one's going to mispronounce the names Tom, Tim, Todd, and Ted, but people named Tom, Tim, Todd, and Ted are a penny a dozen. Meanwhile, people named T-ah (pronounced "Tadasha"), Thyra (is it Theera, Thigh-ra, or Tie-ra?), and Taiven (Tay-ven, or Ty-ven?) stand out in a crowd, but the crowd might ignore them because no one's sure how to pronounce their names. (On this count, perhaps BOHdVF260602's parents were less successful.)

Independently of what they mean or imply, some names are easy to pronounce; they glide off the tongue with ease and sound innately and effortlessly appealing. Other names are hard to pronounce; they challenge your brain before challenging your tongue, teeth, and lips, and when they eventually emerge, you're not sure you've pronounced them correctly after all. Psychologists who study the linguistic properties of these names call the ones that are easy to pronounce *fluent*, and the ones that are difficult to pronounce *disfluent*. If you're trying to decide how fluent a name is, imagine that you're presenting the Oscar for best foreign-language film. You open the envelope and announce, "The Oscar goes to . . ." Some foreign names are very difficult to pronounce for uninitiated English-speakers, but others are easier to pronounce because they're shorter, or share sounds and letter combinations that are common to the English language, or because they feature simpler letter strings. In 1996, the Oscar-winning foreign-language film was *Kolya*, a Czech film produced by Jan Svěrák. Kristin Scott Thomas and Jack Valenti, the category's English-speaking presenters, must have practised hard before announcing the Georgian nominee, *Shekvarebuli kulinaris ataserti retsepti*, directed by Nana Dzhordzhadze. (Actually, many of the films adopt English titles so the presenters don't mar the event with botched pronunciations. In this case, the film was retitled *A Chef in Love,* though Dzhordzhadze's name must have presented its own challenges.)

The most obvious consequence of having a disfluent name is that your parents have invited a lifetime of misspelling and mispronunciation on your behalf. We're all capable of laughing off the occasional error, but sometimes errors have serious consequences. When lesser-known or last-minute candidates enter a political race, their names don't always appear on the ballot form; instead, voters are asked to write the candidate's name by hand, or type the name using a machine that recognizes each candidate's name. Candidates such as George Bush and Bill Clinton may have emerged from a write-in vote unscathed, but Texan house majority candidate Shelley Sekula-Gibbs had less luck in 2006. For starters, some voting machines can't process hyphens, so Sekula-Gibbs became Sekula Gibbs. But the real trouble began when the machines had to be programmed to process misspellings. A bipartisan committee was formed, eventually sanctioning twenty-eight pages of misspellings, from the understandable *Kelly Segula-Gibbs* to the perplexing one-word entry *ShelleySkulaGibbsssss*.

Sekula-Gibbs escaped relatively unharmed, but two heavily favoured candidates in the 1986 Illinois Democratic primary for lieutenant governor were less fortunate. George Sangmeister and Aurelia Pucinski were touted to trounce upstarts Mark Fairchild and Janice Hart. The pundits ignored the fact that many voters know little about their favoured candidates' policy positions and rely instead on irrelevant cues when breaking a tie. On the naming front, pitting the foreign-sounding Sangmeister and Pucinski against the made-for-politics Fairchild and Hart is no more balanced than an arm-wrestling contest between a small child and Mike Tyson. With heavyweight names like Fairchild and Hart, the two underdog candidates swept the race despite their weaker CVs. One voter who was interviewed in the *New York Times* even admitted to voting for Fairchild and Hart "because they had smooth-sounding names". A team of psychologists ran a study that proved the importance of the two names: when mock voters were asked to choose between two candidates based only on their names—George Sangmeister and Mark Fairchild—an overwhelming majority preferred Fairchild. Since most voters knew little about the candidates when they approached the ballot box, it seems fair to assume that at least some of them were swayed by the candidates' names.

It's important to note that these four names differed along other dimensions apart from name fluency, including foreignness and their overlap with appealing English words like *heart* and *child*. These differences mark this anecdote as an interesting but less-than-ideal test of the effect of name fluency on meaningful outcomes. Along with two psychologists at the University of Melbourne, Australia Simon Laham and Peter

Koval, I ran similar analyses that were designed to eliminate the possibility that these effects are driven entirely by the foreignness of disfluent names. We began with the premise that fluent names should act like halos, making the name's owner just slightly more attractive than a fictional similar person with a disfluent name. To test that hypothesis, we examined the relationship between the fluency of five hundred lawyers' names and their positions within the legal hierarchy (from associate to partner). We gleaned those names from ten different US law firms that varied in size and prominence, and asked a group of American adults to rate each name according to how easy it was to pronounce, and how likely its owner was to be foreign.

The results were in equal parts fascinating and disconcerting: lawyers with fluent names seemed to ascend the law-firm hierarchy more often and more rapidly than their disfluently named colleagues. The result couldn't be explained by foreignness, because the effect held when we confined the analysis to lawyers with foreign names, and again when we confined the analysis to lawyers with typical Anglo-American names. A closer look at the data tells the tale. Name fluency doesn't help every lawyer equally, because it's not a miracle-maker. You could be the smartest lawyer with the smoothest name, but if you're a rookie who's just finished your law studies, you're not going to make partner. (Not a single lawyer who'd been employed for fewer than four years was a partner.) The same holds for veterans: by the time you've been practising for three decades, your ability will speak for itself—and most veterans (89 percent) were partners perhaps by virtue of longevity alone. But the effect is strong among mid-career lawyers: after 4–8 years in practice, 12 percent of those with fluent names (names rated 1 on a 5-point pronunciation difficulty scale—half of all lawyers in the sample) were partners, whereas only 4 percent of their counterparts with disfluent names (those whose names were rated at 2–5 on the same scale) were partners. The gap holds when you look at slightly more experienced lawyers; after 9–15 years, 74 percent of the lawyers with fluent names were partners,

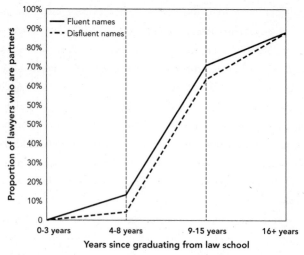

This graph shows the mid-career advantage of having a fluent name. Compared with lawyers who have disfluent names, lawyers with fluent names are 8 percent more likely to be partners four to eight years after graduating, and 7 percent more likely to be partners nine to fifteen years after graduating.

but only 67 percent of those with disfluent names were partners. Quite literally, then, it pays to give your newborn future lawyer as simple a name as possible.

There's a potent moral to the story I've told so far: you're unlikely to be celebrated for having a creative name, but that same creative (and therefore disfluent) name may prime you for negative attention and negative outcomes. It's easy to sympathize with exuberant parents who celebrate the miracle of new life by naming that miracle Keirraih, but when young Keirraih starts school and then work, she's likely to be a magnet for negative attention.

Just as wise parents name their biological offspring with care, wise entrepreneurs choose names for their commercial offspring carefully. Even company names that seem innocuous at first have the potential to give their parents heartburn. In one striking case, the inoffensively named Experts Exchange, an online technology problem-solving company, exposed itself to mockery when it chose the web address www.expertsexchange.com. (The address is now www.experts-exchange .com, and the company has resolved the ambiguity in its favour by choosing the strategically capitalized Twitter handle ExpertsExchange.)

Beyond the obvious dangers of choosing a name with an unintended double meaning, the same fluency effects that shape how quickly lawyers rise to partnership also seem to shape the fortunes of fledgling financial stocks. With my colleague Danny Oppenheimer, a psychology professor at Princeton University, I discovered that young financial stocks tend to perform better on the markets when their names are easier to pronounce. Choosing among stocks that are just about to enter the market is very difficult, because there's so much information to sift through, and none of it predicts the stock's future performance perfectly. A stock with a simpler, fluent name will tend to rise above its disfluently named counterparts for the same reason that a fluently named person might attract law-firm promotions: stock purchasing is inherently risky, and fluency inspires a sense of comfort and familiarity that tempers the inescapable fact that even low-risk stocks sometimes go bust. To test the effect of name fluency on stock performance, we measured the performance of nearly one thousand stocks across the New York Stock Exchange and the American Stock Exchange markets from 1990 to 2004.

In one study, we asked a group of people to imagine they were reading the names of each company at an awards ceremony (the fluency litmus test I described earlier), and to indicate how easy or difficult it would be to pronounce the company's name. At one end of the spectrum were fluently named companies such as Belden Inc., and at the other end were disfluently named companies such as Magyar Tavkozlesi Részvénytársaság (a Hungarian telecommunications company). Not all the disfluent stocks were foreign-owned, and the effect held even when we looked only at American stocks with typically American names. As we expected, the stocks with fluent names fared better than those with disfluent names, especially during their first week on the market. In fact, if you'd invested $1,000 in the ten most fluently named stocks between 1990 and 2004, you'd have come away with $1,153 after just one week, a whopping 11 percent return on your initial investment. In contrast, if you'd invested the same $1,000 in the ten most disfluently named stocks across the same period, you'd come away with just $1,040, a much smaller 4 percent return on your investment.

Of course, there are other differences between fluently and disfluently named companies: service and retail companies might emphasize smoother names more than, say, mining and resources companies, and larger firms might invest more than smaller companies in choosing a catchy name. To rule out the possibility that our effects actually reflected better performance among certain industries or company sizes, we ran a separate study focusing on ticker codes—the brief letter strings that identify each company on the stock market, historically printed on ticker tape alongside stock price updates. To most of us they're gibberish, but to investment experts, they contain multitudes of information. Mention AAPL and investors ask when Apple will release its next blockbuster product; mention HOG and investors ask when Harley-Davidson will release a new motorbike (or *hog* as it's known among enthusiasts). Some ticker codes are transparent (e.g., Google's ticker code is GOOG) and others are more opaque (United States Steel has the coveted single-letter code X). One way of measuring the fluency of a ticker code is to assess whether you can pronounce it as an English word; GOOG is pronounceable, but RSH (RadioShack's ticker) isn't pronounceable according to the rules of spoken English. Sure, you can torture it to sound like "Rish", but it isn't readily pronounceable based on the way we combine vowels and consonants in spoken English.

When we compared the performance of stocks with pronounceable (fluent) tickers with that of stocks with unpronounceable (disfluent) tickers, we found the same results as we'd noticed when we focused on stock names: after just one day of trading, stocks with fluent tickers yielded a roughly 15 percent gain across the New York Stock Exchange and the American Stock Exchange, but those with disfluent tickers yielded only a 7 percent gain. If you're a fledgling company, or a serious investor, an 8 percent bonus makes a very big difference. Predicting stock performance in the short term is notoriously challenging, and financial experts everywhere have long struggled to hit on a solid predictor of early stock performance. This is a powerful result, because it shows that name fluency effects exist even when you eliminate all other information that might be bound up with the fluency of a name. For example, perhaps fluent names like Apple convey more information than disfluent names like Aegon or Aeolus, which tend to be nonsense words or unfamiliar names. This ticker demonstration is striking because fluent and disfluent ticker codes contain basically the same quantity of information (almost none). Moreover, even novice investors can understand the concept of fluency—you don't need a degree in financial mathematics to know that Belden and GOOG are fluent, but Magyar Tavkozlesi Részvénytársaság and RSH are disfluent. Name fluency, then, has the power to shape not only personal outcomes but also the fortunes of investors and companies on the stock market.

Cuddly Names and Powerful Names: the Role of Phonemes

Some simple spoken sounds, or phonemes, emerge easily, while others emerge with some difficulty, but once they're spoken aloud, many of them conjure visual images even if they have no meaning at all. In the 1920s, German psychologist Wolfgang Köhler wrote a classic textbook on how we perceive the world. Köhler argued that people share a common idea about how some nonsensical names would look if they were ascribed to a shape. In one thought experiment, readers were asked to consider which of the following shapes was called a *maluma* and which was called a *takete*.

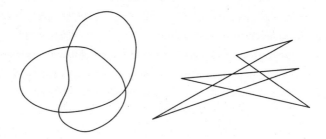

If you're like most people, you've never heard the words maluma or takete, but that doesn't stop you from "knowing" somehow that the smooth, curvy shape on the left is a maluma and the jagged, spiky shape on the right is a takete. Even children who are too young to read are capable of matching rounded shapes to rounded words and hard-edged shapes to hard-edged words. Only a strange, counter-intuitive language would assign the labels the other way round, and so it is that many English words just sound "right". Here's a quick thought experiment: imagine you define the words *stop* and *meander,* or the words *haste* and *dawdle,* but refuse to tell a non-English-speaker which definition belongs with each word. Would she be able to connect the words to their correct definitions? Just as *maluma* seems curvy and *takete* seems jagged, so *meander* and *dawdle* seem soft and slow and squishy, and *stop* and *haste* seem sharp and jagged and immediate. It doesn't make sense, then, to name your sharp, lifesaving pharmaceutical company Baloomba Inc. and your children's party business Zintec Inc., but the names work quite nicely in reverse. I'd be happy to take a new drug manufactured by Zintec and attend a party run by Baloomba, but Zintec sounds like a hard-nosed party-planner and Baloomba seems too whimsical to engage in serious science. Perhaps it's not surprising, then, that a 1979 study found that thirty-eight of the top two hundred US brand names began with the dominant sounds K or C, and that a whopping ninety-three of them contained the K sound somewhere in their names.

The research I've described in this chapter suggests that names are far more important than we might assume based only on intuition. From your name alone, people have some idea of your age, your ethnicity, and whether you're wealthy or poor. They might decide to hire you if your name's easy to pronounce and well chosen, or to relegate you to the bottom of the pile if your disfluent name prompts all the wrong associations. Proper names—the labels we give ourselves and the companies we promote—are not so different from the linguistic labels we give the concepts that fill our lives every day. Labels, like names, shape how we view the world, and as the next chapter shows, the people we label as "black", "white", "rich", "poor", "smart", and "simple" seem blacker, whiter, richer, poorer, smarter, and simpler merely because we've labelled them so.

2.

LABELS

Labels Make a Complex World Simpler

n 1672, Sir Isaac Newton passed a beam of white light through a clear prism and projected the resulting rainbow against the wall of his laboratory. He perceived five distinct colours within the rainbow, which he labelled red, yellow, green, blue, and violet. These labels pleased him for a while, but he believed that colours and musical notes shared a single structure, and that both fell along seven-step octaves. So he returned to his rainbow and decided that a thin sliver of orange fell between thicker bands of red and yellow, and that a subtle strip of indigo fell between the blue and violet bands. The resulting seven-coloured rainbow is the one we know today. Newton's detractors were unimpressed, and they debated the true composition of the rainbow for many years, sometimes claiming that Newton's prisms were cloudy, dirty, or impure, and sometimes arguing that he had seen in the prism too many colours, too few colours, or the wrong colours altogether. But Newton was no more or less right than his critics, because the colours that form the visible rainbow are part of a continuous spectrum. We see distinct colours in the spectrum, but their boundaries are impossible to measure precisely. Regardless, why should it matter whether we use Newton's five-colour taxonomy, his seven-colour taxonomy, or some other variation? The colours don't change merely because we give them different labels, so why should we see them differently?

As it turns out, Newton's choice was far from trivial, because colours and their labels are inextricably linked. Without labels, we're unable to categorize colours—to distinguish between ivory, beige, wheat, and eggshell, and to recognize that broccoli heads and stalks are both green despite differing in tone. To show the importance of colour labels, in the mid-2000s a team of psychologists capitalized on a difference between colour terms in the English and Russian languages. In English, we use the word *blue* to describe both dark blues and light blues, encompassing shades from pale sky blue to deep navy blue. In contrast, Russians use two different words: *goluboy* (lighter blue) and *siniy* (darker blue).

The researchers asked English-speaking and Russian-speaking students to decide which of two blue squares matched a third blue target square on a computer screen. The students performed the same task many times. Sometimes both the squares were light blue, sometimes both were dark blue, and sometimes one of them was light blue and the other was dark blue. When both fell on the same side of the blue spectrum—either light blue or dark blue—the English and Russian students were equally quick to determine which of the squares matched the colour of the third target square. But the results were quite different when one of the colours was lighter blue (or *goluboy* according to the Russian students) and the other was darker blue (*siniy*). On those trials, the Russian students were much quicker to decide which square matched the colour of the target square.

While the English students probably looked at the target blue square and decided that it was "sort of lightish blue" or "sort of darkish blue", their labels were never more precise than that. They were forced to decide which of the other blue squares matched that vague description. The Russian students were at a distinct advantage; they looked at the

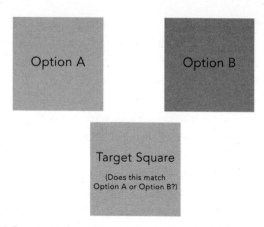

The task from the blue-matching experiment. On each trial, Russian and English students attempted to match a target square to two options. When the two options straddled the border between the Russian colours *siniy* (darker blue) and *goluboy* (lighter blue), Russian students were faster to match the target square to the correct option.

square and decided that it was either *goluboy* or *siniy*. Then all they had to do was look at the other squares and decide which one shared the label. Imagine how much easier the task would have been for the English students if they had been looking at one blue square and one green square; as soon as they determined whether the target square was blue or green, the task was trivially easy. In fact, an experiment published one year later showed that Russian students perceive dark blue to be just as different from light blue as the colour green is from the colour blue to English students. When Russian students located a dark blue square within an array of lighter blue squares, part of the visual field within their brains lit up to signal that they had perceived the odd square. The same brain areas were much less active when English students looked at the same array of squares—except when the odd square was green within an array of blue squares. When the colours had different labels for the English students, their brains responded like the brains of the Russian students. We also know that the Russian students relied on these category names, because their advantage over the English students disappeared altogether when they were asked to remember a string of numbers while they were performing the colour discrimination task. Since their resources for processing language were already occupied with the task of repeating the number string, they weren't able to re-hearse the names of the colours. Without the aid of linguistic labels, they were forced to process the colours just like the English-speaking students. This elegant experiment shows that colour labels shape how people see the world of colour. The Russian and English students had the same mental architecture—the same ability to perceive and process the colours in front of them—but the Russians had the distinct advantage of two labels where the English students had just one. This example is striking, because it shows that even our perception of basic properties of the world, such as colour, is malleable in the hands of labels.

The notion that labels change how we see the world predates the blue-matching experiment by almost eighty years. In the 1930s, Benjamin Whorf argued that words shape how we see objects, people, and places. According to one apocryphal tale, the Inuit people of the Arctic discern dozens of types of snow because they have a different word for each type. In contrast, the rest of the world has perhaps several words—like snow, slush, sleet, and ice. The story isn't true (the Inuit describe snow with roughly the same number of words as we do), but it paints a compelling picture: it's much harder to convey what's in front of you if you don't have words to describe it. Young children illustrate this difficulty vividly as they acquire vocabulary—once they learn to call one four-legged creature with a tail a "dog", every four-legged creature with a tail is a dog. Until they learn otherwise, cats and ponies share the same features, so they seem just as doggish as real dogs.

Cablinasians, Blacks, Whites, the Rich, and the Poor: Categories Resolve Ambiguity

Long before children began confusing domesticated cats and ponies with dogs, humans began labelling and cataloguing each other. Eventually, lighter-skinned humans became "whites", darker-skinned humans became "blacks", and people with intermediate skin tones became "yellow-", "red-", and "brown-skinned". These labels reflected reality no more faithfully than Newton's seven colours reflected the reality of rainbows, and if you lined up a thousand randomly selected people from across the earth, none of them would share exactly the same skin tone. You could arrange them from darkest to lightest and there wouldn't be a single tie. Of course, the continuity of skin tone hasn't stopped humans from assigning each other to discrete skin-colour categories like "black" and "white"—categories that have no basis in biology but nonetheless go on to determine the social, political, and economic well-being of their members.

These racial labels function in part like the colour labels that allowed Russian students to sharpen the fuzzy line that separates darker and lighter blues. They impose boundaries and categories on an infinitely complex social world, but once in place, these boundaries are very difficult to dissolve. When emerging golfing prodigy Tiger Woods appeared on *The Oprah Winfrey Show* in 1997, he claimed that he was not "black" but rather "Cablinasian", a portmanteau word combining his <u>Ca</u>ucasian, <u>bl</u>ack, Native American (American <u>In</u>dian), and <u>Asian</u> heritages. In the United States, golf has long been a segregated sport, with white players relying on the expert advice of black caddies. Woods was railing against the idea that he was simply a black player breaking the mould—in his view he was a complex mix of ethnic backgrounds that were irrelevant to his prowess as a golfer.

Unfortunately, just as Russians see dark and light blue distinctly because they have different linguistic labels, people are apt to resolve racial ambiguity by resorting to racial labels. In a study conducted at Stanford University, an experimenter showed white college students the picture of a young man whose facial features made it difficult to determine whether he was white or black. For half the students, the man was labelled "white", and for the other half he was labelled "black". The students were asked to draw the image in front of them as accurately as they could, so the next participant would be able to match the drawing to the face they had just seen. To sweeten the deal, the student who created the most accurate drawing was promised a $20 cash prize. Some of the students were identified as more likely to endorse racial stereotypes, and those students showed a striking pattern in their drawings. The students who were told that the man was black tended to exaggerate his "typically black" features, whereas those who were told he was white did the reverse, exaggerating his "typically white" features. Although the students from both groups were looking at exactly the same photograph, they perceived the image through a lens that was tinted with the racial label that the researcher provided earlier in the experiment.

The term "tinted lens" borders on the literal here, as a second experiment showed that people believe the same face is darker when its owner is described as black rather than white. Here are three faces from that experiment—one depicting a black man, one depicting a white man,

BLACK AMBIGUOUS WHITE

and the middle face depicting a man who could be plausibly described as either white or black.

Which face looks the darkest? And which looks lightest? Although they're identical in tone, people perceive and later recall the face belonging to the black man on the left as darker than the face belonging to the white man on the right, with the face belonging to the racially ambiguous man in the centre falling somewhere between the two. If you cover up the facial features with your hand and focus only on the foreheads, you'll be able to see that the faces share an identical skin tone. Racial labels are so powerful that we're incapable of judging skin tone accurately in their presence.

Unfortunately, we're also incapable of ignoring social labels when assessing a person's intelligence. In 2005, then Harvard University president Larry Summers attributed the dearth of female science and engineering professors to a "different availability of aptitude at the high end". Three years later, British psychologist Chris McManus made a similar claim about working-class citizens, arguing that the working class lacked the intelligence to be doctors. It's actually very difficult to judge intelligence objectively, especially when the evidence is mixed or inherently ambiguous. In one classic study, two researchers showed that evaluators use labels as a tiebreaker when interpreting this sort of mixed evidence. In that study, Princeton University students decided whether a young Year 5 student named Hannah was performing above, below, or precisely at the level expected of an average student in Year 5. During the first phase of the experiment, the students watched one of two brief videos. In one of the videos, Hannah was shown playing in a landscaped park set in a wealthy neighbourhood. A quick sweep of her school suggested that it was modern and sprawling, graced with sports grounds and an impressive playground. While the students watched the video, they read a brief biographical report on Hannah, which mentioned that her parents were both college graduates and now professionals. This version of Hannah was associated with a series of very favourable labels:

wealth, a good school, and educated parents who were employed as professionals. The other Princeton students were acquainted with a very different and less fortunate version of Hannah. They watched a video of Hannah playing in a fenced-in schoolyard with high-density brick buildings, set amid a neighbourhood of small, rundown family homes. This time, the biographical report described Hannah's parents as high-school (but not college) educated, her father working at a meat-processing plant, and her mother as a dressmaker from home. This time the labels were portentous, suggesting that Hannah would need to overcome socio-economic and educational hurdles before attaining academic success.

At this point, some of the students watched a second video, in which Hannah was asked to answer a series of twenty-five questions from an achievement test. The questions were designed to assess her mathematical, reading, science, and social-science skills. Instead of presenting a clear image of her ability, the video was ambiguous: sometimes she was engaged, answering difficult questions correctly, and sometimes she seemed distracted and struggled with relatively easy questions. The tape was designed to baffle the students, to leave them without a clear picture of her ability.

Hannah's ability was difficult to discern from the video, but some of the students began watching with the labels "wealthy" and "college educated" in mind, whereas the others began watching with the labels "working class" and "high-school educated" in mind. These labels functioned as tiebreakers when Hannah's performance was neither flawless nor disastrous. The students who expected Hannah to succeed saw exactly that pattern of achievement in her responses (ignoring her missteps and distractibility), whereas those who expected less from Hannah saw exactly what the negative labels implied (ignoring her intermittent engagement and mastery of the difficult questions). In the end, the lucky Hannah was judged to have performed above Year 5 level, whereas her unlucky counterpart seemed to perform below Year 5 level. The Hannah study showed that people are suggestible, willing to view the world with the guidance of labels when faced with an otherwise unbreakable tie.

Labels and Associations: why Black and Working-Class Categories are Dangerous

Social labels aren't born dangerous. There's nothing inherently problematic about labelling a person "right-handed" or "black" or "working class", but those labels are harmful to the extent that they become associated with meaningful character traits. At one end of the spectrum, the label "right-handed" is relatively free of meaning. We don't have strong stereotypes about right-handed people, and calling someone right-handed isn't tantamount to calling them unfriendly or unintelligent. In contrast, the terms "black" and "working class" are laden with the baggage of associations, some of them positive but many of them negative. When a person is labelled "black", we're primed to perceive the characteristics that we tend to associate with "blackness" more generally, which is why students drew racially ambiguous faces with typically black features when they were told the face belonged to a "black" person. Participants in the experiment at Princeton similarly associated Hannah's working-class background with diminished intellect, so they tended to emphasize her failings and overlook her strengths when they watched her complete an academic test.

Sometimes, meaningless labels accidentally acquire meaning. By convention, world maps place the Northern Hemisphere above the Southern Hemisphere, though there's no inherent reason to equate cardinal direction with vertical position. Greek astronomer Ptolemy decided that maps should place north above south, possibly because the known world was clustered in the Northern Hemisphere. Naturally, then, the undiscovered parts of the world should lie below the superior, charted territory that constituted the civilized world. Over time, people have come to conflate the two directional systems, perceiving north as above and south as below a central reference point. This association might be trivial if it didn't have commercial consequences. In one experiment, for example, people believed that a shipping company would charge $235 more to transport goods between two locations if they were making the trip from south to north rather than north to south. The reason: the northbound trip seemed "uphill", requiring more effort and possibly more petrol. A second group of people were more willing to drive to a shop located five miles south of the city centre rather than a practically identical shop five miles north of the city centre, again because reaching the northerly shop seemed to demand more effort than did reaching the southerly shop. Meanwhile, a third group preferred to live in the northern part of town, presumably because its "elevated" location rendered it superior to the town's southern suburbs.

In theory, these associations are mutable. Had Ptolemy decided to place Greece, his home, along with the rest of the Northern Hemisphere, on the bottom half of the map, perhaps people would prefer the northbound journey to its more onerous southbound counterpart. In 1979, a young Australian named Stuart McArthur proposed an alternative to the dominant Mercator world map projection: McArthur's Universal

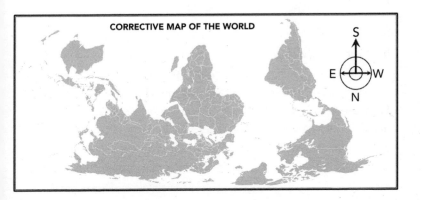

Corrective projection. According to the McArthur map, Australia was restored to its rightful place, both above *and* south of the world's remaining land masses, much like the map on the previous page.

McArthur's map failed to replace the canonical north-above-south projections, but it's hard not to wonder whether children raised under the McArthur system might prefer the ease of heading north to the labour of heading south.

Almost 150 years ago, long after Ptolemy decided that the Northern Hemisphere should lie above the Southern Hemisphere, the Remington company bought the rights to a new typewriter. Instead of placing the letters alphabetically, along three horizontal rows beginning with A and ending with Z, the new layout began with the letters Q-W-E-R-T-Y. The QWERTY keyboard, as it became known, is now the world's dominant keyboard layout. The QWERTY layout was designed to separate frequently used letters, which tended to jam during bouts of rapid typing.

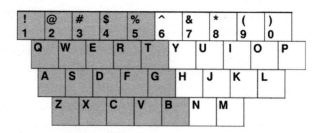

One accidental consequence of introducing a standard keyboard was that millions of computer users would type certain words using their left hands and other words using their right hands. For example, *abracadabra*, *referrer*, and *stewardesses* are left-hand words, whereas *lollipop*, *loony*, and *monk* are right-hand words. (In the keyboard image, the left-typed keys are highlighted in grey, and the right-typed keys are white.) Some words straddle the left–right divide, but you can quantify the right-dominance of every word by subtracting the number of left-typed letters from the number of right-typed letters. It turns out that, since people prefer typing with their dominant hands and most of them are right-handed, they come to prefer concepts with right-dominant labels. In other words, when you ask English-speakers to indicate how much they like real words (or even nonsense words like *plink* or *sarf*), they tend to prefer the words with more right-hand letters than left-hand letters. This effect is especially true for words that were coined after the advent of the QWERTY keyboard—including *n00b*, *yucky*, and *woohoo*. These letter strings are often typed, strengthening their association with the pleasing experience of right-handed typing or the relative difficulty of left-handed typing, so it's not surprising that they show stronger QWERTY effects. Like Ptolemy's decision thereafter to link the northerly direction with upward movement, Remington's adoption of the QWERTY keyboard thereafter consigned words like *wart* to the pile of disliked left-typed words, and anointed words like *punk* to the pantheon of liked right-typed words.

These studies are more than idle curiosities because they tell us something about how racism and prejudice come to infect the adult mind, and how we might prevent them from taking root in the minds of young children. After looking at hundreds of maps that place north above south, adults struggle to shake the notion that north inevitably sits above south. Likewise, adults live in a world that repeatedly pairs race with personality characteristics, so those racial labels are inextricably bound to character traits. Those damaging racial associations haven't yet had time to harden into unshakeable truths for children, so their young minds remain open to other possibilities.

During the height of the civil rights struggle, one astute teacher showed just how willingly children adopt new labels. On 4 April 1968, Martin Luther King Jr was murdered, and the next day thousands of young American children went to school with a combination of misinformation and confusion. In Riceville, Iowa Stephen Armstrong was the first student to arrive at teacher Jane Elliott's Year 4 classroom. As the room filled with students, Armstrong asked his teacher why "they shot that king". Elliott explained that the "king" was a man named King who was fighting discrimination against "Negroes". The all-white class of students was understandably confused, so Elliott offered to show them what it might be like to experience discrimination themselves. The students agreed excitedly, and Elliott staged a demonstration that ultimately led admirers to call her the foremother of anti-discrimination education in the United States.

Elliott began by claiming that the blue-eyed children were better than the brown-eyed children. The children resisted at first. The brown-eyed majority were forced to confront the possibility that they were inferior, and the blue-eyed minority faced a crisis when they realized that some of their closest friendships were now forbidden. Elliott countered the students' resistance by explaining that the brown-eyed children had too much melanin, a substance that darkens the eyes and makes people less intelligent. Melanin caused the "brownies", as Elliott labelled them, to be clumsy and lazy.

To ensure that the brownies would be easy to identify, Elliott asked them to wear paper armbands—a deliberate reference to the yellow stars that Jews were forced to wear during the Holocaust. Elliott reinforced the distinction by telling the brown-eyed children not to drink directly from the water fountain, as they might contaminate the blue-eyed children. Instead, the brownies were forced to drink from paper cups. Elliott also praised the blue-eyed children and offered them privileges, like a longer lunch break, while she criticized the brown-eyed children and forced them to end lunch early. By the end of the day, the blue-eyed children had become rude and unpleasant towards their classmates, while even the gregarious brown-eyed children were noticeably more timid and subservient. The sharper brown-eyed children began to struggle with their work, while the slower blue-eyed children had the gall to criticize the brownies for holding back the class. Elliott had convinced the children that their eye colour was either a label of promise or a mark of shame.

Class ended that Friday afternoon, and the children went home to their families and friends. The following Monday, they arrived at school and Elliott reversed the labels. She told the children that the brown-eyed students were actually superior to the blue-eyed students, and now the "blueys" were labelled with armbands of shame. The students adopted these new roles, but less enthusiastically than they had their original roles. Even the formerly oppressed brown-eyed students occupied their superior position with relative benevolence, perhaps because they had experienced first-hand the sting of a negative label. By mid-afternoon, Elliott abandoned the exercise. The blue-eyed students removed their armbands, and students from both sides of the eye-colour divide hugged and commiserated.

News of Elliott's demonstration travelled quickly, and several weeks later Johnny Carson interviewed her on *The Tonight Show*. The interview lasted a few brief minutes, but its effects persist today. Elliott was pilloried by angry white viewers across the country, and to this day she's unpopular with many residents of Riceville, Iowa, her birthplace and home for many years. One angry white viewer scolded Elliott for exposing white children to the discrimination that black children face every day. Black children are accustomed to the experience, the viewer argued, but white children were fragile and might be scarred long after the demonstration ended. Elliott responded sharply by asking why we're so concerned about white children who experience this sort of treatment for a single day, while ignoring the pain of black children who experience the same treatment throughout their entire lives. Years later, Elliott's technique is still being used in hundreds of classrooms, and even in workplace-discrimination training courses, where adults experience similar epiphanies. Whatever the merits or shortcomings of Elliott's approach, it shows how profoundly labels shape our treatment of other people and how even arbitrary damaging labels have the power to turn the brightest people into meek shadows of their potential selves.

Labels don't just Resolve Ambiguity; They Change Outcomes

Four years before Jane Elliott's classroom demonstration, in the spring of 1964, two psychologists began a remarkable experiment at a school in San Francisco. The study was the brainchild of Robert Rosenthal and Lenore Jacobson, who set out to show that the recipe for academic achievement contains more than raw intellect and a dozen years of schooling. The children attended a school in southern San Francisco identified as the "Oak School", a pseudonym chosen to protect them from the prying eyes of a public that remains fascinated with the study more than half a century later. Rosenthal and Jacobson kept the details of the experiment hidden from the teachers, students, and parents; instead, they told the teachers that the test was designed to identify which students would improve academically over the coming year—students they labelled "academic bloomers". In truth, the test was an IQ measure with separate versions for each school year, and it had nothing to do with academic blooming. As with any IQ test, some of the students scored quite well, some scored poorly, and many performed at the level expected from students of their age group.

The next phase of the experiment was both brilliant and controversial. Rosenthal and Jacobson recorded the students' scores on the test, and then labelled a randomly chosen sample of the students as "academic bloomers". The bloomers performed no differently from the other students—both groups had the same average IQ score—but their teachers were told to expect the bloomers to experience a rapid period of intellectual development during the following year. Spring became summer, and the students and teachers had a three-month holiday.

When the new school year arrived in the autumn of 1964, each teacher watched as a new crop of children filled the classroom. The teachers knew very little about the students, except whether or not they had been described as bloomers three months earlier. Because they were chosen arbitrarily, the bloomers should have fared no differently from the remaining students during the academic year of 1964–65. The students completed another year of school, and just before the year ended, Rosenthal and Jacobson administered the IQ test again to check whether the students' scores had changed since the previous year. The results were remarkable.

The Reception class and Year 1 children who were labelled as bloomers outscored their peers by 10–15 IQ points. Four out of every five bloomers experienced at least a 10-point improvement, but only half the non-bloomers improved their score by 10 points or more. Rosenthal and Jacobson had intervened to elevate a randomly chosen group of students above their relatively unlucky peers. Incredibly, their intervention was limited merely to labelling the chosen students "bloomers" and remaining silent on the academic prospects of the overlooked majority.

Observers were stunned by these results, wondering how a simple label could elevate a child's IQ score a year later. Just as Princeton students perceived Hannah to be smarter when she was wealthier, the Oak School teachers subconsciously emphasized the students' strengths and overlooked their weaknesses. When the teachers at the Oak School interacted with the "bloomers", they were primed to see academic progress. Each time the bloomers answered a question correctly, the answer seemed to be an early sign of academic achievement. Each time they answered a question incorrectly, the error was seen as an anomaly, swamped by the general sense that they were in the process of blooming. During the year, then, the teachers praised these students for their successes, overlooked their failures, and devoted plenty of time and energy to the task of ensuring that they would grow to justify their promising academic labels.

It turns out that labels shape how adults see the world as well, and like the Russian students who discriminated light blue and dark blue more easily because they had separate labels for each colour, people who speak different languages come to see the world at large quite differently. Just consider the idioms people use across the globe. In English, we deride people for being "losers" or "no-hopers", but Germans prefer the more colourful term *Gurkentruppe,* literally a "troop of cucumbers". The German word for turtle is *Schildkröte,* or "shielded toad". These vivid labels are more powerful because they prompt concrete images instead of the weaker, abstract images inspired by their English counterparts. Sometimes words that exist in one language have no equivalent in other languages. In Yagan, an indigenous language on the Tierra del Fuego archipelago, *mamihlapinatapei* means "the wordless yet meaningful look shared by two people who desire to initiate something, but both are reluctant to start", a concept that doesn't exist in quite the same way for English-speakers, who romanticize a first kiss but not the moment before the kiss. Similarly, though English-speakers don't assign gendered labels to inanimate objects, many other languages distinguish between masculine objects and feminine objects. A bridge is masculine to Spanish-speakers and feminine to German-speakers, so in one experiment Spanish-speakers described bridges as big, dangerous, strong, and sturdy, while German-speakers described bridges as beautiful, elegant, pretty, and fragile. Far from merely functioning as placeholders, labels craft the images that populate our thoughts.

Because different languages paint different realities, many of the greatest linguistic insights emerge when anthropologists stumble on dwindling tribal populations with unique languages or dialects. In the early 1970s, anthropologist John Haviland discovered an unusual feature of the language spoken by the Guugu Yimithirr people of far north Queensland, in north-eastern Australia. The language had no words for directions like "left", "right", "in front of", or "behind", but instead the Guugu Yimithirr relied on the cardinal directions *gungga* (north), *jiba* (south), *naga* (east), and *guwa* (west). At first this seems like a trivial difference, but the directional terms that most of us use to specify locations and directions are egocentric: they only make sense if you know where a person is standing, and which way she's facing. As soon as she turns round, an object that sat in front of her now sits behind her. This isn't true of cardinal directions, which relate to the position of the sun rather than the position of a particular person. The Guugu Yimithirr are more familiar with cardinal directions than are English-speakers, so they're able to determine that an object sits to the north or south just as quickly as English-speakers recognize that the object sits in front of or behind them.

Linguist Stephen Levinson visited the Guugu Yimithirr people in the 1980s and described a series of interactions that showed just how differently the Guugu Yimithirr think about physical space. In one case, a local poet advised him to beware of the big ant "just north" of his foot. In another, Levinson asked an elder to describe what he saw in a picture. The elder explained that he saw two girls, one whose nose pointed east and another whose nose pointed south. Of course, had the elder turned 180 degrees to face the opposite direction while holding the image, he would have explained that the girls' noses now pointed west and north respectively.

Not too far away, on the opposite side of Cape York in far north Queensland, the Pormpuraaw Aborigines take a similar linguistic approach to describing time. Instead of imagining that time flows from left to right, or right to left, the Pormpuraaw describe time as flowing like the sun – from east to west. When a Pormpuraawan faces north, time flows from right to left, but when she turns to face south, time flows from left to right. In one experiment, a group of Pormpuraawans were asked to arrange a set of cards showing a man at different ages, from youth to adulthood. As expected, the study's participants arranged the cards in ascending age, ordered from east to west. Those who were facing north arranged the cards from right to left (as in the left-hand panel of the illustration on the following page). Halfway through the experiment, a cameraman who was filming the task explained that he needed to take a different angle, so participants swivelled 90 degrees to face a different cardinal direction (as in the right-hand panel of the illustration). Instead of arranging the cards from left to right relative to their own position, as English-speakers do regardless of which direction they're facing, the Pormpuraawans arranged the cards from east to west again—but this time the cards were oriented from bottom to top rather than from right to left. The linguistic labels of the Yimithirr and Pormpuraawan languages determined how they perceived both physical space and time.

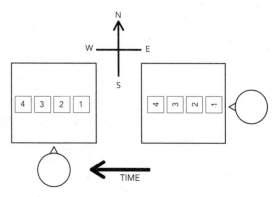

Bird's-eye depiction of a Pormpuraawan completing the card-ordering task, facing north and facing west. Time passes from east to west according to the Pormpuraawan language.

Seeing What isn't really There

Labels go undetected as they frame how we perceive time and space, but they play their most cunning tricks when they paint a scene that doesn't actually exist. In the early 1970s, researcher Elizabeth Loftus began to study how labels distort eyewitness memories. She wondered, for example, whether people who witnessed a car accident recorded and recalled their memories faithfully, or whether their recollections changed depending on how the accident was described. In one classic experiment, people watched a series of car accidents from a Seattle Police Department driving-safety video. After each video, the viewers estimated how fast the cars were travelling before the accident. Everyone saw exactly the same videos, but the questionnaire that they completed used one of five different terms to describe how the vehicles interacted. Some of the viewers were asked to estimate how fast the cars were going when they *hit* each other; others were asked how fast the cars were going when they *smashed*, *collided*, *bumped*, or *contacted* each other. Though everyone saw the same cars involved in the same accidents, their estimates differed widely.

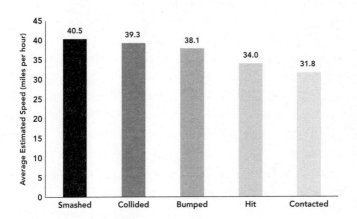

When the accidents were sensationalized, the cars seemed to be travelling faster: in the minds of viewers, a "smashed" car must have been travelling faster than a merely "contacted" or "hit" car. A similar experiment revealed the even more disturbing truth that labels sometimes create memories that are entirely false. A group of college students watched a video of two cars colliding. Some of them were told that the cars smashed, and others that the cars hit one another. A week later they were asked to recall whether they had seen any broken glass following the accident. Almost all of the students who had been told that the cars hit each other correctly remembered that there was no glass following the accident, and only 14 percent mistakenly remembered seeing glass. But among those who had been told that the cars had smashed, almost one-third remembered seeing broken glass. For these students, the sensationalized "smashed" label had replaced reality with a false memory in which the cars spilled glass following the accident. More broadly, this disturbing result suggests that eyewitnesses to a crime or an accident are open to forming false or exaggerated memories depending on how others label the events. The moral of the story is that plaintiffs and defendants should never blithely adopt the descriptions offered by opposing counsel. An angry plaintiff's "smash" is a persecuted defendant's "nudge".

While Loftus investigated how labels changed the way people remembered events in the past, social psychologists began to wonder whether they could also reshape interactions between two people in real time. One question that fascinated the field in the 1970s was why disabled people found social interactions so difficult. Most people aren't cruel and disparaging, but many people with stigmatized disabilities seemed to believe their interactions with strangers were awkward and uncomfortable. On the one hand, a well-intentioned able-bodied person might spend so much mental effort trying to behave "normally" that she had no mental energy left to carry on an easy conversation. On the other hand, the disabled person might be acutely sensitive to every facial expression, turn of the head, or blink of the eyes that might confirm her worst fears: that she's being judged for her disability. Teasing apart these explanations demands creativity. How do you know the root causes for why an interaction isn't going well? Two social psychologists devised a very clever method to show why the label of disability and the stigma of a scar cause such awkward interactions.

The researchers ran their study at Dartmouth College in the late 1970s. Unsuspecting Dartmouth students who had signed up to take part in the study were led into a small room where an experimenter explained that they would be interacting with another person. Before the interaction began, some of the students were told that a make-up artist would paint a scar on their faces. The patient but anxious students stood immobile while a make-up artist applied a fake scar, and then showed them what the scar looked like in a mirror. The students stared briefly at this newly labelled version of themselves. They were essentially the same people, but it wasn't easy to anticipate how the students they were about to meet would respond to meeting a person with a prominent facial scar. After the students looked in the mirror, the make-up artist applied some cream to make sure that the scar would remain in place, and the students walked to another room, where they met their interaction partner for the first time.

The students felt uncomfortable during their interactions, and they were convinced that their scars were attracting unwanted attention. In fact, they spent so much time worrying about the scar that they had no energy left to feign the sort of cool detachment expected of students when they meet one another for the first time. Other students who weren't made up with scars were told that their interaction partner expected them to have an allergy, but allergies make for innocuous labels, and these students sailed through their interactions with ease.

But the experimenters had devised a clever twist: when the make-up artists said they were applying a cream to ensure the scar wouldn't fade, they were actually removing the scar with make-up removal cream. By the time the students began interacting with their partners, their faces were no more flawed than they had been when the experiment began. Still, the label had already done its work: the students were convinced that their partners couldn't stop staring at their scars, and in response their own behaviour jeopardized the success of the interaction. The students' partners agreed: though they weren't told whether the student believed he had been scarred or merely described as allergy-prone, they were able to tell almost immediately which students were led to believe they were scarred. Even in the absence of a real physical blemish—a scar, in this case—people become paralysed by the prospect that others will judge them for the label, and this anxiety is enough to hamper the progress of a fledgling friendship.

Labelling afflicts physically stigmatized people every day, but it has an even darker history in the realm of mental stigmatization, where psychiatric professionals sometimes perceive disorders that aren't actually there. Sigmund Freud's mentor, the French neurologist Jean-Martin Charcot, was one of the most prolific labellers of all time. Charcot's pet diagnostic label was *hysteria*, which he used to describe a broad array of disorders in female patients. To get a sense of just how broadly the term was used, George Beard, a physician during the late nineteenth century, created a catalogue of the symptoms ascribed to hysteria. Beard's catalogue ran for seventy-five pages, and with exasperation he ultimately acknowledged that the list was still incomplete. The list included symptoms from faintness and nervousness to fluid retention and abdominal bloating. Charcot held theatrical demonstrations for his colleagues and students, presenting a "neurotic" woman and describing her symptoms and a range of possible cures. The label lost favour when practitioners decided that its breadth undermined its usefulness, but not before it had done plenty of damage. The treatments included painful abdominal water massages, induced bleeding, and invasive genital stimulation. (Physicians complained so bitterly about having to administer this last form of treatment that the "portable vibrator" was designed to "automate" the process.) Meanwhile, women across the developed world were diagnosed with hysteria to such an extent that the label lost all value. Women under pain of hysteria became second-class patients, and physicians often ignored legitimate complaints that warranted treatment.

The case of hysteria is disturbing, but it feels so remote from contemporary medical mores that it's tempting to feel that psychiatric labelling is no longer a concern. In fact, the reverse is true. With each successive edition of the psychiatric bible—the *Diagnostic and Statistical Manual of Mental Disorders* (or *DSM*)—comes new labels. One dangerous label in vogue at the moment is borderline personality disorder (BPD), which encompasses almost as many symptoms as hysteria did a hundred years ago. BPD entails a subset of chronic anger, feelings of emptiness, impulsivity, unstable personal relationships, and a host of other behaviours. The problem is that these symptoms also explain dozens of other disorders, and psychiatrists have been accused of diagnosing patients with BPD too hastily. Worse still is the stigma that goes along with a BPD diagnosis. BPD is notoriously difficult to treat—in part because the label describes so many different constellations of symptoms—and clinicians respond by distancing themselves from patients who have been diagnosed with BPD. The same patient who would have escaped the stigma of a BPD label before the label became popular now has much more difficulty finding a willing psychiatrist.

BPD isn't the only catch-all label on the market. Since the 1970s, thousands of children have been diagnosed with attention deficit hyperactivity disorder (ADHD), a disorder with a list of symptoms to rival BPD and hysteria. Psychiatrists tend to diagnose ADHD much more often in younger children within each school year, which suggests that some cases of simple childhood immaturity might be mistaken for ADHD. The disorder has spawned a range of overprescribed drug treatments, such as Ritalin and Adderall, which are notoriously popular among healthy but overworked college students and professionals. The mere existence of the labels *hysteria*, *borderline personality disorder*, and *attention deficit hyperactivity disorder* is enough to encourage those diagnoses in the same way that people who adopt the label *disabled* are primed to believe that other people are treating them strangely or unfairly merely because they bear a visible scar.

Labels are immensely powerful, shaping not only what we see but also events that haven't actually taken place. For all their power, though, approximately one-quarter of the world is still illiterate, incapable of reading written labels. The great global common denominator is graphic information in the form of pictures, symbols, and images, which make themselves understood as soon as they attract a casual glance. Arguably more powerful than labels, some symbols communicate with such force that they demand the same care as a loaded gun.

3.

SYMBOLS

Symbols are Magnets for Meaning

The US Naval Amphibious Base, Coronado, sits on Silver Strand between San Diego Bay and the Pacific Ocean. The base was commissioned in 1944 as World War Two came to a close, and by the late 1960s it had begun to outgrow its original design. The navy responded by contracting local architect John Mock to design Complex 320-325, six new buildings that today house sailors from the Seabees division. At ground level, the buildings are nondescript monuments to 1960s barracks architecture. From the air, however, they form an alarming symbol.

Few symbols inspire stronger reactions than the swastika, and many San Diegans were up in arms when they discovered the building's sinister bird's-eye profile. The local Anti-Defamation League and local members of Congress implored the navy to "find a feasible solution". Some creative stakeholders suggested adding strategic walkways to transform the swastika into a completed square, tall stands of trees to obscure the buildings' shape from the air, and even special structures designed to camouflage the building entirely. Navy spokespeople resisted

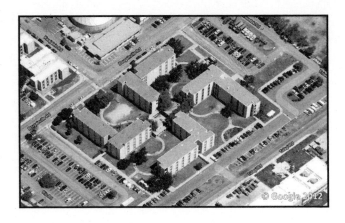

at first, but ultimately they were forced to earmark $600,000 to re-shape the buildings. In a recent interview, architect John Mock distin-guished the "four L-shaped buildings" from a swastika shape and claimed that the original builders and architects knew exactly how the buildings would look from the air. Whether or not the complex forms a true swastika, it's hard to argue that it doesn't bear a striking resem-blance to the tainted symbol.

How does a symbol like the swastika—a simple combination of six straight lines—inspire such strong reactions? Mock's buildings are com-pletely safe, and they don't cause blindness or physical harm when viewed from the air. In fact, until the Nazi Party co-opted the symbol, it repre-sented a range of innocuous mystical concepts. To Buddhists, the symbol represented eternity; to some Hindus, the shape represented the god Ga-nesha; and to the Panamanian Kuna Yala people it represented the octo-pus that created the world. These positive connotations are reflected in its name, which comes from the Sanskrit word for "lucky" or "auspi-cious". So what happened when the symbol became associated with the Nazi Party? Like names and labels, symbols lack meaning until they're associated with existing meaningful concepts. They're powerful because their inherent lack of meaning allows them to represent any concept from a menu of infinite possibilities. A decade after World War Two ended, Gerald Holtom designed the now-famous peace symbol, but imagine how differently people would feel about the symbol if the Nazi Party had adopted it fifteen years earlier.

Gerald Holtom's nuclear disarmament peace symbol, a combination of the semaphore (flag alphabet) signals for *N* and *D*.

Symbols and images are also powerful because we perceive them so effortlessly and so rapidly. A century before Mock designed Complex 320-325, Russian author Ivan Turgenev wrote, "A picture shows me at a glance what it takes dozens of pages of a book to expound." Now shortened to "a picture is worth a thousand words", this aphorism suggests correctly that symbols and other meaningful images have the capacity to inspire quickly extreme reactions, ranging from anger and fear to joy and celebration. They're especially powerful because we process symbolic images very quickly—more quickly than we process the meaning of words—and correspondingly they embed themselves more deeply in our memories.

Symbols, then, are magnets for meaning, and they have the power to shape our thoughts and behaviours just as words and labels do. They accomplish this feat by *priming* (or preparing) us for particular thoughts and behaviours. Since the swastika is now associated with aggression, anger, and general negativity, it should prime us to perceive aggression, anger, and negativity in events that might otherwise seem innocuous. To test this effect, my colleague Virginia Kwan and I asked a group of students to complete two seemingly unrelated tasks. We called the first one a geometric acuity task, a scientific-sounding name for a task in which the students counted the number of right angles in four shapes. Three of the shapes were identical for the entire group of students, but we varied the design of the fourth shape. For half of the students, that fourth shape looked a lot like a swastika, so for those students the concepts of aggression, anger, and negativity should have been particularly accessible. For the other half, the fourth shape was just a series of squares and circles that had no particular meaning.

After the students finished the geometric acuity task, we distracted them with another task for a few minutes, and then asked them to read a supposedly unrelated passage about a man named Donald. The passage described a day in Donald's life, and we purposely described his actions so that they could be interpreted either as innocuous or as evidence that Donald was an aggressive, mean-spirited character. For example, the passage explained that a salesman knocked on Donald's door, but Donald refused to let him enter. Most people refuse to let salespeople enter their homes from time to time (or perhaps most of the time), but if you're viewing Donald's behaviour through a critical lens, his decision to keep the salesman at bay might constitute evidence that he's generally mean-spirited. Later in the day, Donald was queuing to buy tickets to a U2 concert. He started playing poker with some of his fellow U2 fans, and suggested that the winner could take the losers' tickets. A policeman stumbled on the game, which unbeknown to Donald happened to be illegal, and arrested him. The students who read the scenario were asked how severely Donald should be punished and whether he seemed moral and decent, or depraved and offensive.

The students who had seen the swastika fifteen minutes earlier were now reading the passage about Donald with a quietly humming sense of unease. Although many of them claimed not to have noticed the swastika, or that they forgot having seen it by the time they read the passage, it still shaped their impressions of Donald. Those who saw the swastika were far more critical of Donald's decision not to open the door to the salesman, rating his behaviour as 10 percent more immoral on a sliding scale. They were also happier to condemn Donald to criminal punishment for his gambling exploits, similarly suggesting that he deserved a punishment that was approximately 10 percent more severe. In short, the students who were incidentally exposed to a negative symbol found their later impressions tainted by the symbol, even though many of them could barely remember its presence. We see so many symbols throughout the course of the day—particularly in advertisements on billboards, in newspapers, and on TV—that we hardly pay attention to any one symbol floating amid a sea of hundreds of others. Our lack of awareness makes their influence even more insidious as they push us and pull us and shape our thoughts and feelings below the surface of conscious awareness.

Power from Subtlety

Symbols influence us without our consent in large part because our brains constantly process images subconsciously and automatically. While you're concentrating on this book, your brain continues to pick up visual information from the periphery of your visual field. Even images that flash by in an instant, before you've had time to recognize what you've seen, go on to influence your thoughts. Take a look at the array of symbols on the following page for just a few seconds.

You won't have had time to process each one individually, and you're unlikely to remember all of them, but within the space of several seconds they've set off an explosive chain reaction of mental processes inside your head. It's rare to see this many symbols at once, so that chain of thoughts

is quite confused—the heart silhouette might be conjuring thoughts of love, romance, Valentine's Day, perhaps even "I ♥ NY" T-shirts. Meanwhile, the radiation symbol and the skull and crossbones are likely to inspire a very different set of associations, from death and poison to war and famine. Add the other nine symbols to the mix, and you can imagine the feverish propagation of electric impulses coursing through your brain.

There's plenty of experimental evidence for this powerful chain of responses, even when the symbols are displayed so briefly that we don't have time to recognize them. One of these symbols is the now almost universally recognized Apple company logo. The logo doesn't depict just any apple; it's an apple that's come to represent innovation and thinking differently (as the advertising campaign has claimed). Recognizing the symbol's meaning, a group of researchers wondered whether people might actually think differently—or more creatively—when they were very briefly exposed to the Apple logo. In contrast, they expected people who were exposed to the IBM logo to think less creatively, since IBM is associated with intelligence and responsibility, but not particularly with creativity. More than three hundred students were briefly exposed to a series of four different Apple logos or a series of four different IBM logos. The logos were presented so briefly that they were processed subliminally, below the level of conscious awareness, so none of the students had any idea what they'd seen on the screen. To give you a sense of just how briefly the logos were illuminated, each one could have been presented seventy-seven times in the space of a single second—far too quickly for the brain to process their content consciously.

After the students were primed with the logos, they completed a task designed to measure creativity known as the unusual uses test. The test measures how many creative uses people can generate for an everyday mundane object like a brick or a paper clip. Suggesting that a paper clip can be used to bind sheets of paper is uncreative, whereas suggesting that a paper clip can be used as an earring is evidence of creative thinking. (Suggesting that a paper clip can be used to fly you around the world, on the other hand, is both creative and nonsensical, and nonsensical responses aren't rewarded in this test.) As the researchers expected, students who were unwittingly exposed to the Apple logo seemed to think more creatively than their IBM-primed classmates; compared with the IBM-primed students, who generated an average of approximately six uses for the items, the Apple-primed students generated an average of almost eight uses for the same items, and those uses were rated by other students as more creative. Merely exposing people to a symbol that implies creativity for less than a tenth of a second can cause them to think more creatively, even when they have no idea that they've seen the symbol.

While some symbols appear briefly, others appear on the outskirts of the visual field without attracting conscious attention, and even these symbols come to shape our thoughts and feelings. Like the Apple logo, an illuminated lightbulb is associated with insight, recalling Plato's comparison of insight to light illuminating a darkened mind. The glowing lightbulb is an apt metaphor, because it moves from darkness to illumination with the same speed that insight moves the mind from confusion to understanding. In a series of elegant studies, a group of psychologists showed that the relationship between a lightbulb and insight is more than metaphorical. In those studies, university students completed different mental problems that require insight—the sorts of problems that seem impossible to solve right up to the "Eureka!" moment when the solution appears out of the blue. Just as the students were beginning the tasks, the researcher either turned on a naked lightbulb or another form of light that didn't feature an illuminated lightbulb; sometimes the bulb was obscured by a lampshade and sometimes the light came from an overhead fluorescent tube. The students weren't paying conscious attention to the source of light, since every darkened room has to be illuminated somehow, and the process of illumination is too mundane to warrant special attention. Nonetheless, since the symbol of an illuminated lightbulb implies insight, the researchers expected the students to solve the insight problems more easily when primed with the illuminated lightbulb. As expected, the students completed tricky insight-based mathematical, verbal, and geometric problems more often when the experimenter began the session by turning on a visible lightbulb. Here's one of the problems:

Connect the four dots by drawing three connected straight lines without either lifting the pencil from the page or retracing a line, and while ending the drawing at the same dot as it was begun.

●   ●

●   ●

The solution requires a burst of insight, because the lines go beyond the illusory square created by joining the four dots.

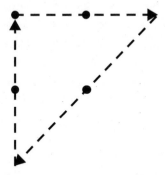

Solution to the geometric insight problem. Forty-four percent of the students who were primed with an illuminated lightbulb solved the difficult problem, but only 22 percent solved the problem when they were primed with a fluorescent light instead.

This is a curious effect; you might imagine that people either have or don't have the capacity for insight into a problem. The researchers argued that the lightbulb primes the concept of insight, which in turn primes past occasions that required insight, thereby putting the students in the right mindset for a new brush with insight. Indeed, part of the trick to solving insight problems is recognizing that they require a particular style of thinking that pursues surprising lateral solutions in favour of obvious but incorrect alternatives. Part of the reason why the illuminated lightbulb primes insightful solutions is that the symbol has one very dominant meaning: the generation of an idea. Other symbols are associated with a wide range of concepts, which makes it far more difficult to predict how they'll influence thinking and behaviour. At the same time, they're capable of producing some of the most powerful effects in human psychology.

Symbols on Steroids, Part 1: Money

In 1991, avant-garde pop duo The KLF was one of the best-selling bands in the world. In February of that year, the band held the number-one spot in the UK singles chart with house anthem "3 a.m. Eternal." But ultimately Bill Drummond and Jimmy Cauty weren't seeking superstardom. They were anarchists at heart, intent on subverting the decadent world they had come to represent. Wielding toy machine guns, Drummond and Cauty walked onto the stage at the 1992 BRIT music awards and fired rounds of blanks into the stunned audience. Later they left a rotting sheep's carcass on the steps of the awards' after-party. With that, they quit the music business.

A year passed while the duo received millions of pounds in royalties from "3 a.m. Eternal" and other best-selling tracks. They considered buying a submarine or an airship, but ultimately founded the art-focused K Foundation. When the prestigious Turner Prize was awarded to sculptor Rachel Whiteread in 1993, the K Foundation announced that Whiteread had also won the foundation's "Worst Artist of the Year" award. When she refused to accept the award's £40,000 prize, Drummond and Cauty threatened to incinerate the money instead. Whiteread accepted the prize reluctantly and donated the full sum to charity.

Still focused on spending their royalties, Drummond and Cauty made a sculpture featuring £1 million in banknotes. None of the big galleries would display the work, so they decided to do the next best thing. Late at night on 23 August 1994, the duo dumped £1 million in £50 notes onto the floor of a boathouse on the Scottish island of Jura. For more than an hour, their friend Gimpo filmed as Drummond and Cauty fed twenty thousand notes into the flames. Most of the notes burned, but a small portion floated up through the boathouse chimney.

Freelance journalist Jim Reid was one of few outsiders invited to the boathouse. When the notes were first revealed, Reid described feeling guilty—as though merely being in the presence of so much money was immoral. Next he felt "the need to do something, not to let it just stand there. Because, of course, I, like anyone else with healthy appetites, wanted it." Reid wrote about his experience in the *Observer* one month later, concluding his article with a list of alternative uses for £1 million. The same million could have fed 800,000 starving Rwandans, or housed sixty-eight homeless families in London for a year, or groomed the then Princess Diana for six years.

Reid's revulsion isn't unusual. When you watch money burn, you feel the extinction of countless possibilities. Nearly two decades later, six psychologists scanned the brains of twenty adult participants as they watched a similar scenario unfold. On a small screen inside the scanner, the adults watched a pair of hands as they either folded a bundle of banknotes or destroyed them. Like Reid, they reported feelings of discomfort and agitation when the notes were destroyed, and their brains told a similar story. The brain's temporoparietal network responds to images of tools, from screwdrivers to hammers, as though it knows they have a functional purpose. Hammers are for hammering as money is for spending and acquiring, and when the adults watched the money being misused, their brains revolted in kind. When the hands cut or tore notes that were more valuable (worth US $100 rather than US $20), the adults' temporoparietal networks responded more vigorously. Money is such a powerful symbol—a means to so many coveted ends—that our brains revolt against the prospect that it might be misused.

There are many *supersymbols*, but one of the most powerful and pervasive is the symbol of monetary currency. There's no particular reason why currency should take the form of notes and coins—societies have bartered with beads, rum, and gemstones—but notes and coins have become symbolic of currency across much of the world today. Poets, singers, and bohemians have romanticized the absence of money for decades, but in truth it's hard to get by without relying on at least a moderate stash. English writer Somerset Maugham put it best, perhaps, when he suggested, "Money is like a sixth sense, and you can't make use of the other five without it." Indeed, it's difficult to enjoy the best food, cologne, artwork, music, and clothing if you don't part with money beforehand.

Noting the critical role of money in our lives, marketing professors have examined the diverse range of responses that notes, coins, and other symbolic reminders of money inspire in people. One of money's dominant functions, as Maugham implied, is freedom and independence, so the researchers expected people to behave more independently and selfishly when primed with symbols of money. In one study, students completed a difficult intellectual task that required them to manipulate twelve shapes to form a large square. The experimenter who explained the task offered to help them if they encountered difficulty, and then left the room so the students could work on the problem uninterrupted. For some of the students, a small pile of money from the board game Monopoly sat on the corner of their desk—a constant, subtle reminder of money. By the time four minutes had elapsed, almost 75 percent of the students who weren't reminded of the money had asked for help; in contrast, only 35 percent of the students who sat peering at the Monopoly money asked for help after four minutes. According to the researchers, the money reminded the students of their independence, delaying their quest for help and prompting them to persevere unaided for just a few more minutes.

Independence and perseverance are positive traits, but like money they have a darker flip side: a reluctance to help or to interact with other people. Dickens's classic *A Christmas Carol* depicts Ebenezer Scrooge, a wealthy banker who thrives on accumulating wealth and avoiding social interaction. Wealth insulates Scrooge from the problems that plague other characters in the book, and it's not until three ghosts visit him that he realizes the folly of his ways. Children vigorously decry Scrooge, a caricature of miserly nastiness, but other people also turn out to have just an ounce of Scrooge in them when they're reminded of money. In one study students played a brief game of Monopoly. Some of the students were left with the Scroogeworthy sum of $4,000, whereas others were left with no money at all. The students who were left with $4,000 then imagined a future of wealth, whereas those who were left with nothing merely pictured what they might do the following day, with no reference to money. A minute later, a minor disaster befell a student who happened to be walking through the lab when she dropped twenty-seven pencils on the floor. The "wealthy" students, content with their $4,000 in Monopoly money and thoughts of a bright financial future, picked up fewer pencils than did the students who weren't primed with the concept of wealth. The "wealthy" students weren't quite Scrooges—most collected some pencils—but they were just a bit less helpful in the wake of their brush with financial excess.

A separate study emphasized the point: in this one, students stared at either a computer screensaver of notes floating in water or fish floating in water. When asked whether they might like to donate some or all of the $2 they were given for participating in the study to a university student fund, the students who watched the money floating across the screen donated only 77 cents on average, compared with the heftier average sum of $1.34 donated by students who watched the fish floating across the screen. It's unfair to label the students "Scrooges", but symbolic reminders of money and wealth certainly nudged them towards selfishness.

Beyond self-sufficiency and independence, money is also symbolically capable of anaesthetizing pain. The *Chicago Tribune* coined the term *retail therapy* on Christmas Eve in 1986 to describe the act of trading money for mood-improving purchases, and comfort-buying drives the consumption of diverse products from single-serve ice cream to romantic comedies on DVD. One innovative company, Bummer Baskets, sells a range of care packages, each designed to assuage a particular variety of pain, dominated by the chocolate-laden Break-Up Basket. Given money's symbolic role in dampening pain, the same market researchers wondered whether students might be numbed to physical pain and social exclusion when exposed to images of money. Electric shocks are a rarity in modern psychological experiments, so the students in the physical pain experiment immersed their hands in a bucket of very hot water for thirty seconds and rated the pain of the experience on a nine-point scale. Those in the social pain experiment played a computer game with two other students who quickly began ignoring them, a potent form of social pain. Before engaging in the two painful tasks, the students completed a cleverly designed "finger-dexterity task". Some of them counted eighty $100 notes, while others counted eighty sheets of blank paper. The students who counted the blank paper found the hot water quite painful— around six on the nine-point scale—whereas those who counted the notes rated their pain at the less severe score of four. Those in the social pain task also felt the sting of ostracism less acutely when they counted money, rating their distress 50 percent less highly on a similar scale. Both physical and social pain seem less painful when we're cushioned by symbolic reminders of money, even when the money isn't real or doesn't belong to us.

Symbols on Steroids, Part 2: Nationalism and Religion

Apart from money, very few symbols have the power to start wars and terminate friendships.

Two exceptions to that rule are symbols of nationalism and icons of religion. Nationalism is embodied in a nation's flag, and flag desecrations feature heavily in anti-nationalist protests. In 2002, Venezuelan president Hugo Chávez narrowly escaped a coup d'état. Chávez had passed dozens of controversial laws in 2001, and a vocal crowd of 200,000 protesters demanded his replacement. The army detained Chávez, while Pedro Carmona, president of the Venezuelan Federation of Chambers of Commerce, assumed the presidency for forty-seven hours, until Chávez's rule was restored. During the attempted coup, Chávez made a number of speeches that local television channels were required to broadcast. Instead of broadcasting the speeches so that they occupied the entire screen, several privately held channels broadcast split pictures that showed opposition protests while Chávez was speaking. One of those channels was Radio Caracas Television International (RCTV). In 2006, RCTV's broadcasting licence expired, and it had to apply to the government for a renewal. The channel had been on air since the early 1950s, but Chávez decided to punish the network for its role in "supporting" the 2002 coup attempt. RCTV's licence was never renewed, and it was forced to broadcast as a guerrilla network, without the government's approval.

RCTV's protest was simple, but powerful and effective: it began broadcasting upside-down images of the Venezuelan flag. Protesters took to the streets, and they, too, carried the inverted flags. Chávez had left the nation in disarray, and the flag's inversion was a powerful emblem of that disorder. The government reacted harshly, forcing the remaining television channels to broadcast a severe message of rebuke. RCTV hadn't torn, burned, defaced, or otherwise damaged the flag, but its inversion was enough to anger the volatile government.

National flags hold similar importance across the globe. In a classic Civil War poem by John Greenleaf Whittier, patriot Barbara Frietchie dissuades Confederate soldiers from destroying the American flag: "'Shoot, if you must, this old grey head / But spare your country's flag,' she said." Other nations share America's fervour. China imposes up to three years in prison for flag desecration, Mexico up four years, and even liberal strongholds such as New Zealand and Denmark legislate against flag destruction. Saudi Arabia's flag is so sacred that in 1994 McDonald's restaurants had to remove takeaway bags bearing the flags of the nations taking part in the FIFA World Cup. In 2002, FIFA designed a ball that featured each participating country's flag, but the Saudis baulked when they imagined players kicking their national symbol.

Flags are the symbolic embodiment of national identity, which explains why so many countries outlaw public flag-burning. It stands to reason, then, that exposing people to their national flag might prime patriotism and national solidarity, but it might also prime the dark sides of those concepts, such as insularity and nationalistic aggression.

First, the good news: priming nationalistic Americans with the US flag reminds them that the United States was founded on the principles of equality and liberty. Three social psychologists invited students at a large American university to complete a brief questionnaire that began by asking how fervently nationalistic they felt towards the United States, and then assessed their attitudes towards Arabs and Muslims. Some of the students sat facing a large American flag, whereas others faced a blank wall instead. The flags didn't affect the students who weren't particularly nationalistic; they reported feeling very little anger or hostility towards Arabs and Muslims regardless of whether they sat facing a flag or a blank wall. But the pattern was very different for the nationalistic students, who were far more tolerant of Arabs and Muslims when they sat in front of the US flag. These results show that flags temporarily remind people of the ideals that define their national identity, and in the case of the American flag, people are transiently more accepting of ethnic and religious minorities.

The American preoccupation with Islam began quite recently, but the land debate between Israelis and Palestinians is biblical in both its origins and its proportions. When conflict simmers for generations, even reasoned argument fails to bridge the chasm that separates the opposing camps. Contemporary Israeli elections are fought and won on the battleground of Palestinian domestic policy. On the right, parties such as Yisrael Beiteinu (Israel is Our Home) refuse to entertain the notion of territorial compromise, while leftist parties like Hadash (the "New" party, or "Democratic Front for Peace and Equality") propose an expansive Palestinian territory. As surprising as it might be that the US flag dampens anti-Muslim sentiment among non-Muslim Americans, it seems like too much to expect the Israeli flag to unite left-wing and right-wing Israelis. A team of social psychologists took up the challenge when they exposed Israeli voters from across the political spectrum to an image of either the Israeli flag or a scrambled version of the flag. The Israeli flag unites all Israelis, whether they're right-leaning or left-leaning, so the researchers expected the voters to converge on a moderate middle ground when they were exposed to the flag. The flag (or its scrambled alternative) was presented very briefly so that the voters were unable to report what they'd seen. After this priming procedure, some of the voters reported their views on contentious political issues, and others stated which Israeli political party they preferred from the menu of a dozen options.

When they were primed with the scrambled flag, the left-wing voters expressed leftist views and the right-wing voters expressed rightist views. For example, the rightists anticipated feeling much sadder when Israel pulled out of the contentious Gaza region, and the leftists believed it was more unfair to an Israeli family's children when that family moved to the Gaza region to protest the withdrawal. But these differences miraculously melted away when the voters were exposed to the flag. The leftists and rightists became moderates, and their views were practically indistinguishable. Even their voting intentions shifted, so that their preferences were again more moderate and largely overlapping. Some weeks later, when the researchers phoned the voters after the Israeli elections, they found the same pattern: those who saw the scrambled flag voted along party lines, but their counterparts who saw the flag tended to vote far more moderately. Incredibly, reminding Israeli voters of their national identity—even below the level of conscious awareness—compelled them to compromise with their political opponents.

Unfortunately, national flags also have the capacity to bring out the worst in people. A team comprising some of the same researchers noticed that the media portrayals of the United States during the mid-2000s suggested that Americans were particularly aggressive. The United States was entangled in the Iraq and Afghanistan wars, and a spate of school shootings and other acts of domestic violence painted a similarly bleak domestic picture. As the researchers expected, Americans who often watched the news seemed to associate the flag with concepts such as war and guns, whereas those who watched the news less frequently had far weaker associations between the flag and aggression. In one study, the researchers subliminally primed a group of American undergraduates with an image of either the US flag or a meaningless configuration of shapes. The students began working on a long and boring task, but after they'd completed eighty trials of the task, an error message flashed on the screen: DATA SAVING FAILURE.

In fact, the experiment was going according to plan; the experimenters had rigged the program to deliver this warning in an attempt to frustrate the already bored and irritated students. The students called the experimenter, who apologized and asked them to begin the task again, from scratch. As far as they were concerned, the eighty boring trials they had already completed had been for nothing. A hidden camera recorded the students' reactions so the researchers could determine whether they responded with aggression or patience. As the researchers expected, the news-watching students who were primed with the US flag were especially aggressive; considering the hidden camera footage, the experimenters rated their reactions as more hostile, angry, irritated, cold, and unfriendly than those of the students who didn't watch the news or weren't primed with the US flag.

These results raise the question of why national flags unite political foes in some contexts and prime aggression in others. Why did left- and right-wing voters come together in Israel when primed with an Israeli flag, while the American-flag-primed citizens who watched news of American military progress became more aggressive? As with so many of the effects in this book, the answer lies in the associations inspired by those primings. A flag for one person might signal national unity, while for another it signals militaristic aggression and nationalistic fervour. Many flags begin as a collection of empty, colourful elements that acquire meaning over time, often inspiring different associations for different populations. While the US flag signals aggressive patriotism for some people, it reminds others that the nation values liberty and equality.

Like nationalism, religious identity is such an important part of how people see themselves that it has the capacity to provoke wars and genocides, hunger strikes and self-sacrifice. Many people are defined in large part by their religious identities, which involve adhering to a set of strongly held group norms. For example, religions prize honesty and integrity, and frown on cheating and impropriety. A few years ago, my colleague Virginia Kwan and I began to wonder whether we could compel people to be more honest by exposing them to religious symbols. We began the study by asking students to estimate the value of four pieces of jewellery. The jewellery included a gold ring, a silver brooch, earrings, and a necklace. The ring, brooch, and earrings were identical for all of the students, but for half the students the necklace featured a diamond-encrusted crucifix, whereas for the other half it featured a diamond pendant. The students who estimated the value of the crucifix were unwittingly primed with the concept of Christianity and its virtuous trappings: honesty and truthfulness.

After the students had estimated the value of the jewellery, they completed a seemingly unrelated questionnaire that was designed to measure their honesty. Some of the questions asked whether the students would admit to engaging sometimes in widespread but socially questionable behaviours (e.g., "I sometimes feel resentful when I don't get my way"), and others asked whether they sometimes failed to commit virtuous behaviours that are almost impossible to uphold all the time (e.g., "I always admit when I make a mistake"). As we expected, the Christian students honestly admitted their shortcomings 70 percent of the time when they were primed with the crucifix, but only 60 percent of the time when they weren't reminded of religion. The non-Christian students behaved just like the unprimed Christian students, admitting their shortcomings about 60 percent of the time regardless of whether they were primed with the crucifix. The symbol obviously didn't have the same resonance for the non-Christian students, so it failed to shape their behaviour as it did the Christian students'.

Unfortunately, religious priming also has a dark side, because it reminds people that they're incapable of fulfilling the impossibly strict standards demanded by orthodox religions. According to the Torah, Jews are expected to uphold 613 commandments, which range from not sprinkling frankincense on the meals of wrongdoers, to breaking the neck of a calf by a river valley following an unsolved murder. Catholic men fail to complete the seven sacraments if they choose not to enter the priesthood, and Scientologists must complete a series of psychological "audits" before they become consummate members of the Church of Scientology. It's no wonder that reminding people of religion primes not only honesty but also self-doubt.

In the late 1980s, psychologists showed one of two images to a group of Catholic students. The researchers flashed the images onto a white screen for such a brief period that it was impossible to perceive them consciously. For some of the students, the image was the solemn visage of Pope John Paul II, whereas the other students were exposed to an image of an equally solemn adult stranger. Later, though none of the students claimed to have seen a face, those who were exposed to the pope's face reported having a substantially poorer self-conception and a lower opinion of their own moral standing. Priming people with religious symbols has paradoxical consequences, because they tend to perceive themselves as relatively immoral beings while simultaneously behaving more honestly.

The Flip Side: Kryptonite to Symbols and Images

It's difficult to measure the power of a symbol like the crucifix or the US flag using strict scientific techniques, but some symbols are so powerful that they inspire reactions without further explanation. Coca-Cola is one of the world's most recognized brands, and the corporation capitalized on its dominance with an audacious billboard advertisement. The ad featured a silhouette of the company's famous contour bottle below the words "Quick. Name a soft drink". The brand's name was absent from the billboard, but its bottle was so well recognized and its name so strongly associated with soft drinks that "Coca-Cola" immediately came to mind. In some sense, this is the holy grail of advertising: a brand that becomes so strongly associated with a product category that people begin to refer to the whole category by the brand's name. But the power that comes from widespread familiarity also brings with it a symbol's greatest weakness: minor tweaks to the symbol that turn out to have grave consequences.

Companies regularly rejuvenate their brands by replacing old logos and packaging with "improvements". Brand makeovers are delicate, because there's a fine line between rejuvenation and failure. In the 1980s, Coca-Cola panicked when a sample of blind taste testers preferred a few sips of Pepsi to a few sips of Coke. The company unveiled New Coke to much fanfare in 1985, but consumers weren't looking for a newer version of their old favourite. The launch failed, Coca-Cola compromised its crushing market dominance, and consumers refused to rest until the classic Coke formula returned to supermarket shelves. In fact, part of the reason they preferred Pepsi was because it was slightly sweeter than Coke, and people respond positively to sweetness in small doses. Had the testers consumed an entire can of each product, as they did later, the results would have been quite different. What tastes pleasantly sweet after one sip becomes cloying after a dozen sips. Part of the reason people continued to buy Coke ahead of Pepsi was that they enjoyed drinking an entire can of Coke more than they enjoyed drinking an entire can of Pepsi.

People rail against these obvious changes to beloved symbols and brands, but what happens when the changes are so subtle that most people ignore them? One of the most powerful symbols today, as we've already seen, is monetary currency. Every few years, the US government updates notes and coins, though many of the changes are quite subtle. The US Treasury has introduced numerous currency updates, unveiling plans to produce a new series of banknotes covering all denominations from $5 to $100 in August 2008, while the US Mint announced that thirty-eight "Presidential" $1 coins would be released between 2007 and 2016. A similar announcement in 1999 preceded the release of fifty "US State" quarters between 1999 and 2008. The Treasury's official motivation for these updates seems somewhat frivolous: to "return . . . circulating currency to its position as an object of aesthetic beauty". People have come to associate money with its capacity to purchase goods, so my colleague Danny Oppenheimer and I wondered whether the purchasing power of money might be compromised by these changes. Put simply, would people perceive currency as slightly less valuable when we introduced a series of small tweaks to existing notes?

We asked a group of American commuters to estimate how much they could purchase with different forms of American currency. In one study, each person estimated how many of each of ten inexpensive items—such as thumbtacks, paper clips, pencils, and white paper napkins—they could purchase with $1. We gave half the adults a questionnaire featuring a photocopy of a real $1 note, and the other half a very similar questionnaire, with one important difference: the $1 note depicted at the top of the questionnaire was subtly altered so that it looked similar but not identical to the original. The adults who were looking at the photocopy of the fabricated $1 note also estimated how much they could purchase with $1. To give you a sense of how the two notes looked, they are shown side by side on the following page.

The commuters spent very little time looking at the photocopied note, but it still shaped their estimates of the note's purchasing power. Those who completed the questionnaire featuring the real note esti-

Real (left) and fake (right) dollar notes from the purchasing estimate study. There are half a dozen minor differences between the two notes, but not a single adult who responded to the questionnaire noticed that the fabricated note had been altered.

mated that they could purchase an average of twenty-two of the inexpensive items, whereas the adults who completed the questionnaire featuring the altered note estimated that they could purchase an average of only twelve of the items. That's a huge difference—and keep in mind that not a single person noticed that the fabricated note wasn't real, even when the experimenter asked them whether they noticed anything strange about the note. The symbol of money is very powerful—it can make us independent and selfish and insensitive to physical pain—but it's also quite fragile: as soon as you tweak currency, even subtly so that people don't notice the difference, it starts to lose its symbolic association with value.

The forces that shape the world within our heads—names, labels, and symbols—derive much of their power by association. In chapter 1, Hurricane Katrina tugged just a bit harder at the heartstrings (and purse strings) of Kims, Kevins, and Kaylas because they associated the storm's name with their own. In chapter 2, people were happier to travel to a shop five miles south of their town than to an identical shop five miles north of their town, having come to associate southerly journeys with the ease of moving downhill—a relic of gazing at hundreds of maps that depict north above south. And, in this chapter, the literal illumination of a lightbulb led students to illuminate metaphorically the hidden solution to a tricky mental problem. In each case, a feature of the environment activated related concepts in the minds of the people who encountered those features, prompting unexpected thoughts, feelings, and behaviours that come to make sense once you trace a mental path from the original word or image to the final outcome.

Just beyond the world that exists within our heads is the world that exists between us: Earth's seven billion inhabitants. Association plays a big role in this world, too (consider how difficult it is to dissociate your impressions of identical twins), but other people also shape how we think, feel, and behave through complex biological processes. While men produce more testosterone when surrounded by beautiful women, new mothers produce more of the hormone oxytocin when their babies are near, and each of these biological responses goes on to influence how they behave. While men become more reckless in the wake of a testosterone spike, mothers become fiercely protective of their babies. This sensitivity to the presence of other people—whether strangers or loved ones, whether they're alone or in groups, and even the mere suggestion of another person's presence—is enough to change how we behave. Chapter 4 opens by discussing how being alone differs from being surrounded by others, and how adding or subtracting people from the environment changes how we behave across a huge variety of situations.

PART TWO

THE WORLD
BETWEEN US

4.

THE MERE PRESENCE OF OTHER PEOPLE

It's in the Eyes

For several years, the staff in the psychology department at Newcastle University in the north of England took tea and coffee from the kitchen without contributing to the honesty box on the counter. A notice nearby asked drinkers to pay a small fee for their beverages—30 pence for tea, 50 pence for coffee, and 10 pence for milk—but the pile of coins inside the honesty box accumulated slowly, while tea, coffee, and milk supplies shrank rapidly. Something needed to be done, and three academics in the department decided to tackle the problem using the best tool at their disposal: a research intervention. As students of human behaviour, they recognized that people are guided by weak moral compasses that function much more effectively under surveillance. Unfortunately, honesty-box contributions were anonymous, and it would have been expensive and overzealous to install a camera. Instead of forcing everyone to comply under the gaze of constant surveillance, the researchers devised an intervention that merely made people feel as though they were being watched. For a ten-week period, they displayed ten different pictures above the price list for one week each, alternating between images of a pair of eyes and images of flowers. The researchers measured how much milk was consumed as an index of coffee and tea consumption, and counted how much money was in the honesty box at the end of each week. The intervention was a remarkable success. When the image featured a collection of flowers, drinkers paid an average of only 15 pence per litre of milk consumed, whereas they paid 42 pence per litre when the image displayed a pair of eyes. The mere suggestion that someone was watching compelled drinkers to contribute nearly three times more cash to the honesty box.

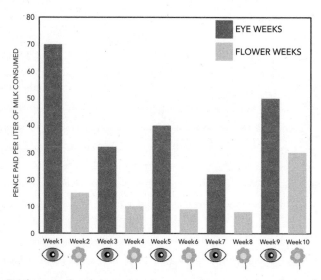

Drinkers contributed almost three times as much to an anonymous honesty box when the price list featured a pair of eyes (dark grey bars) rather than flowers (light grey bars).

Two hundred miles south of Newcastle, the West Midlands police department was justifiably curious about the research. The department was responsible for policing Birmingham, the second-largest city in the UK, and the Newcastle University intervention appeared to be both inexpensive and effective. Within months, the police department launched Operation Momentum, putting up a string of posters featuring a pair of piercing eyes with the slogan "We've got our eyes on criminals". Local officers described the campaign as a great triumph, claiming a 17 percent reduction in robberies, and swiftly launched its sequel: Operation Momentum 2.

As French philosopher Jean-Paul Sartre noted sixty years ago, as soon as we imagine we're being watched, we start to notice how we're behaving, and we begin to imagine how other people might respond if they were watching. We're far more forgiving of our own moral shortcomings—like failing to pay a small sum for tea and coffee—than we imagine other people might be, so the same acts that seem appropriate in isolation seem unacceptable when viewed from an observer's perspective. Today few of us spend more than a few hours alone, so our thoughts and actions come to reflect the presence of the family, friends, and strangers who surround us. So much of the way we think and behave is moulded by these interactions with others that it becomes very difficult to imagine the people we'd become during a week, a month, or even a year of social isolation. For small groups of people across time, that hypothetical has become a temporary or permanent reality, and the results have almost always been alarming.

Damaged by Social Isolation

As in Rudyard Kipling's story of Mowgli, a boy who was raised by a pack of wolves in the jungle, some people are raised without any human contact at all. Stories of feral children are legend, though few of them are supported by strong evidence. Marcos Rodríguez Pantoja spent twelve years living with wolves in the mountains of southern Spain, until he emerged miraculously at the age of nineteen. Robert, a Ugandan boy, survived a massacre that killed his parents in the early 1980s, and lived for three years with a troop of vervet monkeys. Perhaps the most famous and disturbing case of the twentieth century was "Genie", a girl whose parents forced her to spend the first thirteen years of her life strapped to a chair in a dark room in Los Angeles. When Genie was discovered in 1970, she was incapable of speaking, making eye contact, or engaging in basic social interactions. Instead of walking, she held her hands out in front of her body and shuffled erratically, and instead of speaking, she made animalistic sniffing and spitting sounds. Although Genie learned to speak in short sentences, she never overcame the initial period of isolation. As her psychologists noted, children acquire most of their social and linguistic skills during a critical window early in their lives. Children who grow up without human contact tend not to acquire those skills, and just as people struggle to learn new languages after childhood, they rarely learn to engage in basic social interactions.

Because their social muscles wither without regular exercise, even people who are raised with plenty of social contact struggle during prolonged isolation. In the mid-1950s, social psychologist Stanley Schachter recruited five young men to participate in a small experiment on social isolation. Each man was confined to his own room, a comfortable "cell" furnished with a table, a chair, a bed, a lamp, and toilet facilities. The rooms contained no books or magazines or TV, and a researcher left food for the men at the door without making social contact. Schachter told the men that he would pay them for their time, that they were free to withdraw from the experiment at any time, and left them alone as time began to elapse.

Just twenty minutes later, one of the men frantically rapped on his door and asked to be released. Even this brief period of social isolation was too much for him to bear, so Schachter paid him and allowed him to leave. Of the four remaining men, three lasted two days. One of those men claimed that his two days in isolation were among the most difficult days of his life, and he vowed never to repeat the experience. Another told Schachter that he felt increasingly uneasy and disoriented as time wore on. The third was unfazed but requested to be released after two days, while the final man remained happily isolated for eight full days.

Not everyone responds to social isolation in the same way, but for many if not most people, the experience is disorienting, unsettling, and no less acute than the hunger and thirst that come from a prolonged fast. As the space race intensified during the 1960s, a young French adventurer named Michel Siffre decided to contribute to the cause. Siffre offered to spend two months deep underground in a dark cave to simulate the isolation that astronauts might experience during solo missions. In the summer of 1962, Siffre descended to a depth of 375 feet inside a subterranean glacier in the French-Italian Maritime Alps. The cave was humid and cold, and though Siffre suffered from hypothermia, he emerged with his mental faculties largely intact. Apart from losing track of time and a brief spell of madness in which he sang wildly and danced the twist, his thinking remained clear and he was eager to conduct a more extensive experiment.

Ten years and countless hours of planning later, Siffre spent six months in a cave near Del Rio, Texas. This second cave was warm and comparatively comfortable, and Siffre amused himself by reading magazines and books and conducting scientific tests. But then, on day seventy-nine, he succumbed to a prolonged bout of depression after his record player broke and mould and mildew began to destroy his magazines and scientific equipment. He pondered suicide, only to befriend a mouse that renewed his will to live. Sadly, when he tried to trap the mouse in a casserole dish, he accidentally crushed and killed it, and wrote in his journal that "desolation overwhelms me". Even Siffre, who had volunteered to enter the cave, emerged disoriented, confused, and profoundly depressed, another victim of the ravages of social isolation.

Cases like Siffre's voluntary confinement are too rare to warrant sweeping conclusions, but thousands of prisoners have experienced similar disorientation and discomfort during periods of enforced solitary confinement. In the early 1980s, psychiatrist Stuart Grassian examined a group of inmates who had spent between eleven days and ten months in solitary confinement at a prison in Massachusetts. The men experienced hallucinations, profound depression, confusion, perceptual distortion, memory loss, and paranoia. A decade later, psychologist Craig Haney studied a hundred inmates at the Pelican Bay supermax prison in California. Many of the prisoners spent years in isolation, emerging with a combination of "chronic apathy, lethargy, depression, and despair". Between 80 percent and 90 percent of them were "irrationally angry", confused, and socially withdrawn—symptoms that affect only a few percent of the general population. Dozens of studies have drawn similar conclusions, and many of them have found that isolated prisoners struggle to distinguish between reality and fiction. Psychologists have compared the effects of social isolation to the process of deterioration that victims experience when they're poisoned by slow-acting snake venom. At first, isolation breeds agitation—the sort of agitation that seasonal hunters in remote parts of the world refer to as "cabin fever". Cabin fever isn't pleasant, and sufferers will expose themselves to bitter blizzards rather than face another hour alone in a small space. After agitation come hallucinations, acute anxiety, and even psychosis: a complete psychological break from reality. Chronic social deprivation is also one of the primary causes of premature death in people who are otherwise healthy.

Why is prolonged social isolation so profoundly damaging? Apart from the depression that sets in when people are forcibly isolated, one reason is that we tend to lose our sense of reality when we're unable to confirm our version of the world with that of other people. Does it make sense to slaughter, cook, and eat cows? What about domestic dogs? Are men considered stylish when they don long powdered wigs? Leather jackets? Three-piece suits? The answers to these questions are impossible to determine in the absence of social contact, because they're entirely determined by social norms or standards that differ across time and cultures. People born in China and the United States have the same digestive systems, and people born in the 1700s and 2000s have the same sensory systems, yet their preferences diverge under the influence of very different social contexts. You can imagine how Anne Shapiro, an American woman who awoke from a twenty-nine-year coma in 1992, felt when she emerged into a completely different world from the one she left in 1963, on the same day President John F. Kennedy was assassinated. Similarly, a prisoner who began a twenty-nine-year prison term in 1963 would have rejoined a world now populated with computers, cordless phones, and colour televisions. To those of us who have lived through these years in good social company, these changes are gradual and manageable, but to people who have lived in comparative isolation, they're monumental shifts that demand new and improved conceptions of reality. In fact, much of what we consider to be real is a direct product of standards determined by the people around us.

Deriving Reality by Comparing Yourself with Other People

In some settings, your understanding of reality is independent of other people. For example, try to answer these questions:

Question 1: Is your body comfortable, or would you be more comfortable with the help of heating or air-conditioning?

Question 2: Is the room you're in light enough, or would you be more comfortable under the glow of an extra lamp?

Even if you live alone in a shack, thousands of miles from civilization, you can answer these questions quite easily. Humans and other animals know instinctively whether the ambient temperature is comfortable and whether the environment is bright enough to enable them to see.

Now try this very different question:

Question 3: Given the amount of electricity you use to power the heat-ing, air-conditioning, and lighting in your home, are you being good to the environment?

There's an important difference between this third question and the first two questions. This one is much more difficult to answer in the absence of social standards. Even if you knew that your household used 5,000 kilowatt-hours of electricity last year, how would you evaluate the environmental impact of that figure? Like so many questions that tap into behavioural norms, it's very difficult to assess your behaviour with-out the help of comparison standards. (The average US household con-sumes 11,500 kilowatt-hours per year, so 5,000 is an impressively modest figure.)

Historically, energy bills have been restricted to an unhelpful sum-mary of each household's usage figures, so consumers have struggled to measure their consumption behaviour against an informative yardstick. Part of the problem is that energy companies face the same obstacle that hobbled the Newcastle University psychology department: in the absence of constant feedback, they're unable to encourage people to consume less electricity. Like the psychologists who encouraged socially conscious be-haviour with a strategically placed pair of eyes, one energy company en-couraged people to scrutinize their actions both cheaply and effectively.

Opower was founded in Virginia in 2007 by two long-standing friends. The company promised to improve communication between en-ergy providers and consumers by harnessing the tools of behavioural sci-ence. As of 2012, Opower had contracts with more than fifty utility companies across twenty-two US states. Each month, Opower sends a report to each household containing not just the standard consumption figures, but also a simple summary of the household's electricity use compared with the rest of the population. The most important part of the report is the Last Month Neighbor Comparison, which features two pieces of information: how much energy you're using relative to your efficient neighbours, and a description of your use as "more than average", "good", or "great".

Consumers who achieve "greatness" by using considerably less electricity than their neighbours are rewarded with two smiling faces, whereas those who are merely good are greeted with a single smiling face. Opower has been incredibly successful, reducing energy consumption in catchment areas by an average of 2.5 percent per person—a long-term saving of almost a billion kilowatt-hours across the United States since the company's inception. What's made Opower so successful is its recognition of two critical factors: first, that people don't know how to evaluate their energy without knowing how much electricity other households are consuming; and second, that people respond to the virtual acclaim and criticism that comes from simple social cues like smiling faces. More recently, the company has released an iPhone app that allows users to compete with their friends for the title of "most energy-efficient". The real or even imagined presence of fellow energy consumers drives competition, and people respond by curbing their appetite for electricity.

What Opower has done for environmental change, Turkish soap opera *Noor* has done for cultural change in the Arab world. Some writers have claimed that *Noor* (Arabic for "light" and the main character's name) may someday be considered the origin of "the Islamic world's accidental cultural revolution". In 2006, Saudi Arabian TV channel MBC bought the rights to the soap opera about a young woman named Noor who marries into a wealthy family. The characters quickly became surrogate family members in households across Saudi Arabia, and later in other parts of the Arab world. Some of them violated deeply held conservative norms by drinking wine with dinner and engaging in premarital sex, but the relationship between Noor and her handsome, progressive husband, Mohannad, showed viewers the marital benefits of gender equality. Mohannad was consistently loyal and attentive, supporting his wife's career as a fashion designer and as an equal partner in their marriage. Dozens of other TV stations around the world bought the rights to the show, and it began subtly to reshape how people thought about their relationships. Mohannad and Noor became two of the most popular babies' names in Saudi Arabia. Formerly submissive wives began to demand that their husbands treat them with the respect that Mohannad accorded Noor. Meanwhile, as the divorce rate rose by 10 percent in the United Arab Emirates, officials came to believe that the increase was partly due to the prominence of empowering soap operas such as *Noor*. According to interviews, many of these divorces were initiated by women who were unhappy in their marriages, but only realized that they had the power to escape after watching similar situations on TV. A soap opera in Brazil taught women to seek contraception, and fertility rates in areas that received the satellite signal fell dramatically, while they remained stable in nearby areas that were beyond the signal's reach.

Like the Saudi women who watched *Noor*, we're all born into one reality, oblivious to the countless alternate realities that exist in other parts of the world. Without the presence of people who express the possibilities of a different set of norms, we continue to think, feel, and behave within the invisible boundaries that have shaped us since birth. The good news for social progress is that we're instinctively programmed to mimic other people—to mirror their behaviour and to learn how to tackle problems with fresh insight.

Mimicry, Problem-solving, and Social Connection

In the early 1930s, psychologist Norman Maier began to wonder how people solve problems that require creativity. Maier brought sixty-one students into his lab at the University of Michigan, and asked them to find as many solutions as they could to a simple physical problem. Two cords of identical length hung from the lab's ceiling, and Maier asked the students to tie the cords together. The room also contained a number of other items, including pliers, extension cords, a table, chairs, and poles. When the students grabbed one of the cords and tried to walk across to the other cord, they realized that they couldn't quite reach the second cord without using the props in the room. Some of the solutions were simple, so most of the students described them without much difficulty. For example, the second cord could be anchored to a chair halfway between the two cords, allowing the students to bring the first one over to the second. One of them could also be lengthened with the extension cord or pulled closer with the pole.

The last remaining solution was much trickier, though, and only 39 percent of the students arrived at the solution without help: one of the cords could be converted into a pendulum if affixed to one of the smaller, heavy objects in the room. The students could then swing the pendulum, grabbing the attached cord as it approached the second cord. When most of the students couldn't solve the problem unaided, Maier gave them a subtle hint at the solution that became one of the first demonstrations of social learning. As time passed, he began pacing the room, occasionally grazing one of the ropes with his shoulder and setting it in motion. The rope swung gently, but Maier refrained from discussing the hint, and the students continued to ponder the problem. Less than a minute after witnessing Maier's subtle hint, two-thirds of the students who hadn't yet solved the problem jumped up and excitedly described the pendulum solution. Almost all of them denied having seen that the experimenter jostled the cord, and even if he had brushed against it, they were sure that it hadn't prompted the solution. Instead, they were convinced that the solution came to them unaided, a product of mental effort rather than gentle prompting. Although Maier was more interested in problem-solving than in social mimicry, he also concluded that people learn from subtle cues without recognizing that they're mimicking the behaviour of others.

Consciously mimicking or aping another person is taboo in social settings, but unconscious mimicry is rife. Former England soccer manager

Steve McClaren departed England to coach Dutch side FC Twente in 2008. Several months later, McClaren was interviewed before a game, and instead of responding with his normally fluid British accent, he spoke in a halting form of English that made him sound Dutch. His grammar was strangely off-kilter, and he skipped words that native English-speakers would normally use. British fans responded by plastering a YouTube video of the interview with dozens of derisive comments. A group of computer scientists also found that when two people talk on the phone while walking, they tend to synchronize their footsteps even without the help of visual feedback, relying instead on the rising and falling tones of their partners' voices. Even infants as young as nine months of age begin mimicking other people, leading psychologists to argue that mimicry is an innate, evolved form of social glue that binds people together.

Psychologists call this the chameleon effect. Chameleons primarily change colour to signal their intent to mate or fight, and mimicry in humans appears to serve a similarly social purpose. In one classic series of experiments, two students visited a research lab to complete a simple task that required them to interact for a few minutes. Unbeknown to one of the students, the other student was actually a member of the experimenter's team who was instructed to adopt a specific string of mannerisms. With some of the students she smiled, with others she refrained from smiling, and with some she rubbed her face several times, while with others she shook her foot incessantly. The students didn't notice these subtle behaviours (as they told the experimenter later), but a videotape of the interaction showed plenty of mimicry. When the trained actor smiled, the students smiled three times as often; when the actor rubbed her face, the students rubbed their faces twice as often; and when she shook her foot, they shook their feet twice as often. In another, similar experiment, an actor either mirrored the students' behaviour or adopted neutral mannerisms that bore no resemblance to those of the students. When the students later reflected on these interactions, they felt that the interactions went more smoothly when they had been mimicked. Not only do people naturally mimic one another, but those actions go on to create social bonds between strangers that form the foundation of future friendships.

Humans are suckers for mimicry, because unconscious imitation is one of the few clear signals that other people admire you enough to emulate your gestures. Watching someone as they mimic you is also a rare opportunity to evaluate your behaviours through the lens of an outsider, which Sartre described as at once exhilarating and frightening. For some people, some of the time, there's nothing more exciting than performing before a large audience, but much of the time there's nothing more mortifying than standing in the spotlight of another person's gaze. According to one story, that statement is literally true; thousands of Americans who were surveyed claimed that public speaking was their biggest fear, with death a long way back in second place.

Performing before a Crowd: the Highs of Social Exhilaration and the Lows of Social Anxiety

Of the 100 billion people who have ever lived, Usain Bolt may be the fastest. On a Saturday evening during the 2008 Beijing Summer Olympics, the Jamaican sprinter demolished the hundred-metre world record—the pinnacle of athletic achievement. Bolt's performance was devastating. In a post-race interview, American eighth-place finisher Darvis Patton drew a line between Bolt and the rest of the field. "It's not even close," Patton said. "It's everybody catching up with Usain Bolt. He's a legend in his own right. The guy's a phenomenal athlete. He's a freak of nature." Underscoring his dominance, Bolt slowed to celebrate his victory twenty metres from the finish line, and discovered that one of his shoelaces happened to be untied. A team of Norwegian astrophysicists, lamenting

Bolt's decision to decelerate before the end of the race, calculated that his time of 9.69 seconds might have been lowered to 9.51 seconds had he continued running apace. This revised time challenges the belief held by several prominent scientists that humans will one day run a theoretical minimum time of 9.48 seconds—but probably not before the year 2500.

Some athletes inhabit a Zen-like state before they run, but Bolt lives to run in front of "audiences who love" him. While his competitors gaze myopically at the finish line, Bolt dances playfully before each big race. Bolt's tendency to warm to crowds may be one reason why he runs so fast at big events.

Perhaps the first experiment ever conducted in the field of social psychology suggests that humans are often faster and stronger when they test their speed and strength in the company of other people, rather than alone.

That study, conducted at Indiana University in the late 1890s, was the brainchild of Norman Triplett, a cycling enthusiast and a sports aficionado. In dozens of experiments he pushed cyclists to ride as fast as they could on stationary bikes, occasionally leaving them alone in the lab and free from distraction, at other times pacing them against a motor-driven cycle, and sometimes asking them to ride in the presence of other cyclists. Across his observations, Triplett noticed that the cyclists tended to ride faster when other cyclists rode nearby. One cyclist rode a mile in 2 minutes 49 seconds when alone, but managed to ride the same mile in 2 minutes 37 seconds in the company of four pacing cyclists; similarly, he rode ten miles in 33 minutes 17 seconds while riding alone, but rode the same distance two minutes faster when riding with several pacers. Triplett acknowledged that his observations were far from rigorous, so he conducted an experiment to show that the effect persisted in a tightly controlled lab study.

Triplett recruited forty children, ages eight to thirteen, to complete his study in 1897. He measured how quickly the students could wind a fishing reel so that a small flag attached to the line travelled a distance of sixteen metres. The task was simple but novel, and none of the children had played with fishing rods before the experiment. They performed the task both alone and in the presence of other children, and Triplett noticed that they wound the reels faster in the presence of others. He concluded that an audience enables people to "liberate latent energy" not normally available when they perform alone. Peering 110 years into the future, Triplett might have attributed Usain Bolt's remarkable performance to a combination of natural talent and—a critical special ingredient—the presence of a supportive, energy-liberating crowd.

Science doesn't always tell simple stories, and other researchers challenged Triplett's groundbreaking results well into the twentieth century. While some researchers replicated Triplett's effect—now known as the *social facilitation* effect—others found the opposite effect, known as *social inhibition*. Joseph Pessin and Richard Husband asked participants in their study to learn a simple maze either blindfold and alone or blindfold in the presence of other people. The blindfold participants traced their fingers along the maze, and reversed each time they encountered one of ten dead ends. Instead of performing better in front of an audience, Pessin and Husband's participants completed the maze more quickly when they were alone.

Inconsistencies such as these persisted for years, until social psychologist Bob Zajonc (pronounced like *science* with a leading *z*) proposed a solution: it all depends on the nature of the task. Audiences accentuate our instinctive responses and make it more difficult to override those responses in favour of more carefully considered alternatives. For Usain Bolt, there's nothing more natural than running, and the children in Triplett's experiment devoted little thought and attention to the frantic winding of the experimental fishing reel. In contrast, learning a maze is difficult, and it requires concentration. Pessin and Husband's maze learners were probably distracted by the knowledge that they were being watched, and feared making a mistake in front of an audience.

Zajonc avoided experimenting with humans at first, choosing to observe the behaviour of seventy-two cockroaches instead. With a small team of researchers, he devised two minor athletic tasks that required the cockroaches to scuttle from a brightly lit area in a small box to a more appealing darker compartment. Some of the cockroaches completed a simpler task, in which they ran along a straight runway from the glare of the box to the darkened goal compartment. The remaining cockroaches completed a more difficult task, traversing a more complex maze before they could escape the light. Some of the cockroaches completed these tasks alone, but the researchers also built a small audience box to force some of the athletic cockroaches to compete in front of an audience of roach spectators. Just as the researchers predicted, the cockroaches were much quicker to cover the straight runway when watched by an audience, reaching the darkened goal compartment an average of twenty-three seconds more quickly when they were performing before a crowd. But the cockroach athletes responded very differently to an audience when they were faced with the complex maze, reaching the goal seventy-six seconds more quickly when they were alone. The same audience that pushed the cockroaches to perform the simpler task more quickly also delayed them when the task was more complex.

In the early 1980s, social psychologists found evidence for Zajonc's theory in humans when they watched the behaviour of competent and novice pool players. Strong players, who sank 70 percent of their shots while playing alone, made 80 percent of their shots in the presence of four onlookers. Meanwhile, weaker players who made only 36 percent of their shots alone, sank a lowly 25 percent when observed. The stronger players were energized by the presence of onlookers, but the same audience distracted the already overloaded weaker players. As writers and school students will similarly testify, there's nothing more disconcerting than having a reader or a teacher gazing over your shoulder as you try to simplify a clunky sentence or complete a tricky maths problem.

More Competitors Breed
Less Competition

All audiences aren't created equal, and Zajonc and Triplett were almost always interested in passive audiences—those made up of observers who had no real stake in the performers' success or failure. The cockroaches in Zajonc's maze and the cyclists who trained together were never competing directly with the performer, never willing his loss at the expense of their win. But many observers are also competitors, observing precisely because they're taking part in the same competition. When Usain Bolt crouches before a race, he's also observed by seven other athletes who occupy the lanes to his left and right. Does it matter whether Bolt pays attention to all seven competitors, or perhaps just his strongest rival? Would he perform differently in a head-to-head two-man race, as star athletes Michael Johnson and Donovan Bailey did when Bailey beat Johnson for the title of "world's fastest man" in 1997? Should football managers motivate their players by reminding them of the entire league of teams, or should they focus instead on one team at a time? Are students better off completing standardized tests in a small hall, with only a handful of other students, or will they perform better surrounded by hundreds of fellow test-takers? These are important questions for all sorts of people, from athletes to students.

We don't have answers to all of these questions yet, but psychologists have examined the relationship between SAT scores and the number of test-takers in each venue. For each US state, they calculated the number of students who were taking the SAT in 2005, and divided that figure by the number of test-taking venues in the state. The outcome of that simple equation represented the average number of test-takers in each venue. After crunching the numbers, the researchers found that the students in states with more test-takers per venue tended to perform more poorly. In other words, the students scored better on the SAT when they were surrounded by fewer competitors. Of course, states differ in lots of ways, so it's possible that the higher-density states were poorer and had fewer venues, or that the students were merely more distracted while taking the test. To address these concerns, the psychologists ran other studies where students completed tests alone, but believed they were competing against a large pool or a small pool of fellow students. In one experiment, students completed a quiz in twenty-eight seconds when they believed that they were competing against ten other students, but completed the same quiz in thirty-three seconds when they believed they were competing against a larger pool of a hundred students.

This result might seem surprising. Shouldn't people respond to *more* competition by putting in *more* effort? That simple relationship seems compelling, but when people are overwhelmed, their motivation wanes and sometimes they disengage completely. It's easy to focus your energy on the opponent across the tennis net or the team at the opposite end of the field, but it's much more difficult to focus on the entire population of competitors in the tournament or league all at once. We derive a lot of our competitive spirit from these sorts of mental comparisons, weighing our own performance against the performance of others, and we're more likely to commit to the task when those social comparisons are vivid, rich, and motivating. Indeed, a similar process explains why people donate more money to charity when they focus on just one child in need, rather than the overwhelming need of millions of starving children: it's much easier and more rewarding to commit mental and emotional energy to an easily imagined limited cause than it is to commit energy to a cause that's so vast that your efforts are unlikely to put a dent in the edifice of need.

It's tempting to think of people as lazy, expedient, and exploitative when they appear to slacken in the presence of competitors and team members. In truth, though, people are seldom aware of these effects, many of which only begin to make sense when you examine them through the nuanced lens of human psychology. One of the most puzzling behavioural patterns is the tendency for a crowd of people to ignore an emergency that, as isolated individuals, they would address with urgency. Journalists lament the decline of humanity each time this happens, but a small group of insightful psychologists have offered another, more compelling interpretation.

Too Many Cooks Ignore the Broth

The tragedy unfolded in 2011, just before sunrise on a mid-April morning in Queens, New York. A man and a woman who apparently knew each other fought with increasing venom, and a homeless Guatemalan man named Hugo Alfredo Tale-Yax intervened to help the struggling woman. Her male companion turned on Tale-Yax and stabbed him several times in the torso. For ninety minutes, Tale-Yax lay in a growing pool of his own blood as dozens of passers-by ignored him, took photos, or stared briefly before continuing on their way. By the time firefighters arrived to help, the sun had risen and Tale-Yax had died.

Tale-Yax's death inspires a predictable stream of responses, beginning with contempt for human nature and ending with questions about how and when humans lost their humanity. Were we better citizens fifty years ago? Or ten years ago? Does New York attract particularly callous residents, or are good people turned vile after spending too long in the city?

Some of the answers are disturbingly clear. Bystander non-intervention is not merely a product of postmillennial depravity, and similar incidents have been reported as far back as the 1960s. One incident that attracted widespread media attention (and the attention of a couple of talented social psychologists) was the stabbing to death of Kitty Genovese, also a Queens resident, in 1964. The details of the attack remain contentious, but the basic facts are distressing. As Genovese arrived home from work at 3.15 a.m., an assailant stabbed her in full view of at least a dozen apartment residents. None of the residents called the police during the attack, which lasted half an hour, and Genovese ultimately died in the ambulance on her way to Accident & Emergency. The passers-by who ignored Tale-Yax behaved just as their counterparts had half a century ago.

The effect may not be new, but that doesn't explain why our moral compasses seem to be broken. There are at least two explanations for bystander apathy: either there's something wrong with our moral wiring, or our moral wiring is fine and there's something special about these situations that causes us not to respond. Both of those explanations appeal to experts. According to psychologist Michael Bradley, interviewed in an ABC news story, there is indeed something wrong with our moral wiring: "We have this kind of 24/7 pounding of violence. We now know that that pounding of violence actually causes brain changes where people start not to distinguish between real violence and cyberviolence. We're actually rewiring our brains not to react to violence and pain the way we should." Simply put, it takes a lot for us to respond to violence, because what used to warrant a response no longer registers on our violence-detecting radar. Violent video games, films, and TV shows have dampened our sensitivity to real-life violence, so public stabbings don't register as strongly as they used to.

That explanation sounds plausible, but it doesn't explain why bystander apathy predates the rise of violent media or why, as researchers have shown, bystanders aren't equally apathetic across different situations. If bystanders are apathetic only sometimes, it seems less likely that our wiring is faulty than that certain situations lessen our tendency to intervene.

The first proponents of the situational explanation were social psychologists John Darley and Bibb Latané. Darley and Latané observed the media storm that followed the Genovese murder, and were convinced that commentators and the media were oversimplifying the story. Instead of blaming New York City or the inherent heartlessness of New Yorkers, Darley and Latané set out to determine whether specific features of the situation might have dissuaded the onlookers from intervening. Their key insight was that the very feature that made the situation so shocking—that there were *so many* observers and not one of them intervened—ironically explained why the observers were so apathetic in the first place.

To understand their insight, imagine this situation: you and a stranger are stranded on a desert island. Apart from the two of you, there isn't another soul for miles. All of a sudden, the stranger collapses to the sand and lies motionless. How strongly do you feel the need to intervene? If you're like most people, your drive to help the collapsed stranger is overwhelming. It's very difficult to imagine carrying on with your day while your fellow castaway lies unconscious nearby. Now imagine a slightly different situation: this time, there are ten of you on the same island. You're all strangers, and none of you is trained as a doctor. Again, one of the other castaways collapses to the sand. How strong is your desire to help? Surely, if you don't help, one of the other castaways will intervene? And what if there were a hundred people on the island? Is your desire to help even weaker? As Darley and Latané observed, the responsibility to help is compelling when you're the only potential source of help, but that same sense of personal responsibility is much weaker when it's divided among several potential helpers.

In the late 1960s, Darley and Latané conducted a series of experiments that demonstrated this diffusion-of-responsibility principle. In one experiment, New York University students visited the psychology lab to discuss the difficulties of college life with other students. The experimenter explained that the discussion would take place over an intercom system, rather than in person, a decision apparently designed to preserve the students' anonymity, encourage them to share their views honestly, and shield them from embarrassment. Students could only speak one at a time, as the microphone system shut down as soon as someone else was speaking. Darley and Latané varied the size of the discussion groups, so that some of the students spoke to just one fellow student, others to two others, and others still to a larger group of five. Apart from the naive

New York University students, the other students on the intercom were
fully briefed on the experiment's aims, and how it would proceed. The
discussions were uneventful as the students shared their initial views.
But then, during the second round of comments, one student began to
speak loudly and incoherently as if he were suffering a seizure. In fact,
Darley and Latané had paid him to read from the following script over
a period of two minutes:

> I-er-um-I think I-I need-er-if-if could-er-er-somebody er-er-er-er-er-
> er-er give me a little-er-give me a little help here because-er-I-er-I'm-
> er-erh-h-having a-a-a real problem-er-right now and I-er-if somebody
> could help me out it would-it would-er-er s-s-sure be-sure be good . . .
> because -er-there-er-er-a cause I-er-I-uh-I've got a-a one of the-er-sei
> er-er-things coming on and-and-and I could really-er-use some help
> so if somebody would-er-give me a little h-help-uh-er-er-er-er-er
> c-could somebody-er-er-help-er-uh-uh-uh [choking sounds] . . . I'm
> gonna die-er-er-I'm . . . gonna die-er-help-er-er-seizure-er-[chokes,
> then quiet].

The naive students listened in stunned silence as the fit continued,
forced to decide whether to fetch help. As Darley and Latané expected,
their responses differed dramatically depending on whether they believed other students were available to help. When they were engaged in
a one-on-one discussion with the struggling student, 85 percent of them
helped before the seizure ended, waiting for an average of 52 seconds
after he first indicated signs of difficulty. In contrast, when they believed
another student was listening to the unfolding seizure, only 62 percent of
them helped before the seizure ended, waiting on average for a full 93
seconds. Worse still, and more consistent with the number of bystanders
who ignored the Kitty Genovese and Hugo Tale-Yax tragedies, only 31
percent of the students helped before the seizure ended when four others
were available to help, now waiting for an average of 166 seconds—

nearly three minutes. By this time, the seizing student had grown silent after struggling to shout the words "I'm gonna die". The students certainly took the seizure seriously—many of them yelled, "My God, he's having a fit!" as soon as it began—but they were far less likely to help when the presence of other potential helpers diffused their sense of responsibility first.

In contrast to the seizure in this experiment, some emergencies are ambiguous. Was Hugo Tale-Yax just another homeless man sleeping awkwardly, or was he in trouble? Surely, it didn't help that each new bystander on the scene watched as countless others passed by without stopping to investigate. In a second experiment, Darley and Latané wanted to show that people interpret the inaction of others as a sign that there's no emergency at all. Students sat in a waiting room and completed a questionnaire before they were due to participate in an experiment in another part of the building. Sometimes the students sat alone in the waiting room and sometimes they sat with several others. After a few minutes, the experimenters turned on a smoke machine in an adjacent room, and smoke began to filter through a vent into the room where the students waited for the next phase of the experiment to begin. The waiting room slowly filled with smoke, and the students were compelled to notice that an unexplained source in the next room was producing smoke.

When the students sat in the room alone, they were quick to alert the experimenter to the thickening pall of smoke. But when they sat with other students, they glanced around nervously at one another and often failed to respond at all. You can imagine the scene: four students putting on a front of serene detachment as the room becomes so thickly filled with smoke that they can hardly see the questionnaires on their laps. Darley and Latané explained that the students weren't sure whether the situation was an emergency at all. It's a classic stalemate: no one wants to cry "emergency" when there's no emergency at all, so everyone continues to sit by coolly as the room fills with smoke.

Although it's useful to understand how people respond to a generic audience—or to bystanders, as in the case of Darley and Latané's work—that's only half the story. The second half rests on knowing more about the audience members: how they look, whether they're male or female, and whether they're loved ones or strangers. How do men respond to the presence of beautiful women? Why is it that people are able to withstand more pain when they're looking at pictures of loved ones? Why are well-intentioned police officers still more likely to mistake a mobile phone for a gun when it's cradled in the hand of an innocent black man rather than an innocent white man? Without knowing more about the people in our midst, it's difficult to say just how they'll affect our thoughts, feelings, and behaviours.

In the middle of the twentieth century, a young American psychologist named Abraham Maslow connected the dots between the people in his life and their effects on his behaviour. He noticed that different people activated different needs, and so was born Maslow's famous hierarchy of needs. But Maslow's insights had begun to form many years earlier as he endured the hardships of growing up young, poor, and Jewish in 1920s Brooklyn.

5.

THE CHARACTERISTICS OF OTHER PEOPLE

The Social Motives

rooklyn wasn't an easy place for Jews at the turn of the twentieth century. When young Abraham Maslow wasn't avoiding gangs on his way to school, he was in conflict with anti-Semitic teachers in the classroom. Life wasn't much better at home, where Maslow struggled to get on with his mother. Years later, he described her as narcissistic, prejudiced, friendless, incapable of love, and slovenly—a cocktail of deficiencies that loomed large in years to come because they had plagued his childhood. Despite these hardships, Maslow was an optimist, and like many first-generation European Jewish immigrants, from economist Milton Friedman to virologist Jonas Salk, he believed in the liberating power of education. Maslow didn't have many friends, so he spent most of his time indoors, reading and gradually developing an interest in the relatively young discipline of human psychology. Many of his contemporaries were fixated on rats in mazes, but Maslow soon found their research trivial, and instead he decided to explore the complexities that made humans different from other animals.

Maslow's greatest achievement came in 1943, when he published an opus titled *A Theory of Human Motivation*, a catalogue that drew heavily on his difficult childhood in describing the goals and motives that make humans tick. Maslow claimed that once humans were assured of air, food, water, and sexual reproduction—the most basic physiological needs—they would seek safety from harm, just as his parents had done when they fled czarist persecution a few years before his birth. After safety, they would seek friendship, family, and love—the social comforts that had eluded Maslow as a child. When those basic needs were met, they would turn their attention to gaining respect and achieving success at work, before finally embarking on the final motive: self-actualization. Maslow had always believed that education would free him from the shackles that confined most people to ploddingly mundane lives. With admiration, he watched as people like Albert Einstein achieved moral clarity and followed their creative and intellectual passions, presumably having satisfied their more basic lower-order needs.

While, seventy years later, psychologists continue to debate the structure of Maslow's hierarchy, few disagree that his motives guide a diverse array of human actions. During that seventy-year period, thousands of researchers have found their own creative and intellectual passions in trying to understand how we satisfy those motives. They've learned that while most animals rely on limited social interaction to achieve their goals, humans sometimes consciously and often unwittingly exploit social connections to satisfy their own motives. The story begins with the most basic goal—genetic survival through sexual reproduction—and the tendency for male chess players to adopt far riskier tactics when playing against beautiful women.

The Sexual Motive: Chess-playing Beauties, Recklessness, and Lap Dances

Chess isn't in the canon of sexy sports, but fast-living French grand-master Vladislav Tkachiev tried to campaign for its inclusion when he and his brother Evgeny founded the World Chess Beauty Contest in 2005. The brothers invited female chess stars from around the world to submit their most alluring photographs so that a selection of male players who made up the Arbiters' Board could anoint a queen. The photos flooded in. Russia's Alexandra Kosteniuk, an international favourite, gazed coquettishly from behind a loaded chessboard. Laoura Hachatrian wore so little clothing that her concerned boyfriend insisted on censoring the bottom half of the original shot. Natalia Pogonina, a Liv Tyler lookalike, stood behind her guitar and pouted. The sport's adherents also include Carmen Kass, a bona fide supermodel and former president of the Estonian National Chess League. Kass had been the face of Christian Dior's J'Adore perfume, and also ran unsuccessfully for a position in the European Parliament.

The physical presence of a competitor shouldn't matter much in the cerebral domain of chess, but it has an enormous impact on performance. Experts will tell you that playing against a computer is very different from playing against a human opponent who makes identical moves. Even Vladislav Tkachiev blanched when he faced legend Garry Kasparov, who "looked a metre taller" than Tkachiev, though they were the same height. And what happens when men play against the sirens of chess—the Carmen Kasses and Alexandra Kosteniuks? Chess players are extreme rationalists, but that doesn't mean their genes aren't constantly geared towards fulfilling Maslow's lowest-order motive: genetic survival through sexual reproduction. The males of some species fight to the death in search of potential mates, but male chess players approach a similar goal with greater subtlety.

Like all heterosexual men, male chess players who are exposed to beautiful women produce more testosterone, which sets off a cascade of biological responses that encourage them to pursue Maslow's sexual motive. One of those responses is the tendency to take risks in an attempt to impress attractive members of the opposite sex, which shows that the male has sufficient resources to gamble some of them on a risky bet. A group of European economists wondered, then, whether male chess players—normally conservative and patient during important matches— might adopt riskier strategies when facing attractive female opponents.

The researchers collected data from hundreds of chess games to examine what happens when male competitors face beautiful female opponents during tournament play. The competitors in the sample were accomplished chess players between the ages of twenty-five and thirty-four who played actively between 1997 and 2007. A group of adults rated the attractiveness of each player based on an official head shot, while the researchers devised two measures of riskiness during a match: preference for a risk-averse draw, and the riskiness of each player's opening gambit. Draws are risk-averse, because two accomplished chess players are capable of directing the game to a draw with little risk of losing and very little hope of winning the match. Some opening moves are also riskier than others. Statistics show that players who adopt the risky Morra gambit, which requires sacrificing some pieces and exposing others early in the game, draw only 20 percent but lose 45 percent of the resulting games; in contrast, those who choose the safer Alapin gambit, protecting their valuable pieces with weaker pawns, draw 35 percent and lose only 33 percent of those games. The researchers found that male competitors adopted riskier opening gambits and assiduously avoided draws when they were seated across from attractive female opponents. Unfortunately for these bamboozled men, risky play comes at a cost, and they tended to lose many more games than their clearer-headed counterparts.

What is it about pretty women that distracts male chess grandmasters (and men more generally) from the job at hand? The answer to that question comes from an ingenious study conducted at a skateboarding park thousands of miles away in Brisbane, Australia. The inspiration for this research comes from a simple but staggering statistic: men are more than three and a half times more likely to die from all accidental causes than are women. Evolutionary psychologists believe that, just as male lions and elephants risk their lives in dominance contests, men are more likely to die accidentally because they take greater risks to impress women. According to the theory of evolution, our male ancestors competed for the affections of our female ancestors, and the successful among them mated and raised offspring. In other words, the roughly three billion men who populate the planet today are the lucky offspring of generations of males who procreated in part because they rose above the herd of their weaker, poorer, more apprehensive counterparts. So the two social psychologists reasoned that men should be especially likely to take risks in the presence of an attractive woman—precisely the effect that the European economists found among male chess experts.

Instead of investigating the behaviour of chess experts, the psychologists trained their attention on male skateboarders. They approached almost a hundred skateboarders at a park in Brisbane, and asked them to perform a series of easy and difficult tricks. Difficult tricks carry some risk of injury, so although they're more rewarding when completed, they're also more dangerous. Skateboarders often minimize these risks by aborting tricks before they're completed rather than exposing themselves to physical harm. At first, the men performed the tricks in front of a male experimenter, but later some of them repeated the tricks in front of an attractive eighteen-year-old female experimenter. Regardless of the experimenter's gender, they completed most of the easy tricks with aplomb, rarely failing or aborting those tricks. But the story was very different when they attempted the difficult tricks. Although the skateboarders completed the more difficult tricks successfully in front of the attractive female experimenter, her presence nudged them to fail many more and abort far fewer tricks. In the presence of an attractive female, men were more willing to take risks and less willing to abandon a trick that approached failure. Immediately after the skateboarders completed their tricks, the experimenter collected and analysed their saliva—a popular method of measuring testosterone levels. As expected, the men who performed in front of an attractive female had significantly higher testosterone levels, and the higher those testosterone levels, the more likely the men were to follow through with poorly executed tricks. According to the logic of mating behaviour, the attractive female experimenter activated the hapless skateboarders' mating instincts, leading them to produce testosterone, which in turn undermined their willingness to abort tricks that were doomed to fail. Of course, those same men also completed more difficult tricks successfully, which suggests that minor mishaps are sometimes a fair price to pay for ultimately impressing an audience of attractive females.

The men in these experiments were obviously influenced by feminine beauty, but how do we know that they were motivated by sexual desire rather than merely succumbing to distraction? In late 2006, three psychologists tackled that question when they interviewed eighteen topless dancers who worked at an Albuquerque gentlemen's club. The paper began by describing the economics of lap dancing, the atmosphere inside the club, and the club's typical patrons because, as the authors recognized, "academics may be unfamiliar with the gentlemen's club subculture". Lap dancers in the US earn most of their income from tips that generally range between $10 and $20, but male patrons have plenty of leeway. Some tip as little as $1, while others surrender wads of $20 notes. Patrons also give larger tips when they're more attracted to the dancers—an evolutionary throwback in which the man tries to impress the woman by flaunting his resources. In an evolutionary sense, this ostentatious behaviour is wasted if the man seduces a woman who can't become pregnant, but not all women can bear children, and even fertile women are capable of conceiving for only six or seven days each month.

Since spending their resources is costly, men are more likely to succeed in the mating game if they spend on women who are capable of conceiving. So if the men were subconsciously reserving generous tips for fertile women—those who could at least theoretically satisfy Maslow's sexual motive—the researchers expected the dancers' tips to rise as they approached the fertile oestrus phase, and to fall during the non-fertile menstrual and luteal phases. Meanwhile, those who were taking the contraceptive pill were likely to attract smaller tips without the same day-to-day cyclical variance that affected those who weren't taking hormonal contraceptives. When the women reported their day-to-day earnings at the end of the sixty-day experiment, the results were striking. For each five-hour shift, women who were not taking the pill earned an average of $335 during the fertile oestrus phase, $260 during the infertile luteal phase, and only $185 when they were menstruating. According to the researchers, the men were picking up on subtle, "leaked cues" when the women were fertile. As you might expect, then, these dramatic variations were absent among women who were taking the pill, and they rarely earned more than a relatively modest baseline of roughly $250 per shift. These results suggest that men are more ostentatious and willing to part with their resources in the company of women who are biologically capable of satisfying Maslow's survival mating motive.

Having addressed their basic survival needs, Maslow believed, people turn to the second tier in his motivation hierarchy: safety. Shelter and security seem like basic inalienable human rights, but the human drive for safety comes with dark costs. We're a generous species, capable of great acts of kindness and sensitivity, but we're also a fearful species prone to acts of prejudice and discrimination. In theory, the United States grants the vote and equal rights to ethnic and racial minorities, but minorities are still haunted by the relics of its xenophobic past.

The Safety Motive: a Partial Explanation for Racism?

In 1964, Dr Martin Luther King granted an interview to the BBC's Bob McKenzie on his way to collect the Nobel Peace Prize in Oslo. During the interview, McKenzie asked King a controversial question that drew an optimistic response:

> Bob McKenzie: Robert Kennedy, when he was Attorney General, said that he could imagine the possibility of a Negro President of the United States within perhaps 40 years. Do you think this is at all realistic?

> Dr King: . . . I am optimistic about the future. Frankly, I have seen certain changes in the United States over the past two years that surprise me. I've seen levels of compliance with the Civil Rights Bill and changes that have been most surprising. So, on the basis of this, I think we may be able to get a Negro President in less than 40 years. I would think this would come in 25 years or less.

Forty-five years later, Barack Obama became the first black president of the United States and collected his own Nobel Peace Prize. King's prediction wasn't too far off, though Bobby Kennedy was closer to the mark. Obama's presidency heralded a new age in the United States, but a small band of jubilant social commentators went too far when they claimed that the nation was now "post-racial". In truth, xenophobia—the fear of difference—is a deeply ingrained component of being human, and racial prejudice persists in part because people see difference as a barrier to personal safety.

One of the classic demonstrations of ingrained xenophobia comes from a series of studies conducted by social psychologist Bob Zajonc in the late 1960s, a year before he published the social facilitation studies I described in chapter 4. Zajonc began by showing the photos of twelve strangers who were graduating from a nearby university to students at the University of Michigan. During the first phase of the experiment, each student saw some of the photos twenty-five times, some of them five or ten times, some of them only once or twice, and some not at all. Later, when asked how much they liked the men depicted in the photos, the students had a strong preference for the men they had seen more frequently. In fact, they rated the men they had seen twenty-five times as 30 percent more likeable than the men they had seen only once, which shows that familiarity signals safety, which in turn overcomes our innate human tendency toward xenophobia.

Though the fear of difference is deeply ingrained, the nature of discrimination has changed. Today it's far more subtle than it was in Martin Luther King's 1960s, when clear lines distinguished opulent white buses, schools, and restaurants from allegedly inferior black buses, schools, and restaurants.

Take the critical question of whether black males still experience discrimination at the hands of the US justice system. In a series of elegant experiments, social psychologists have shown that black criminal defendants are at a disadvantage even in the absence of overt discrimination. In one experiment, white undergraduate students were exposed to pictures of either fifty black or fifty white male faces, each for a tiny fraction of a second. The pictures were flashed on the screen so quickly that none of the participants knew they had seen faces, let alone whether the faces belonged to black or white males. Still, this process, known as subliminal priming, has remarkable effects on how people think. Even when they're unable to identify the content of the images, those images rest quietly just below the level of conscious awareness, shaping their subsequent thoughts, behaviours, and feelings. In this case, after the students saw the black or white faces, they were asked to identify a series of objects. Some of those objects were crime-related (e.g., guns), whereas others were unrelated to crime. Each object was displayed first as a noisy, scrambled image, similar to the snowy black-and-white images on a TV with poor reception. As the figure shows, below, those degraded images became progressively clearer with each frame, so that they were eventually identifiable. The students were able to identify the crime-related objects after only nineteen frames when they were primed with the black faces, whereas they took more than twenty-six frames to identify those same objects when primed with white faces. (The primes had no effect when the students tried to identify the objects that weren't related to crime—they took roughly twenty-three frames regardless of whether they were primed with black or white faces.) This result tells us that exposing people to black male faces—even briefly and without their awareness—readies them to perceive crime in the world at large.

FRAME 1   FRAME 20   FRAME 41

A degraded picture of a gun from an experiment on race and object detection.
The image becomes progressively clearer with each frame.

This result is disturbing, because it suggests that people harbour strong mental links between black males and crime—but it doesn't directly answer the question of whether this association actually disadvantages black males in the real world. To answer that question, the same researchers turned to a database of death-penalty cases tried in Philadelphia between 1979 and 1999. In a provocative paper entitled "Looking deathworthy", they showed that when the victim was white, black men who looked stereotypically black were dramatically more likely to receive a death sentence than were black men who looked less stereotypically black. Whereas stereotypically black men tended to receive a death sentence in 58 percent of all cases, black men who did not look stereotypically black received a death sentence in only 24 percent of all cases. These results held even when the researchers carefully removed the effects of other variables that may have inflated the difference, like the defendants' and victims' socio-economic status.

This striking result suggests that our quest for safety, and our resulting fear of difference, has fostered a justice system that discriminates against black defendants. Put simply, under some circumstances a black man who looks "more black" is 33 percent more likely to receive the death penalty than is a black man who commits the same crime but looks less stereotypically black. Inequalities like these illuminate the sad truth that our hidden, unconscious attitudes towards minorities evolve far more slowly than our overt spoken attitudes. Many of those ugly views are so well hidden that we're not even aware that we hold them.

In the early 2000s, when social psychologists asked college students whether they knew of the stereotype that "black people are like apes", only 9 percent of them claimed to know of the stereotype. The researchers weren't content to rest on spoken responses alone, so they ran a series of studies that revealed a more sinister truth: regardless of whether or not the students were consciously aware of the stereotype, their decisions were clearly swayed by the association between black people and apes. In one study, students who were subliminally primed with images of apes were more likely to focus on black faces than on white faces later in the experiment. They were also more likely to perceive the police beating of a black man who resisted arrest as more justifiable than did other students who were not exposed to images of apes, or who made similar judgements about the beating of a white man. The briefest flash of an image of apes was enough to shift people's attention towards black faces—clear evidence that they associate the two concepts—and, more distressing still, to weaken their reactions to the police beating of a black victim. In the world at large, this last result is especially troubling, because people are less likely to treat others with respect if they harbour hidden associations between those people and animals. In a final study to hammer home that very point, the researchers found that newspaper articles had referred to black defendants in death-penalty cases using ape-related words (*ape*, *monkey*, and *gorilla*) four times as often as they did when referring to white death-penalty defendants. When the researchers looked deeper, they also found that the black defendants who were ultimately sentenced to death attracted twice as many ape-related descriptions as did the black defendants who were spared the death sentence. Unfortunately, we're largely incapable of eliminating these hidden prejudices from our judgements. The United States has come a long way in the past century—not least in twice democratically electing Barack Obama to the highest seat in the land—but associations between black people, crime, and animalism still persist.

Of course, racial xenophobia extends beyond the borders of the United States, and beyond attitudes towards black people. During the month of July 2005, London was under siege. On 7 July, fifty-two people were killed during a series of coordinated suicide attacks, and two weeks later, on 21 July, another four would-be terrorists failed to detonate bombs designed to kill dozens more. The four men of "Middle Eastern appearance" managed to escape, and London's Metropolitan Police Service responded by launching its largest-ever manhunt operation. The day after the manhunt began, a series of tragic events culminated in the murder of a man who was mistaken for one of the attempted bombers. These events were difficult to comprehend without an understanding of how prejudice clouds our capacity to perceive the world as it really is.

On the morning of 22 July, police followed a man as he left his home. According to later reports, he was wearing a suspiciously thick jacket given the mild weather, and he appeared to live in a building associated with the bombers. As time passed, a growing squad of police officers joined the pursuit, and when the man left a bus and ran towards an Underground train station, they were convinced they had only one choice. Witnesses described seeing several officers following the man onto the train, cornering him, pushing him to the ground, and finally firing seven shots into his head at point-blank range.

The victim was Jean Charles de Menezes, a twenty-seven-year-old Brazilian electrician who was described by his friends and family as a gentle family man. Menezes was not Middle Eastern and did not have the "Mongolian eyes" his pursuers described. Surveillance footage showed that he was not wearing a suspiciously thick puffy jacket after all, but rather a thin denim jacket that seemed appropriate given the mild morning weather. Witnesses disagreed about whether he ran towards the train, but public-transport users routinely run towards trains. These ambiguities, innocuous in isolation, were enough to convince police that they were pursuing a man who was seconds away from detonating a hidden bomb. Police officials opened several inquiries, but none of the officers faced disciplinary action, and a coroner's inquest ultimately ruled that the death was suspicious but not unlawful.

As the word suggests, prejudices prepare us for interactions that we're yet to have, and we rely on them because we believe that people who are different from us are more likely to threaten our safety. Of course, they're often misleading and mistaken, and those mistakes sometimes produce tragic consequences. As the death of Jean Charles de Menezes illustrates, preconceived notions sometimes prepare us for precisely the wrong kinds of snap judgements. When faced with ambiguity—whether a surprisingly thick jacket conceals a bomb, or why a person is running towards a departing train—our prejudices tend to break the tie, resolving the scene before us so that it confirms those pre-existing beliefs.

Sometimes life imitates research, which is precisely what happened several years before the Menezes tragedy. Social psychologists at the Universities of Colorado and Chicago devised an engaging computer game to illustrate the difficulties that police face when deciding whether or not to shoot a potential assailant. In a series of photos, male youths posed holding either weapons or innocuous items such as wallets and mobile phones. Students and adults sat in front of the computer, and their job was to decide whether or not to shoot the series of youths on the screen. The "winners", who quickly shot the assailants and just as quickly allowed the innocents to go unharmed, received cash prizes, so players were motivated to take the experiment seriously.

The researchers added an important tweak to the game: some of the males in the pictures were black and some of them were white. The game was difficult, and players struggled to decide whether to shoot or withhold fire. But as the researchers expected, the game was especially difficult when it contradicted the players' pre-existing prejudices. All too often, mirroring the Menezes case, players tended to shoot the innocent black males who were holding wallets and cell phones and to allow the armed white males to go free. They were also much slower to respond in these cases, as the obvious conflict between their prejudices and the image on the screen could only be resolved with great mental effort. Some years later, two psychologists in Sydney, Australia showed the same effect with men wearing Muslim headgear: students tended to shoot young men holding coffee cups and bottles more often when those men wore turbans than when they were bareheaded. Their post-11

Images from the University of Colorado shooter-detection computer game.

September 2001 prejudices prepared them to shoot even when the turbaned target was innocent.

Prejudice arises in part because people are innately averse to novelty and difference, both of which threaten our quest to fulfil Maslow's safety motive. Consequently, we form associations between groups and character traits, like friendliness, animalism, laziness, rudeness, ostentatious displays of wealth, aggressiveness, and dangerousness. Sometimes these associations keep us safe from novel threats, but often they're also hurtful, and they explain a diverse constellation of distressing behaviours, from biased death-penalty decisions to dangerously itchy trigger fingers.

The Power of Love(d Ones)

Moving beyond the often destructive human drive for safety, Maslow turned to the sunnier motives of love and friendship. Despite his turbulent childhood, he remained optimistic about the power of social connection. By the age of twenty he had married his first cousin, Bertha, and fifteen years later social affiliation occupied a central position in his hierarchy of motives. Maslow had a vague sense of love's ineffable power, but now, sixty years later, scientists believe they have a far deeper understanding of the biology that underpins the experience of love—so much so, in fact, that a New York company has begun to sell the power of love in the form of Liquid Trust.

According to its website credo, Vero Labs is a New York City-based company "dedicated to researching and developing innovative products that help foster and enhance human relationships". One of those products is a nasal spray known as Liquid Trust. Vero Labs' website suggests that the product enhances human relationships in three simple steps. First, users apply the Liquid Trust spray while they're getting dressed before important meetings or social events. Second, when people encounter the wearer, they unconsciously inhale Liquid Trust. And third, those people unwittingly develop a strong feeling of trust for the wearer.

Liquid Trust sounds like a creature of science fiction, but it's both real and at least theoretically capable of synthesizing trust between two people. The mechanism that explains how Liquid Trust encourages bonhomie is supposedly grounded in science, and its adherents are convinced that it works as advertised. It contains a single active ingredient, oxytocin, which is the same chemical that compels mothers to care for their newborn babies. Although oxytocin plays a prominent role in childbirth and breastfeeding, recent research suggests that it also encourages people to trust one another, and to suspend their evolved tendency to distrust strangers just long enough to enable them to build close relationships. The Vero Labs website includes testimonials from satisfied customers, like G, a part-time barman who claimed that his tips increased fivefold when he began using Liquid Trust.

There's good evidence now that oxytocin's effects are far from straightforward, but the hormone's power is hard to question. In one classic study, researchers sprayed either a small dose of oxytocin or an inactive placebo into the noses of male university students in Zurich. Both sprays were odourless, and the only difference between them was the presence of the hormone in the oxytocin spray. After the students inhaled one of the sprays, they played an economic game that measured how strongly they trusted a series of strangers. According to the rules of the game, the students were given a small sum of money, which they could keep or give to a stranger whom they had not met before the experiment began. Any money handed over to the stranger was tripled, and the stranger had the opportunity to reward the original student by sharing some or all of that newly multiplied money. Handing over the money was risky, though, because roguish strangers might keep it all for themselves, so the students were forced to trust the stranger if they were going to hand over their money. The students who inhaled oxytocin were more trusting, transferring 17 percent more money to the strangers than did the other group of students who inhaled the placebo spray. Merely inhaling a small quantity of oxytocin was enough to weaken the students' natural suspicions, encouraging them to trust strangers who might otherwise have triggered suspicion.

If a small dose of inhaled oxytocin promotes trust in strangers, you can imagine how oxytocin affects new mothers when it floods their brains in larger, naturally occurring doses. Breastfeeding mothers experience such dramatic reductions in stress that they barely release cortisol—a hormone that normally responds quickly to stress—when they're exposed to strong physical stressors. They also become calmer, more interactive, and less anxious than their usual selves, more willing both to protect and bond with their newborn babies.

Oxytocin and, by extension, Liquid Trust sound like panaceas designed to overcome the ills of a chronically distrustful modern world, but the hormone doesn't always promote the same warm responses. Most of the early research on oxytocin considered how people respond to their newborns and their lovers, so the hormone seemed universally to inspire love and affection. More recently, though, researchers have turned their attention to more distant social acquaintances, and the results are very different. Although oxytocin promotes positive responses towards ingroup members—people of the same race, ethnicity, nationality, or religion—it produces weaker or even negative responses towards people who inhabit social out-groups. In a recent experiment, social psychologists found that Dutch students were quicker to link positive words with Dutch names and negative words with German or Arab names when they inhaled a small dose of oxytocin. In other experiments, the students were given a classic philosophical dilemma: would they save five anonymous people who were stuck in a cave by detonating a bomb that would kill one person who was stuck in the cave's entrance? In some cases, the person blocking the exit had a typical Dutch name, like Maarten, and in others he had a typical Arab name (Mohammed) or German name (Markus). The students who inhaled the placebo were equally likely to

sacrifice the Maartens, Mohammeds, and Markuses, but those who inhaled oxytocin were less likely to sacrifice Maartens than they were to
sacrifice Mohammeds or Markuses. Oxytocin led them to value the life
of a fellow Dutchman above the life of an Arab or a German. Instead of
promoting indiscriminate affection, oxytocin engendered warmth towards in-group members but not towards out-group members.

Loved ones are the ultimate in-group members, especially capable of
fulfilling Maslow's affiliation motive, but sometimes they aren't around
to deliver a timely dose of oxytocin. The good news is that romantic
partners don't need to be physically present to act as psychological painkillers. As the old film trope goes, soldiers prize nothing more than photos of their loved ones when they go to war, and recent research suggests
that people are wise to gaze at these photos during difficult times.

In one experiment, a UCLA neuroscientist tested whether women
could withstand pain more effectively when they were looking at photos
of their long-term romantic partners. The experimenter applied a series
of "thermal stimulations"—painfully warm probes—to the forearms of
twenty-eight women who were in romantic relationships that were more
than six months old. During some of the probes, the women looked at
photos of their romantic partners; for others, they looked at photos of a
male who was a stranger but belonged to the same ethnic group and was
just as attractive as their partner; for others still they stared at objects, like
a chair, or at a small black shape on the computer screen. The probes
were always a bit painful, but they were rated as 5 percent less painful
when the women looked at photos of their partners. In fact, the photos
dulled the pain slightly more effectively than did actually holding their
partner's hand, which suggests that imagined social support sometimes
dulls painful experiences just as effectively as does real live social support.

Photos of loved ones are powerful painkillers because they activate
two critical regions in the brain. The first region, known as the ventro-
medial prefrontal cortex (VMPFC), sits just above the eyes at the front of
the brain. The VMPFC has attracted plenty of attention among neuro-

scientists recently, and their understanding of its function continues to grow. In the context of pain reduction, the VMPFC signals safety and the absence of risk—much like the hormone oxytocin—which to some extent overrides bodily experiences of pain. Although the physical experience at the probe site doesn't differ, the VMPFC dampens the sensation of pain by metaphorically whispering that everything is going to be fine. Meanwhile, pictures of loved ones also activate reward centres in the brain, which distract us from otherwise painful experiences. Activated together, the VMPFC and these reward centres diminish visceral pain by inducing security, conveying the absence of risk, and producing a generalized sense of well-being.

Maslow was right to emphasize the importance of love, affection, and friendship, not just because they're responsible for psychological well-being but also because they affect us on a deeper, biological level. Oxytocin engenders the sort of trust necessary to form social bonds between mothers and babies, and sometimes pushes wary adversaries to overcome an intractable détente. Meanwhile, merely seeing or thinking about loved ones activates brain regions that dull the sting of physical pain. Having discussed the importance of love and affection, Maslow turned to the upper echelons of his model: the motivation to feel morally virtuous, and to fulfil whatever defines our own personal potential.

The Top of Maslow's Hierarchy

> For children are innocent and love justice, while most of us
> are wicked and naturally prefer mercy.
>
> — G. K. Chesterton

Apart from Albert Einstein and a few esteemed acquaintances and colleagues, Maslow had a hard time identifying people who were self-actualized. He believed that it takes a lifetime to experience the sort of self-acceptance and moral clarity that defines self-actualization, so he might have been surprised by the results published in a paper sixty years later. While Maslow focused on middle age and maturity, the researchers who published the paper recognized that the innocence of childhood is among our purest symbols of moral clarity.

In some of the experiments, one group of participants wrote about a pleasant childhood memory in as much detail as they could muster. Some of the memories focused on playing with friends or learning to ride a bike, and in each case the memories evoked warm images of childhood. The remaining participants also invoked memories of the past but focused instead on pleasant memories from high school. The researchers reasoned that memories of high school are no more or less pleasant than fond memories of childhood, but they don't evoke the same sense of innocence that diminishes as we enter adolescence. Later in the experiment, the researchers asked the participants whether they wanted to donate a chunk of their pay for completing the experiment to a charity for Japanese earthquake survivors. Many of the participants were generous, but overall they donated far more to the charity when they had previously recalled childhood memories—40 percent of their pay, rather than just 24 percent when they had recalled memories of high school.

In other studies, people who remembered their childhood were more willing to help the experimenter with a task after the experiment officially ended, and they also became more critical of immoral behaviour in others—a sign that their own moral standards were elevated when they recalled the innocence of childhood.

The researchers also wanted to show that these differences were driven by thoughts of innocence and virtue, so they asked all the students to complete a series of word fragments. For example, they had to form the first words that came to mind when they saw the three fragments: P _ R _, M _ R _ _, and V _ R T _ _. Students who were focused on innocence, having been primed by childhood, should have been more likely to think of the words PURE, MORAL, and VIRTUE, rather than alternatives like PORE, MURKY, and VORTEX, and that's exactly what the researchers found. Those who focused on childhood memories completed 65 percent of the fragments with innocence-related words, whereas those who focused on high school completed only 42 percent of the fragments with innocence-related words. In other studies, the researchers showed that these effects persist among people who think back on childhood as a difficult period in their lives. It wasn't just the pleasantness of childhood, but rather the innocence, that gave them the sort of moral clarity that Maslow described when he imagined the state of self-actualization.

Childhood inspires moral clarity because it allows us to think back to a time before morality became complicated. As we mature, our moral decisions acquire the baggage of compromise and conflicting principles. Children know that stealing is wrong, so they won't absolve a sick pauper who steals medicine for his wife—but the decision is far more complicated for an adult. Popular culture might suggest that you look inward to decide what's truly right, and researchers have found that people are indeed more honest when they're forced to stare at their own mirror images. When you've behaved badly, your mirror image judges your moral bankruptcy. In Oscar Wilde's *Picture of Dorian Gray*, Dorian is a handsome man who remains youthful as he commits increasingly immoral acts. Meanwhile, a portrait of Dorian that sits in his attic magically grows more and more hideous as though reflecting his progressively uglier soul. Like Dorian Gray's portrait, the image that looks back at us from a mirror makes us introspective and self-possessed, and when we commit immoral acts, our mirror image seems to judge us.

In the mid-1970s, two social psychologists asked students at a large university to spend five minutes completing a brief test designed to measure the complexity of their thoughts. The students had to unscramble a series of anagrams, but there was no way they could finish the entire series within the allotted five-minute period. The researcher told the students that a bell would ring after five minutes, and that they shouldn't continue working past the bell, since that would be cheating. Some of the students completed the test across from a large mirror and heard themselves speaking through a tape recorder, whereas others couldn't see themselves while they worked on the anagrams and heard someone else's voice on the tape recorder. Meanwhile, the experimenter looked through one-way glass and counted how many of the students continued to work past the five-minute bell. The results were staggering: only 7 percent of the students who saw themselves in the mirror cheated, whereas a massive 71 percent cheated when they weren't forced to look at themselves as they decided whether to behave honestly. When people consider behaving badly, their mirror images become moral policemen.

It's hard to know whether the students were more honest because they heard their own voices or because they saw themselves in the mirror, but other researchers have shown that people behave more virtuously after simply looking in the mirror. A group of social psychologists ran a series of studies in the late 1990s designed to show that people claim to behave more morally than they actually do. Their approach was simple and elegant. Students were told that they were going to assign themselves and a student partner, whom they hadn't met, two different tasks. One of the tasks was appealing because it entailed a possible reward, and the other was less appealing since there was no reward. Having learned of the two tasks, the students were asked whether they or their partner should be assigned to complete the appealing task. Obviously the students preferred to assign themselves to the appealing task and their partners to the unappealing task, but they also recognized that it would be fairer to toss a coin to decide who would undertake each task. The laws of probability state that if the students were using the coins fairly, roughly half of them should have been assigned to the positive task, and the other half should have been assigned to the negative task.

Though all of the students tossed the coin, the researchers found that 85 percent of the students assigned themselves to the positive task, suggesting that the coin was merely a prop that allowed them to defend the fairness of the desired outcome. Since they weren't supervised, you can imagine how the students interpreted a negative outcome: if they lost the first toss, perhaps they decided that the outcome should rest on a best-of-three scenario.

The researchers tried the task again, this time placing the students in front of a large mirror. Forced to stare at their reflections as they tossed the coin, the students were perfectly fair, assigning their phantom partner to the positive task exactly 50 percent of the time. Incredibly, the students claimed they reached their decision fairly in both situations, but only the students who sat in front of a mirror actually obeyed the outcome of the coin toss.

The people we encounter every day vary along countless dimensions, though many of them enable us to fulfil the motives that Maslow identified in his hierarchy. Some are strangers, some are acquaintances, and some are so deeply entwined with our identity that it's hard to imagine being the same person without them. Some are in-group members, sharing our race, ethnicity, religious affiliation, and linguistic background, and others occupy groups that differ from our own. When these people are present, either physically or merely because they're occupying our minds in passing, we think, behave, and feel differently. The deeply stored associations we've formed between people and character traits linger. Running alongside these associations, the same encounters inspire a galaxy of biological responses. Some of those responses are helpful, but others place awkward hurdles on the path towards our goals and desires. These responses are miraculous, and they start with hormones and brain processes that begin well below the surface of conscious awareness.

Each of the social interactions discussed in the past two chapters also exists within a larger, overarching cultural context. Cultures are groups that share a common set of views, values, goals, and practices—from huge global regions to sports teams and knitting circles—and each culture has its own idiosyncrasies. Some cultural contexts cradle us gently, providing social support and a sense of camaraderie, and others help us to understand the world by casting it through a culturally tinted lens. This cultural lens influences what we see so profoundly that it goes on to shape how we think about almost everything imaginable, from objects and people to abstract concepts like mathematics, honour, and art.

6.

CULTURE

Seeing Objects and Places through a Cultural Lens

n the late 1800s, German psychiatrist Franz Müller-Lyer designed one of the world's most famous visual illusions. The illusion became popular because it was easy to recreate and very difficult to shake. It began with a simple question: which of the following two vertical lines is longer?

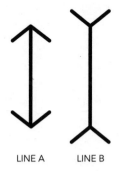

LINE A   LINE B

If you're like almost everyone whom Müller-Lyer tested, Line B will appear longer than Line A. In fact, the two lines are identical in length, as this doctored version of the illusion shows:

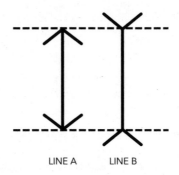

LINE A   LINE B

For decades, vision researchers assumed that the illusion told us something fundamental about human vision. When they showed the illusion to people with normal vision, they were convinced that the line with the inward-pointing arrows would always seem longer than the line with the outward-pointing arrows. That assumption wasn't really tested before the 1960s, because until then almost everyone who had seen the illusion was WEIRD—an acronym that cultural psychologists have coined for people from Western, Educated, Industrialized, Rich, and Democratic societies.

In the early 1960s, three researchers remedied that oversight when they showed the illusion to two thousand people from fifteen different cultural groups. The illusion deceived the first few groups. Adults living in Evanston, Illinois perceived Line B to be on average 20 percent longer than Line A, while students at nearby Northwestern University and white adults in South Africa similarly believed that Line B was between 13 percent and 15 percent longer than Line A. Then the researchers journeyed farther afield, testing people from several African tribes. Bushmen from southern Africa failed to show the illusion at all, perceiving the lines as almost identical in length. Small samples of Suku tribespeople from northern Angola and Bete tribespeople from the Ivory Coast also failed to show the illusion, or saw Line B as only very slightly longer than Line A. Müller-Lyer's eponymous illusion had deceived thousands of people from WEIRD societies for decades, but it wasn't universal.

How was it that African Bushmen and tribespeople were immune to the illusion, when they shared the same visual and neural anatomy as the Westerners who couldn't shake the sense that Line B was longer than Line A? In the absence of biological differences, the answer was, of course, cultural. In contrast to most Western societies, the Bushmen, Suku, and Bete lived in worlds with very few straight lines. Their houses, often made of thatch, were either rounded or devoid of the hard lines that dominate Western interiors, and they spent most of their time gazing at natural scenes of grassland, trees, and water that similarly lacked geometric angles.

Why should this have mattered? Because over years and years, people who live in hard, geometric interiors become used to judging the size of objects based on the rules of three-dimensional visual perspective. For example, if you were inside this room and you had to decide which of the two walls highlighted with thick black lines, A and B, was taller, which would you pick?

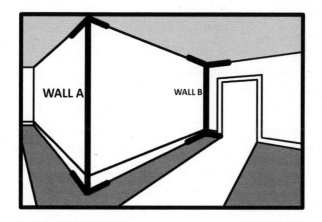

From years of living indoors in structures with perpendicular walls, you know without even paying attention that the two walls are the same height. Wall A is closer to you, so it casts a larger image on your retina, at the back of your eye, but you're so familiar with the basic principles of perspective that you correct for that difference. The lines that Wall A creates where it meets the floor and ceiling are similar to Line A in the Müller-Lyer illusion, and the lines that Wall B creates are similar to Line B. When you see configurations like Line A, you're reminded of objects that are close to you and aren't actually as large as they appear; in contrast, configurations such as Line B remind you of objects that are far away and are actually larger than they appear. In your head, you make those corrections automatically, so Line B looks longer than it is (just as Wall B is taller than it looks), and Line A looks shorter than it is (just as Wall A is shorter than it looks). These intuitions are bound up in cultural experience, and the Bushmen, Suku, and Bete didn't share those intuitions because they had rarely been exposed to the same geometric configurations.

Many of these cultural differences stretch back millennia. Ancient Greek philosophers, who formed the basis for much modern Western philosophy, tended to analyse objects in isolation from their contexts, whereas ancient Chinese philosophers were far more concerned with the relationship between an object and its context. Thousands of years later, these differences continue to express themselves in how Westerners and East Asians perceive the world.

In one experiment, researchers asked Chinese and American students to study a series of photos that featured a central object against a background. For example, one of the photos featured a tiger standing by a stream in a forest, and a second photo featured a fighter jet against an alpine backdrop. Later, the experimenters showed the students a new series of photos and asked them whether they had seen the object in the foreground during the first phase of the experiment. Most of the students were pretty good at the task, answering correctly on 70 percent of the trials. But there was one notable exception: when the experimenters presented the objects against new backgrounds (like moving the tiger from the forest to a grassy plain, or placing the jet against a cloud-filled sky), the Chinese students struggled with the task. Their accuracy dropped below 60 percent, so they were almost guessing whether they had seen the focal object earlier in the experiment.

The reason for their difficulty became clear when the researchers examined their eye movements as they memorized the images. The American students devoted most of their attention to the focal object, and spent considerably less time focusing on its background. While the Americans gazed at the objects through Aristotelian eyes, the Chinese students viewed the scenes through a Confucian lens, focusing as much on the background as on the object. The Chinese students were confused when the objects appeared in new backgrounds, because they had formed memories of the objects in context, while the Americans had paid very little attention to the backgrounds at all.

Seeing People through a Cultural Lens

Cultural legacies have a similar influence on how we perceive people and social interactions. Just as Chinese people are more likely than Americans to focus on objects rather than their backgrounds, so they also believe that people are overlapping entities who relate to the other people in their lives. Westerners (people from the United States, Canada, Western Europe, Australia, and New Zealand, for example) are more likely to believe that they are distinct from other people, so even when they become very close to friends or loved ones, they still see themselves as individuals. This philosophical belief, known as *individualism*, is very different from the East Asian (Japanese, Chinese, and Korean, for example) belief in *collectivism*, which implies that everyone is interconnected, that our identities overlap, and that our actions should benefit the group as a whole above any one individual. Although people from both cultural groups recognize that they're at once individuals and members of a group, the individual component looms larger for Westerners, while the collective component carries relatively more weight for Easterners.

In one series of experiments, researchers asked American and Japanese students to interpret the emotions of a cartoon man who stood in front of a background filled with four other male and female cartoon characters. Sometimes all five shared the same emotional expression, but at other times the figure at the front seemed to have a different expression from those of the figures behind him, as in the case below.

When the students were asked to judge the central character's emotions—whether he was happy, sad, or angry—72 percent of the Japanese students said that they were unable to ignore the emotions of the people in the background, while only 28 percent of the American students had the same reaction. Of course, the Japanese students then rated the happy character as less happy, the sad character as less sad, and the angry character as less angry when the four characters in the background expressed different emotions. As in the study that featured tigers and fighter jets, the Japanese students spent plenty of time looking at the four faces in the background, whereas the Americans focused almost exclusively on the expression of the large face in the foreground.

Americans take the virtues of liberty and individual freedom for granted, but since East Asians pay so much attention to collective well-being, culture researchers have questioned whether they might emphasize the values of harmony and conformity over uniqueness and independence. One analysis measured the use of uniqueness and conformity in over three hundred newspaper and magazine ads in the United States and Korea. Some of the publications focused on business and social commentary (*Money* and the *New York Times* in the United States and *Business Weekly* and *Deep Fountain* in Korea), while others targeted women and youth. While almost every advertisement in Korea promoted the values of tradition, conformity, and following trends, nearly every advertisement in the United States emphasized choice, freedom, and uniqueness. One Korean ad claimed, "Seven out of ten people are using this product", a statement that might repel US consumers. In contrast, an ad in the United States noted, "The Internet isn't for everybody. But then again, you are not everybody", a sentiment that might offend the collectivist sentiments of Korean consumers.

These ads also reflect how collectivists and individualists actually behave. One of the most famous research programmes in the history of social psychology was Solomon Asch's investigation of human conformity in the United States during the 1950s. Asch had grown up in Poland during the early 1900s before moving to Brooklyn, New York with his parents in 1920. As a boy sitting at his parents' table on Passover, Asch asked why a glass that his father had filled with wine sat untouched in front of an empty seat. His father replied that the glass was reserved for the prophet Elijah, and at that moment young Solomon was convinced that the level of wine in the glass declined slightly. Asch's early fascination with suggestibility and influence became a lifelong interest in conformity and propaganda, particularly in the wake of the horrors of

World War Two. So he designed a study to test the limits of human conformity. In his standard experiment, seven people sat in a room and completed a simple task: to determine which line on the right matched the length of the line on the left.

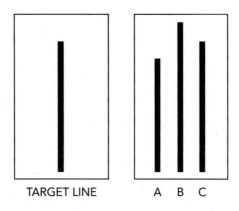

TARGET LINE   A   B   C

The task is trivial, because the answer is very clearly Line C, but there was a twist in the experiment's design. The last person to respond aloud was a naive participant who had no idea what the experiment was designed to test. He also had no idea that the other six participants were plants who had been instructed by the experimenter to claim, unanimously, that the correct answer was Line B. So as the experiment progressed they casually called out, "Line B", while the experimenter recorded their responses. The naive participant became increasingly agitated, wondering at first whether he had misunderstood the instructions and then whether the other people in the room were playing a prank. But none of them wavered, and then it was his turn to respond. Across hundreds of trials, Asch found that roughly 30 percent of all American participants conformed, responding with the same manifestly incorrect "Line B" response that the others in the room delivered, one after another. This result is powerful because it shows that although Americans generally place a premium on the individualistic values of uniqueness and self-reliance, they still succumb to the pressures of social influence.

As with the Müller-Lyer illusion, it took researchers some time to investigate the effect in other cultures, but eventually they administered Asch's experiment across the globe. The results were similar in other individualistic countries, from the UK to Holland, but they were dramatically stronger in collectivistic countries. Japanese participants conformed up to 50 percent of the time, Ghanaians 47 percent of the time, and Fijians 58 percent of the time. Conformity—a route to social harmony—occurs sometimes in the individualistic United States, but it's far more likely to occur within cultures that value collectivistic ideals.

These striking differences between individualists and collectivists are reflected in their distinct ancient philosophical styles, but why did ancient Greeks pursue individualistic philosophies while Confucians pursued collectivistic philosophies? Researchers still argue about the ultimate origins of individualism and collectivism, but one fascinating (and contentious) recent theory suggests that these tendencies might reflect the concentration of disease-causing microbes. Collectivistic societies are likely to thrive in pathogen-rich areas of the world, because collectivists tend to fear outsiders more than individualists, and they're less likely to take the sorts of risks that might encourage disease. This xenophobic attitude towards outsiders may have benefited collectivistic societies, because it shielded them from alien diseases that their bodies weren't equipped to fight. In contrast, individualists were more likely to stray from the group and to interact with outsiders, encouraging new diseases to ravage their own groups when they returned from adventures beyond the fold. Over time, then, collectivistic cultures thrived in pathogen-rich areas of the world, while their individualistic counterparts fell to the ravages of disease. Meanwhile, individualistic cultures thrived in areas with fewer dangerous pathogens. They tended to be more industrious, adventurous, and creative, so they dominated their collectivistic counterparts as long as they weren't threatened by communicable diseases.

A study in 2008 showed just this pattern when a team of American and Canadian psychologists compared microbe levels in historically individualistic and collectivistic areas of the world. The researchers divided the world into almost a hundred regions, and consulted two expert culture researchers to assess the level of individualism and collectivism in each area. The experts rated each region on a scale of 1 (very collectivistic) to 10 (very individualistic). Individualistic regions included the United States (which scored 9.55), Britain (8.95), and Switzerland (7.90), whereas China (2.00), Nigeria (3.00), and Portugal (3.80) were relatively collectivistic. Lying between the extremes were regions including Romania (5.00), Spain (5.55), and South Africa (5.75). The relationship between the two critical measures was very strong, as the regions with historically higher pathogen levels tended to be far more collectivistic, historically, than the areas with lower pathogen levels. The researchers concluded that the pressures of the environment may have shaped specific longer-term cultural patterns in each region of the world.

While researchers still debate the origins of collectivism and individualism, culture continues to shape how people think about more than just the physical and social worlds. Cultural experience also shapes how we construe abstract concepts, such as the relationships between numbers, the best way to paint a portrait, and whether to fight or flee in response to personal insults. We become so comfortable with our own cultural understanding of these abstract concepts that we come to assume that our views are privileged or inevitable. But even hard-edged concepts such as mathematics are open to cultural reinterpretation. In the late 1980s, when one researcher came upon a group of poor Brazilian children who sold sweets on the streets, he learned that the Western approach to teaching addition and subtraction isn't the only option.

Seeing Mathematics, Art, and Honour through a Cultural Lens

Wealthy ten-year-olds in the West learn how to add and subtract in school, while poor ten-year-olds in many parts of the world are forced to teach themselves the same concepts as a matter of survival. In Recife, a large urban area in north-eastern Brazil, poor children sell sweets and fruit on the street from a very young age. They wade into the deep waters of commerce without any schooling, and the submissive and uncertain among them are vulnerable to con artists and customers who try to pass a two-real note for a five-real note (the real is the Brazilian unit of currency). The children quickly learn to add and subtract, and to distinguish between bargaining and giving away their wares too quickly. In the 1980s, a number of researchers descended on Recife and discovered that these children had developed a sophisticated understanding of mathematical concepts that their privileged Western contemporaries acquired only after years of education. The researchers asked the child sellers to complete a number of mathematical tasks that they also presented to children of the same age at a local public school, and in a nearby rural area. In one task, they were asked to add seventeen notes that totalled 17,300 cruzeiros (the currency at the time; now replaced by the real). And in another they were asked to determine whether they could earn more revenue per bag by selling each bag of Pirulitos—Brazilian sweets—for 200 cruzeiros, or seven bags for 1,000 cruzeiros.

The Recife schoolchildren and rural children who weren't selling sweets and fruit struggled to add the notes, answering only 30–50 percent of the questions correctly. But the sellers answered a whopping 82 percent of the questions correctly. Even their errors were smaller, usually falling no more than 200 cruzeiros from the correct answer, whereas the other children were significantly less accurate. The sellers were also far better at the revenue-calculation task. Seventy-eight percent of them correctly noted that selling one bag of Pirulitos for 200 cruzeiros generated more revenue per bag than selling seven bags for 1,000 cruzeiros. The schoolchildren answered the question correctly only 50 percent of the time, and only 24 percent of the rural children who weren't working as street vendors gave the correct response.

When the experimenters asked the street vendors how they had performed so impressively, they explained how they broke the larger numbers into smaller components. Instead of trying to add the seventeen notes one after another, for example, they split them into convenient groups—one 500-cruzeiro note, two 200-cruzeiro notes, and one 100-cruzeiro note came to 1,000 cruzeiros, and those notes could be set aside while the remaining thirteen notes were added. They similarly explained that if one bag of Pirulitos was worth 200 cruzeiros, they could sell two for 400, three for 600, four for 800, and five for 1,000 cruzeiros— a smaller number than they would have to give up in a trade of seven bags for 1,000 cruzeiros. Despite lacking a formal education in mathematics, these children had lived in a culture that forced them to acquire their own skills. While they quickly learned to add and calculate the profit in different trades, they were no better at reading numbers off the page or comparing the size of different numbers—tasks that weren't important in the day-to-day requirements of street selling.

Mathematics and art seem to occupy opposite ends of the cultural spectrum—one universal and enduring, the other localized and always changing—but they also occupy considerable common ground. Leonardo da Vinci the artist was also Leonardo da Vinci the mathematician, and his *Mona Lisa* and *Last Supper* paintings appeal to the eye in part because they obey certain mathematical laws of visual harmony. Like a number of classical East Asian sculptures and buildings, their proportions conform to the so-called golden ratio, where their longer side is approximately 1.618 times longer than their shorter side. The golden ratio, first proposed by Pythagoras in the fifth century BC, is supposed to hold universal aesthetic appeal, and dozens of cultures adopted golden proportions when designing buildings and producing art.

Despite the universality of the golden ratio, cultures don't always agree on what makes an artwork appealing. In a survey of almost five hundred famous Western and East Asian portraits, researchers found that the subject's face covered an average of 15 percent of the canvas in Western artworks, and only 4 percent in East Asian artworks. In a similar analysis of Facebook profile pictures, 12 percent of a sample of Texan and Californian users displayed photos of their faces without any background, while fewer than 1 percent of a sample from Hong Kong, Singapore, and Taipei chose similar close-ups that focused on their faces and excluded the background.

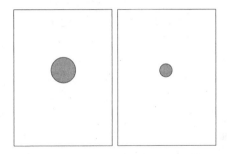

Average ratio of subject's face to canvas size in Western (left) and East Asian (right) museum portraits.

These aesthetic ideals aren't just cultural relics. When the same researchers asked American and East Asian students to draw a scene featuring a house, a tree, a river, a person, and a horizon, the American students created simpler drawings that emphasized the house and person, while the East Asian students focused more on the background and added 74 percent more contextual detail than the American students. When the same students later took photos of four models, the Americans filled the frame with the models' faces. In contrast, the East Asian students emphasized the models' bodies and the room's background, oc-

cupying only a third as much of the canvas with their faces. A broad
sample of people within each culture, from naive students to artistic luminaries, appeared to hold the same aesthetic preferences.

Artworks are also enlightening because they reflect a culture's ideals
and preoccupations. East Asian artists have long celebrated noble warriors who die in the name of honour, a concept that doesn't feature in
Western artworks. Japanese masterpieces, for example, depict samurai
warriors who failed to uphold their honour committing *seppuku*, an act
of ritual suicide. The concept of honour isn't entirely absent from US
culture, though, and certain regions of the United States emphasize honour more than others. In those regions homicide, though universally con-
demned in abstraction, is more likely to be excused in practice when the
killer's honour, or the honour of a loved one, is threatened.

Imagine, for example, that you own a business, and you're looking to
hire a new employee. Letters of interest pour in from dozens of well-
qualified applicants, but one letter stands out from the rest. The applicant
is a hard-working twenty-seven-year-old man who seems to be a good fit
for the job, but he discloses an event from his past that causes you some
concern:

There is one thing I must explain, because I feel I must be honest and
I want no misunderstandings. I have been convicted of a felony,
namely manslaughter. You will probably want an explanation for this
before you send me an application, so I will provide it. I got into a fight
with someone who was having an affair with my fiancée. I lived in a
small town, and one night this person confronted me in front of my
friends at the bar. He told everyone that he and my fiancée were sleeping together. He laughed at me to my face and asked me to step outside if I was man enough. I was young and didn't want to back down
from a challenge in front of everyone. As we went into the alley, he
started to attack me. He knocked me down, and he picked up a bottle.
I could have run away and the judge said I should have, but my pride

wouldn't let me. Instead, I picked up a pipe that was lying in the alley and hit him with it. I didn't mean to kill him, but he died a few hours later in hospital. I realize that what I did was wrong.

How do you respond? Do the circumstances that the applicant describes mitigate the severity of his actions, or are they irrelevant to your assessment of his culpability? Does he deserve to apply for the job, or would you refuse to consider him for the position?

In the mid-1990s social psychologists Richard Nisbett and Dov Cohen delivered hundreds of bogus applications with precisely this paragraph to chain stores scattered across the United States. The stores were loosely divided among three distinct regions: southern states (e.g., Tennessee, Alabama, and Mississippi); western states (e.g., Arizona, New Mexico, and Wyoming); and northern states (e.g., New York, Massachusetts, and Michigan). With a basic understanding of US culture—and a history of watching US TV shows—you'll recognize that those regions have distinct cultural mores.

Over the months, responses poured in from the chain stores, and they followed an interesting pattern. Compared with northern stores, those in the south and west were somewhat more willing to offer jobs to the contrite applicant, and the tone of their letters was more conciliatory and flexible. Many of them referred to the applicant's conduct with understanding and empathy, whereas stores in the north either tended to ignore his conduct or referred to it disapprovingly. One particularly understanding letter from a southern store owner vividly illustrates the sort of thinking inspired by the culture of honour:

As for your problem of the past, anyone could probably be in the situation you were in. It was just an unfortunate incident that shouldn't be held against you. Your honesty shows that you are sincere . . . I wish you the best of luck for your future. You have a positive attitude and a willingness to work. Those are qualities that businesses look for in an employee. Once you get settled, if you are near here, please stop in and see us.

The south and west are associated with entrenched family rivalries, spaghetti westerns, and a general emphasis on traditional gender roles. Southern and western men are more likely to be excused if they respond violently to the sorts of events described in the researchers' job letter. This so-called *culture of honour* is absent from the northern states, where men aren't laden with the same cultural expectations. Northern men have the option of avoiding violence without compromising their integrity.

You might wonder, at this point, whether Southerners and Western-ers are just more accepting of violence; perhaps their responses have nothing to do with the culture of honour or the nature of the crime. The researchers were concerned about that, too, so they sent out another se-ries of letters in which the applicant admitted to stealing cars in his youth to support his family. Again, he expressed remorse and the desire to move on with his life. For that crime, which had nothing to do with honour or face-saving behaviour, stores from all three regions responded with the same degree of tolerance.

The same patterns emerged in a second study, when Nisbett and Cohen offered to pay college newspaper interns to write a story about a violent incident. According to the background fact sheet, a young white male named Victor Jensen stabbed a second young white male who rid-iculed him at a party and called his sister and mother "sluts". When the interns at universities in the south and west wrote about the incident, they were more likely to justify Jensen's behaviour, and temper their blame by mentioning that Jensen was provoked to respond violently. The interns at northern universities were less forgiving, construing Jensen's behaviour as recklessly impulsive rather than the natural response to a brazen attack on his honour.

As young southern and western males mature, they learn to perceive personal threats through a magnifying lens. Incidents that might otherwise provoke puzzled amusement take on a life of their own, demanding equivalent or escalated responses. These responses reflect a deeply entrenched culture of honour that traces its origins to early settlement, as far back as the seventeenth century.

According to researchers, several factors explain why the culture of honour arose in some but not all regions of the United States. Northern states were largely settled by farmers who had the benefit of stronger legal systems from early settlement. Meanwhile, the south and west were inhabited by ranchers and herders to a greater extent, and their livelihood could be threatened at any moment by thieves and poachers. Crimes were difficult to punish in the expansive south and west, especially when they were first settled, so herders were forced to take matters into their own hands. Meanwhile, warmer weather and poverty only encouraged violence and vigilantism. Thus were born the violent retaliation and long-running family rivalries that characterize today's culture of honour. Although some experts dispute this causal chain, there's no doubt that settlers in the colonial south and west embraced duelling, the notion of gentlemanliness, and military law far more deeply than did their northern counterparts. As those practices were passed from generation to generation, the culture of honour gained a foothold that continues to distinguish violent retaliatory responses in the south and west from tamer responses in the north.

Although the concept of honour seems like a relic from a more traditional era, men who grow up in the culture of honour continue to respond differently to men who mature in other parts of the country. In a series of experiments, the same psychologists observed how southern and northern men responded to insults that potentially threatened their masculinity. In each experiment, college-aged men were asked to walk from one college classroom to another via a long, narrow corridor. As they walked down the corridor, some of the men were forced to pass another male student walking in the opposite direction—a plant put there by the experimenters. When they passed the plant, he bumped them and muttered the word "asshole" under his breath. Other men who were taking part in the experiment walked down the corridor without incident as the student made way for them without speaking.

The insulted men were obviously surprised by the student's hostility, but Southerners and Northerners responded very differently. When two nearby observers examined the men's responses, they found that 85 percent of the students who grew up in the south were more angry than amused, whereas 65 percent of the students who grew up in the north were more amused than angry. When the students got to the room down the corridor, they were asked to complete a story in which a male had been insulted (in a way not dissimilar to their own recent experience). Three-quarters of the Southerners completed the story by suggesting that the insulted man would respond with his own insults or violence, but only 41 percent of the Northerners suggested the same hostile outcome. In other studies, the experimenters measured the students' hormonal responses, finding that the insulted Southerners experienced dramatic rises in cortisol and testosterone, hormones associated with stress and aggression respectively.

Meanwhile, in a third experiment, the students were told to walk back down the same corridor. This time, they were forced to pass yet another male plant who was tall (six foot three) and imposing (weighing 17 stone). Observers carefully watched how the student responded to this simulated game of "chicken", and found that all Northerners and Southerners who hadn't been insulted gave the large male a wide berth of two or three feet. In contrast, the insulted Southerners refused to move until they were almost bowled over—they moved, on average, when the oncoming juggernaut was little more than a foot away. Later, insulted southern males also behaved more aggressively when dealing with a much smaller experimenter—a man who was five foot six and weighed 10 stone—and responded to a questionnaire by admitting that they felt their manhood had been challenged. Whereas Northerners barely registered the insult, Southerners attempted to reassert their masculinity by responding with a constellation of aggressive behaviours.

Later studies suggested that the culture of honour leads to even graver ends, as Southerners are more likely to die young of accidental causes associated with risk-taking and machismo. Each culture has its own particular insecurities, so the insults that undermine a man's honour in one culture are dismissed as glancing blows in another. The southern preoccupation with honour illustrates how ancient fears and insecurities later express themselves in vaguely related contexts, sometimes hundreds or thousands of years after those insecurities first emerged. These same fears come to shape how people in that culture experience physical and mental illness—and many of the symptoms that emerge affect just one small cultural enclave while sparing everyone who lives beyond the reach of those peculiar cultural anxieties.

Cultural Maladies

The insecurities that produce aggressive displays of masculinity in some cultures also inspire culture-specific maladies that affect isolated pockets of the population. *Anorexia nervosa* sufferers who restrict their eating and fear gaining weight are concentrated in the wealthiest regions of the world, where thinness is a compelling cultural ideal. The disorder is almost unheard of in poorer countries, and it barely existed before the 1950s. Meanwhile, women in the Middle Ages suffered from nervosa's medieval cousin, *anorexia mirabilis*. These women similarly refused food to the point of death, but they were motivated by religious rather than aesthetic ideals. In a culture where asceticism was the key to religious enlightenment, fasting was next to godliness.

As the two versions of anorexia show, culture-bound disorders reflect the deep-seated fears and concerns that plague a cultural group at a particular point in time. One of the most famous recent cases is the West African genital-shrinking epidemic known as *koro*. Between 1997 and 2003, a koro epidemic spread through six West African nations and generated dozens of news articles. One article in the *Nigerian Vanguard* described the ensuing alarm:

> Panic has gripped residents of the Plateau State capital [Jos], following cases of disappearing organs ostensibly for ritual purposes. No fewer than six of such cases have been reported in the last one week in different parts of the state capital, involving males and females whose organs allegedly "disappeared" upon contact with organ snatchers. A middle-aged man was almost lynched yesterday along Rwang Pam Street, after he allegedly "stole" a man's private part through "remote control". The victim allegedly felt his organs shrink after speaking to the suspect, who reportedly asked for directions.

While delusions affect people from every imaginable culture, koro sufferers were experiencing a specific symptom that had rarely been seen in other parts of the world. Psychologists noted that two West African cultural beliefs may have contributed to the so-called penis-napping epidemic. The first was the tendency to attribute unexplained events to malevolent witchcraft. The same unexplained events in other parts of the world might prompt question marks and head-scratching, but West Africans are relatively quick to blame unwanted events on supernatural intervention. The second belief was that witches and other supernatural beings would steal and eat a man's penis or a woman's womb, sometimes holding it hostage until a financial bribe was offered. When the afflicted patients were examined, however, their organs seemed to be intact, despite frantic claims that their genitals had disappeared entirely. In the end, doctors explained that koro sufferers were enmeshed in a bout of mass hysteria, converting a frenzy of anxiety into the earnest delusion that their genitals were disappearing before their eyes. Of course, in another culture—one less fixated on the fear of genital shrinkage—these delusions would have been quite different, reflecting that culture's own specific fears and preoccupations.

Culture-specific maladies abound, and each reflects the conditions that define the lives of its sufferers. A relatively new set of phobias has emerged in East Asia, where the demands of social etiquette are sometimes overwhelming and inflexible. Sufferers of *jiko-shisen-kyofu* are deeply afraid that their own glances will displease or offend others, while *sekimen-kyofu* sufferers fear the consequences of blushing in public. Both phobias are unique to East Asia, since blushing and lingering glances are mere peccadilloes in the rest of the world.

Meanwhile, Newfoundlanders who awaken paralysed in the night are said to experience old hag syndrome, since they imagine that a large disembodied woman is sitting on their chest. The hag, a malevolent mythical woman, occupies an important place in Newfoundland folklore, so locals sometimes conjure her image during episodes of sleep paralysis. People experience sleep paralysis elsewhere in the world, but they explain and understand the sensation very differently. In all, twenty-five such culture-bound syndromes appear in the official diagnostic and statistical manual of the American Psychiatric Association (the *DSM*), and the list is likely to grow when the association releases its next edition of the manual in 2013.

When the American Psychiatric Association talks about culture-specific maladies, what does it mean by culture? National identities impart culture—as in the case of the East Asian phobias—but culture also comes from smaller geographic regions, sports teams, and friendship circles. The people who occupy those groups share a common set of beliefs about the world, and those beliefs colour their values, hopes, and anxieties. Humans the world over have the same basic biological make-up— the same brains, eyes, and ears—but the way we experience the world varies dramatically. In the case of culturally bound maladies, cultural beliefs prepare people to experience a particular constellation of symptoms. While West Africans believed their genitalia were being "snatched" in the late 1990s, anxious East Asians were more likely to fear the prospect of violating deeply held politeness norms. Although both groups experienced completely different symptoms, those symptoms made perfect sense in each context.

The cultural differences described in this chapter—from how we see the world to our peculiar culture-bound maladies—seem to imply that culture is immutable; that once you're immersed in one culture your thinking will be bound for ever by that culture's norms and mores. Historically that may have been true, because people lived in isolated communities that rarely interacted with other communities nearby. Today, of course, the world is a very different place, with billions of people migrating within and across the world's two hundred countries.

Biculturalism: Immersion in Two Different Cultures

The US Census, which counts and categorizes the country's population every ten years, is far more sensitive to the possibility that people identify with multiple cultures than it was just twenty years ago. In the 1990 census, respondents were forced to identify with a single ethnic group, while in 2000 and 2010 respondents could associate themselves with more than one ethnic group. Indeed, over 6 percent of the population—more than two million people—identified with two or more ethnic or racial groups in 2010.

Bicultural people—those who have lived for extended periods in two cultures—experience the world very differently from monocultural people, who have only lived in one culture. In an interview, Andrew Lam, a Vietnamese-American writer, described the experience of identifying with two very different cultures. Lam's father was a general in South Vietnam, and he ensured that his family escaped to the United States when the Vietnam War began to escalate. (The general joined the rest of his family after the South Vietnamese army surrendered.) Lam vividly remembered his first American meal, a ham sandwich and a glass of milk, and the experience of shivering during the Southern California winter—a mild winter by American standards, but far colder than the balmy tropical climate Lam enjoyed as a child. These superficial differences are matched by deeper cultural differences. Whereas Americans prize verbal affection—the phrase "I love you" holds a special place in familial and romantic relationships—Vietnamese tend to demonstrate their love through gestures. Lam's mother would cook his favourite meal when he visited, and he would finish the entire meal to show his appreciation. Lam's father was taciturn and only once told his son how proud he was, when Andrew won a prestigious journalism award. Lam also described the shock of moving from a collectivistic culture, where the good of the community is paramount, to an individualistic culture where he had to learn self-focused phrases like "follow your dream" and "look out for number one".

American and Vietnamese cultures are very different, and it's difficult to reconcile conflicting cultural beliefs. You can't, for example, put your own personal dreams first while also putting your community's well-being above your own, unless you happen to dream of serving your community. As a result, bicultural people like Andrew Lam are forced to engage in what psychologists call frame-switching. According to the theory of frame-switching, you can perceive the world either through the frame of one culture or through the frame of the other. This is captured in visual illusions like the Necker Cube, the left-hand illustration below.

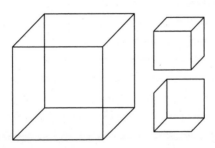

The Necker Cube lacks depth cues, so you can see it either as a cube facing downward (the top-right figure) or a cube facing upward (the bottom-right figure), but not both at the same time. The same is true of biculturalism. Although many bicultural people come to feel comfortable in their new cultural home, their minds are for ever bifurcated, split between the norms of their original culture and their new culture. All it takes to flip the switch back to the "old country" is a simple reminder of how things used to be.

In a series of experiments, psychologists capitalized on one robust difference that separates Western from Chinese thought: the way each culture explains social events. Suppose, for example, that you see a person driving recklessly through a red traffic light. Westerners are more likely to criticize the person, assuming he generally cares little for the safety of others; in contrast, East Asians (Chinese included) are more likely to believe that the driver has been forced to drive fast because he's in the midst of an emergency. Perhaps he's transporting someone to hospital, or perhaps he's been summoned to collect a sick child from school. In other words, the person is behaving badly because he's responding to situational constraints, and not because he's chronically irresponsible.

In one experiment, the researchers showed bicultural people a series of images that were related to one of the two cultures that constituted their bicultural identity. Westernized students in Hong Kong, who were familiar with both Chinese and Western culture, were shown either images of an American flag, Abraham Lincoln, and Superman (Western primes) or images of a stone monkey, the Great Wall of China, and a Chinese opera singer (Chinese primes). Later the students completed a range of questionnaires designed to detect whether their patterns of thought more strongly reflected Chinese or Western cultural mores. When the bicultural students in Hong Kong read a story about an overweight boy who went out for dinner with his friends and ate a sugary, high-calorie cake, they interpreted the boy's behaviour differently depending on whether they were primed with American or Chinese images. When primed with the American images, they tended to blame the boy, suggesting that he probably had poor self-control, but when primed with Chinese images, they believed the boy was in a difficult situation, and he was probably pressured to eat the cake. Guided by the primes, the students viewed the world through the cultural lens that came to mind most readily.

Multiculturalism: Skimming the Surface of Many Cultures

Not everyone spends time immersed in two different cultures, but plenty of people dip their toes into many cultural environments. With the rise of international travel, the Internet, and globalized consumerism, people are exposed to dozens of cultures without having to emigrate. Some of the consequences of cultural exposure en masse are perhaps unsurprising. When the American TV show *Beverly Hills, 90210* debuted in France in 1993, it had a dramatic effect on child-naming practices. Three of the show's main characters were named Dylan, Brandon, and Brenda, names that were non-existent in France before 1993. By the mid-1990s, all three names had mushroomed in popularity, and Dylan had become the sixth most popular boy's name in France. Another main character named Kelly had very little influence on naming practices, probably because that name had already grown popular when the American TV show *Santa Barbara* introduced a character named Kelly to French screens in 1985. Obviously this influx of non-French names (Dylan, Brandon, and Brenda are Welsh and Irish) comes at the expense of French names, which are cast aside in favoor of more exotic, star-studded alternatives. Indeed, a number of French intellectuals decried the rise of these names, claiming that they were partly responsible for a rapid dilution of French culture at the end of the twentieth century.

Other effects of cultural exposure are more surprising and subtle, and they arise when people begin to learn the meanings of novel cultural concepts. Westerners were once unfamiliar with the Chinese Taoist *yin-yang* symbol, but it has become a popular feature in new age and surf culture, and almost everyone who responded to a recent survey I ran with my colleague Virginia Kwan recognized the symbol (shown below). The yin-yang symbol depicts the interconnectedness of opposing forces, like night and day, dark and light, and female and male. It also suggests that these opposing forces are balanced and always changing, so that the sky, for example, will inevitably oscillate between darkness and light as time passes. Westerners were once collectively ignorant about the meaning of the yin-yang, but a growing number of non-Asian Americans recognize that the symbol implies change, balance, and constant movement between opposites.

The Chinese Taoist yin-yang symbol.

Since Americans are now more familiar with the yin-yang symbol, we were curious to see how they responded when they were subtly exposed to the yin-yang while making various judgements. In one experiment, we asked people to imagine that they were weather forecasters trying to predict whether it would be sunny or rainy following a string of sunny or rainy days. The bulk of the questionnaire was identical for each of the students taking part, except that half the questionnaires featured a tiny yin-yang symbol at the top of the page, whereas the other half featured a tiny map of the continental United States. (The yin-yang and map symbols were subtly included as part of a stationery-company logo, as though the questionnaires had been printed by a company that used one of those symbols as its logo.)

Although few of the students remembered seeing the symbols after completing the questionnaire, their weather predictions varied dramatically depending on whether they were exposed to the yin-yang or the American map. Since the yin-yang symbol implies change and balance, the students who were exposed to it predicted many more changes in the weather than did students who were exposed to the map. The white American students adopted thought patterns that are more typical among Chinese people when they were exposed to the yin-yang symbol. Later, when we looked at weather prediction trends in the United States and China, we found that Chinese forecasters predicted many more changes in weather patterns across the globe than did American forecasters, which suggests that the cultures have different ideas about how much the weather changes.

We found the same pattern when we asked workers in Manhattan's Wall Street district to complete a stock investment questionnaire. The workers were given a fictional sum of $1,000 to invest across nine stocks. Some of the stocks had clearly appreciated in recent times, experiencing unambiguous gains over the six months preceding the investment decision. Others had performed ambiguously, sometimes appreciating and sometimes depreciating, but overall performing more poorly than the first set of stocks.

Since Americans expect trends to continue, we expected the participants to prefer stocks that had experienced recent gains, except when a yin-yang symbol reminded them that "what goes up must come down". When we asked, they overwhelmingly preferred the previously appreciating stocks—except when our research assistant arrived wearing a T-shirt that featured a small yin-yang symbol. As in the weather prediction studies, the yin-yang primed them to consider the possibility that the

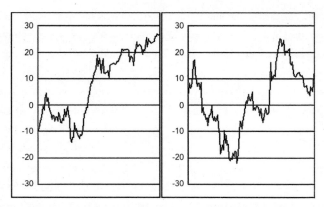

Examples of stock charts from the financial investment study. The chart on the
left represents an unambiguously appreciating stock, and the chart on the right
represents a stock that experienced mixed fortunes.

appreciating stocks might experience a change in fortune, so they invested $160 less in those stocks than did participants who were ap-
proached by a research assistant wearing a plain white T-shirt. The effect
was also stronger the more broadly respondents had travelled, and the
more they knew about the meaning of the yin-yang symbol. The simple
lesson here is that even Americans who have only lived in one area of the
United States are susceptible to cultural influences, because they're increasingly exposed to the sorts of foreign cultural symbols that their ancestors rarely or never encountered before the advent of globalized
entertainment, the Internet, and inexpensive international travel.

Culture is a powerful and pervasive ingredient of thought, determining not only how we interpret transient events such as weather and stock
market changes but also how we experience diseases and personal
threats. Cultures are powerful in part because they're ubiquitous, envel-
oping us in norms, mores, and ideals from birth to death, and partly
because we rarely turn our minds to their influence. While names, symbols, and social interactions soak up some mental energy, we move from
one cultural environment to another even as our attention is drawn else-

where. We can't help but live in a particular country, interact with a particular group of people, or pursue a particular set of interests, and the experience shapes us until we no longer recognize that our worldview is a combination of these diverse and distinct cultural norms.

In the last three chapters I've described how the social world—the world between us—shapes a diverse range of outcomes. Some of these effects have biological origins, from the latent energy released by an audience in chapter 4, to the risk-promoting consequences of testosterone and the mother–child bonding inspired by oxytocin in chapter 5. Others are a matter of experience inspired by cultural habits, which explains why psychiatric illnesses, artistic preferences, and conceptions of honour differed across cultures in this chapter.

Even broader than the world between us is the expansive physical world that surrounds us—a world that contributes to some of the most striking quirks in human thinking and behaviour. The physical world—ambient colours, locations, and weather conditions—hides in plain sight precisely because it forms a constant backdrop against which we live our ever-changing lives. Instead of consciously processing the colour of every object, the nature of every room, and the temperature as it changes across time, we wisely conserve our limited mental resources for complex tasks that demand focused attention. The next chapter begins with an account of one such cue: a new form of lighting that began as an attempt to beautify an ageing city, but ultimately came to address some of the city's biggest problems.

PART THREE

THE WORLD *AROUND* US

7.

COLOURS

The Policeman's Blues

At the turn of the millennium, the government in Glasgow, Scotland appeared to stumble on a remarkable crime-prevention strategy. Officials hired a team of Glaswegian contractors to beautify the city by installing a series of blue lights in various prominent locations. In theory, blue lights are more attractive and calming than the garish yellow and white lights that illuminate much of the city at night, and indeed the blue lights seemed to cast a soothing, ethereal glow. Months passed and the city's crime statisticians noticed a striking trend: the locations that were newly bathed in blue experienced a dramatic decline in criminal activity. Just as the West Midlands police force clamped down on crime with billboards depicting human eyes, the blue lights in Glasgow, which mimicked the lights on the top of police cars, seemed to imply that the police were always watching. The lights were never designed to stem crime, but that's exactly what they appeared to be doing.

Word of the miraculous constabulary power of blue light travelled quickly. The police force in Nara Prefecture, Japan installed a series of

152 blue lights at several crime hotspots. The crime rate fell by an impressive 9 percent, but the blue lights had other, unanticipated benefits: the suicide attempts that plagued Japanese train stations and crossings ceased altogether—not a single attempt was reported along the Central and West Japan Railway Company lines between 2006 and 2008. Even littering and rubbish dumping seemed to decline in blue-lit areas, and blue lights were hailed as a panacea for several of society's most stubborn ills. Some enterprising minds even suggested replacing standard lights at gang hangouts with the pinkish lights that dermatologists use to inspect teenage skin for acne. What better way to encourage teen gang members to disperse than to emphasize their flawed complexions?

Amid the jubilation, researchers began to question the link between the blue lights and the range of reported benefits. Some suggested that the blue lights were brighter or attracted more attention than yellow and white lights, which merely displaced crime, suicide attempts, and littering to more dimly lit locations. Though researchers continue to question whether the lights were beneficial because they were blue, or rather because they attracted attention, several rigorous studies have shown that the colour blue has remarkable effects on the human body.

In one study, two researchers visited a sawmill in Montreal, Canada. Sawmill workers grade freshly cut pieces of timber and then cut the graded timber into boards for construction projects—exacting tasks that impose high costs when the workers make mistakes. Many sawmills operate throughout the night, and workers are sometimes forced to alternate between day and night shifts. This schedule wreaks havoc on a worker's circadian rhythm, the same biological pattern that causes jet lag when people travel from one time zone to another. Seasoned international travellers know how difficult it is to resist the urge to sleep when jet lag takes hold, and that same state of exhaustion causes countless accidents among shift workers. The researchers approached one such group and suggested an inexpensive, novel remedy: exposure to blue-green light. Blue-green light waves are the shortest visible light waves, and they trigger a range of biological functions that regulate circadian rhythm. Natural light is rich in these blue-green short waves, which is why sunlight is an excellent natural cure for jet lag. To test their theory, the researchers purchased a series of special lights that bathed the night-shift workers in a blue-green glow as they worked. When the shift ended the following morning, the workers wore special amber glasses to block out all blue and green light, thereby confusing their bodies into believing that they were working during the day and leaving work at night. The effects were remarkable. By the fourth day of the trial most of the workers felt more alert, as their error rate declined from 5 percent to just 1 percent.

Few people alternate between night shifts and day shifts, but a similar problem is said to affect millions of people across the world: seasonal affective disorder (SAD), or the winter blues. People who suffer from SAD tend to become depressed and listless for long periods during the winter, which also explains in large part why the disorder affects only 1 percent of Floridians but 10 percent of New Hampshirites. Among the many proffered solutions, blue-green light therapy stands alone as perhaps the least intrusive, and sufferers can purchase special lamps and lightbulbs for little more than the cost of a standard desk lamp. The good news is that dozens of researchers have documented the effectiveness of the remedy, which has the same effects as genuine sunshine: diminished depressive symptoms and renewed energy. This research is generally sophisticated and rigorous, but colour therapy began as a far less meticulous pursuit.

The Inauspicious History of Colour "Science"

Very few people have strong intuitions about quantum physics, brain surgery, and organic chemistry, because those fields are too

technical to invite naive theories and misguided insights. They're pro-
tected from uneducated opinions because physicists, surgeons, and chem-
ists focus on tiny, abstract concepts such as quarks, strings, neurons, and
molecules. In contrast, the subject matter of colour science is vivid and
ubiquitous, and even novices have basic theories about the role of colours
in human psychology. As pioneering colour scientist Kurt Goldstein
noted during a speech in the early 1940s, "That colours influence organic
life does not need special proof. Looking around at the colourfulness of
all living things, one becomes immediately aware of this fact."

The early science of colour therapy was as unscientific as Goldstein's
claim. One paper in the *Bulletin of the Massachusetts Association for Occupational Therapy* in 1938 printed as gospel the observations of a single
nurse and her attendant at Worcester State Hospital. They claimed that
magenta briefly sedated disturbed patients, blue had a similar but longer-
lasting effect, and yellow and red stimulated depressed and melancholy
patients. The observations were fascinating, but they weren't supported
by rigorous experimental testing.

Then, in the mid-1940s, two army surgeons introduced Auroratone
films, a new method of colour treatment for depressed and shell-shocked
patients. The films featured a combination of ever-changing psychedelic
colours and soothing soundtracks—some including songs specially written for the purpose by Bing Crosby. The films mesmerized patients because they were colourful, but probably more so because their viewers
belonged to a generation that had only recently discovered television. According to one report, patients stared transfixed as Crosby sang "Going
My Way" over a swirling melange of colours. One twenty-six-year-old
patient known as Patient A had been in North Africa and southern
Europe during the last few years of World War Two. He was injured in
December 1944, and recovered at the hospital that first tested the Auroratone method. Before he watched the films, physicians described Patient
A as "very confused, agitated, restless, and untidy about his person". He

wept and spoke like a child, and experienced "vivid hallucinations and grandiose delusions". In October 1945, almost a year after his original injury, two attendants guided the restrained man to a seat in front of the hospital's Auroratone screen. Along the way, he tried to strike another patient, and the attendants had to use all their strength to keep him restrained. As soon as the film began, Patient A became a different person. He spoke coherently and politely, enjoyed the film in silence, and claimed for the first time that he wanted to go home. When the film ended, only an hour after his earlier violent outbursts, he walked to his room quietly and without restraints. Patient A was joined by Patients B, C, D, E, and F, who were also sedated by the Auroratone films, each claiming that he was calmed by the film's "pretty colours" when debriefed after the therapy session. Something about the films was working, but no one ever bothered to check whether it was the colour palette, the way the colours swirled on the screen, whether the films would have been just as effective in black and white, or even whether the music was the major factor. Eventually Auroratone went the way of so many other faddish therapies and fell out of favour.

During the same era, a physician named Felix Deutsch described a series of fascinating case studies that added to the confusion. In one case, a woman came to him suffering from tachycardia (heart palpitations) and shortness of breath. Her resting pulse rate was 112 beats per minute, 40 beats higher than the ideal rate of 72 beats per minute. Deutsch responded by placing the patient in a red room for four brief treatment sessions. After one session, her pulse dropped from 112 to 80 beats per minute. After four sessions, her pulse rate dropped to 74, and remained there long after the session ended. She explained that the red room had produced a warming sensation, alleviating the sense of choking that had plagued her for days. Deutsch was delighted, but the plot thickened when another patient arrived with dangerously high blood pressure. This patient spent time in a green room rather than a red room, and her results were just as miraculous. After seven sessions, her blood pressure had fallen from 250/130 to a still unhealthy but no longer critical 180/110 (a normal reading is 120/80). While the warmth of red comforted one patient, the coolness of green comforted another, and failing to run meticulous tests, Deutsch was never able to explain why two apparently opposing colours had the same therapeutic effects. One possibility is that the patients were responding positively to attention from a kind and devoted expert, rather than to the treatment itself. Other psychologists had called this phenomenon the Hawthorne effect some years earlier, when workers at a factory known as Hawthorne Works had worked harder and more diligently when researchers both brightened and dimmed the factory floor's lighting. Apparently, the level of illumination was irrelevant; the workers who were normally ignored by superiors were suddenly the focus of attention, and they responded with a burst of enthusiasm. In the end, Deutsch's findings failed to establish that either red or green rooms dampen racing heart rates and high blood pressure any more than they showed that patients will sometimes respond to any form of treatment if they expect to feel better.

The modern science of colour research is richer and far more rigorous than it was in the days of Auroratone films and hit-or-miss colour treatments. According to today's colour psychologists, colours play a powerful role in human decision-making for two reasons. The first reason is that colours affect us physically, as the sawmill workers showed when their body clocks adapted better to shift changes under blue rather than white or yellow light. The second reason is that we associate colours with almost every imaginable pleasant and unpleasant object that populates our planet, which might explain why crime rates declined in Japan and Scotland when local authorities introduced blue streetlights that mimicked the lights on top of police cars.

How Colour Affects Us, Part 1:
Colours and the Human Body

In 1921, Swiss psychologist Hermann Rorschach introduced a psychological test that remained popular for more than fifty years. Patients who completed the Rorschach test were asked to describe what they saw in ten inkblots that looked something like moths, humans, and other animals. Patients who were slow to perceive two humans interacting in one image were said to suffer from social anxiety, and those who saw a threatening male in another were said to have trouble with men and authority. The unreliable test waned in popularity as psychologists introduced superior alternatives, but not before it paved the way for a string of fascinating colour experiments.

In the 1950s, two psychologists noticed that a small group of schizophrenic patients responded peculiarly to two of the Rorschach plates. When shown images two and three, the patients went into a so-called colour shock, sitting in dumbstruck stupor while the tester waited for a response. Unlike the other images, these featured small red blotches alongside the dominant black blots. Images two and three weren't the only images with colourful elements, but something about the stark red patches inspired an unusual response.

The psychologists became curious, so they created a room with a white light and a red light, which they controlled with two separate switches. They recruited nearly a hundred people to participate in an experiment, half of whom were nearby university students—the "normal" group—and half of whom were schizophrenic patients from a nearby state hospital. Each group conducted a series of tests while bathed in both white and red light, and the experimenters measured the difference in their performance under the two colours of light. One of the tests was a thirty-second tremor test, in which the experimenters measured whether the participants' hands were shaking while they tried to remain completely still. Both groups shook more vigorously under the red light, but the effect was especially pronounced among a small group of the schizophrenics. Some of them shook uncontrollably, complaining that their hearts were racing, and that they felt "shocked" by the light. Others complained that they felt sick to their stomachs, and another muttered that "part of my brain, heart, and kidneys were right with God at times but not under this light". The experience obviously frightened many of them, a few jerking in surprise and another urinating uncontrollably when the room was first bathed in red. A second study showed similar results among "normal" males who were exposed to red light but not blue light, suggesting that it wasn't merely the strangeness of non-white light that produced erratic responses. This time, the participants were more anxious and hostile when the light was red rather than blue or white, and their visual cortex—the part of the brain that responds to colour—was more active under the red light. Their heart rate and blood pressure also escalated, showing that the red light had strong physical effects.

While red environments elevate blood flow and nervous-system responses inside our bodies, they also appear to change how we see the world looking outward. One researcher described how a woman suffering from cerebellar disease struggled to walk upright. According to early observations, her gait was unsteady, she wobbled when she walked, and sometimes she became dizzy and fell over without the aid of a wall or another person. Sometimes her dizziness was debilitating, and at other times it wasn't as acute, enabling her to walk with relatively little difficulty. With the help of her physician, she came to realize that she was especially dizzy when she wore red dresses. When she wore green or blue, she was calmer and her symptoms subsided.

The same researcher described other similar cases, which convinced him that the colour red was a genuine physical menace. Red similarly throws off physical judgement even in people without existing medical disorders. People appear to write more erratically in red light than in green light, and their writing becomes less coherent when they write with red ink rather than blue, black, or green ink. When asked to estimate the length and weight of sticks and other objects, people are far more accurate under green than red light. They tend to suffer from *macropsia* and *micropsia*—the illusion that objects are larger or smaller than they actually are.

These effects aren't just idly fascinating; they also influence how we experience our lives every day. The same red that agitates people in a scientific laboratory also agitates them when they load web pages with red backgrounds. In one series of experiments, people felt more agitated while waiting for a red or yellow web page to load than when the same page had a blue background. This agitation made them impatient, so they believed that the yellow and red pages took longer to load than the blue page did, though both pages loaded at the same speed. Later they also claimed that they would be less likely to recommend the site to a friend.

Through the fog of elevated heart rates and distorted perceptions of time and space, researchers have struggled to explain precisely why the colour red incites physical rebellion. Colour science is nothing without number-crunching and comparing how people react to different-coloured rooms, lights, and computer monitors, but sometimes the most striking insights come from simple verbal responses. For decades, researchers have asked test subjects why they responded so intensely to the colour red, and dozens have replied that it disturbs them because it reminds them of blood and, consequently, injury, illness, and even death. Colours are powerful, not just because we respond to them physically but also because they remind us of the objects that embody them—red blood, blue sky, yellow sun, and green grass.

How Colour Affects Us, Part 2: Links between Colours and Everyday Objects

Almost a century ago, a Japanese psychologist became curious about the colour preferences of young people. How old were they when they developed strong colour preferences? Could they explain why they liked some colours more than others? Were those explanations accurate? Children are difficult test subjects, so the researcher began by giving them coloured crayons. Though he continued to focus on their colour preferences (most of them liked the primary colours: red, yellow, and blue), he noticed something interesting about their drawings during the experiment's opening interaction. Instead of haphazardly drawing whatever came to mind, they seemed to draw very different objects with different colours. With black crayons they almost always drew buildings, cars, and other inanimate objects, very rarely drawing people, animals, or natural scenes. With coloured crayons, they drew people and animals, apparently associating vibrant colours with life.

People across the world have very different associations with the same colours, which also suggests that these links are a product of the environment as well as inbuilt biological preferences. Most people across the world favour blue—the so-called *blue phenomenon*—but that's also because it's universally associated with clear skies and calming oceans. The few countries that associate blue primarily with sadness—Hong Kong, for example—also tend to rate it less favourably. People in the United States like black, possibly because they associate it with strength and masculinity, while it's less popular in Colombia, where it implies sadness and formality. Colour associations are especially powerful in the realm of foods, where red implies the richness of cherries, apples, and red meat, and purple implies that something's amiss (unless you're eating acai berries, one of the few natural foods that take on a purplish hue).

Whether colours influence us physically, or because they prompt us to think of related concepts, they shape our thoughts, feelings, and behaviours across a huge range of contexts. As the rest of this chapter shows, the same colour sometimes has very different effects across different contexts. Red traffic lights, stop signs, and flashing lights warn motorists to be vigilant, while the same colour red stirs thoughts of romantic passion and affection. Indeed, no context means more to humans, biologically and sentimentally, than the context of love and sex, and a team of psychologists has taken up the mantle of determining which colours maximize (and minimize) the prospects of mating success.

Colours in Love

The burgeoning world of online dating is now estimated to be worth more than £3 billion globally. As the market matures, online daters are learning the importance of crafting a strong profile while avoiding the pitfalls that plague more careless subscribers. In late 2009, dating site OkCupid released a report that described the dos and don'ts of online dating. For example, daters who send messages with *netspeak* terms like "ur," "r" and "u" attract responses to fewer than 10 percent of their opening messages. (The average response rate is roughly 32 percent.) "How's it going?" is more successful (53 percent), but "hi", which lacks the force of a direct question, fares more poorly (24 percent).

OkCupid's report is silent on the matter of colour, but several enterprising social psychologists have picked up the slack. It's not immediately obvious which colour should maximize romantic success. Blue is the most popular colour in the world, grey and black are associated with dominance and power, green is supposed to be soothing, and red is typically associated with love in popular culture.

In one experiment, five young women spent the day hitchhiking near a famous peninsula in Brittany, France, their safety monitored by several hidden observers. The women changed their shirts throughout the day, choosing randomly from a menu of black, white, red, yellow, blue, and green. Female drivers weren't particularly sympathetic, stopping only 5–9 percent of the time regardless of the colour of the hitchhikers' T-shirts. Male motorists, on the other hand, were more considerate and more discerning: whereas only 12–14 percent of all male motorists stopped when the women wore black, white, yellow, blue, or green, 21 percent stopped when the women wore red shirts. Since only men were swayed by the colour red, the researcher argued that red enhances romantic appeal specifically, rather than platonic attraction more generally.

A similar experiment two years later suggested that the result wasn't a fluke. Sixty-four French women who had posted ads on a personals website agreed to participate for a year in a study to test this question. Each woman created an ad featuring a colour photo of her face and upper body, over which she wore a plain-coloured T-shirt. For nine months the ads weren't changed at all—except for the colour of the women's tops. Every two weeks the experimenter digitally altered the colour of each woman's top, choosing from the same six colours available to the female hitchhikers in the earlier experiment. Then they watched and waited while the women recorded the emails they received from thousands of interested men. As in the hitchhiking study, the women were far more popular when their shirts were red. During the nine-month period, 14–16 percent of their emails arrived when they wore the black, white, yellow, blue, and green shirts—but 21 percent arrived when they wore the red shirt.

In explaining why red enhances sexual appeal, researchers reach back to the world of lower-order animals, where rich displays of red tend to promote sexual success. The reasoning behind this relationship differs for males and females. Female animals display their biological readiness for mating with vivid patches of red on their genitals, chest, and face. As females approach ovulation, their elevated oestrogen levels promote blood flow, which in turn reddens their skin. Like lower-order animals, women experience reddening of their skin as they approach ovulation, and whenever they're sexually excited or aroused. It's no coincidence, then, that femmes fatales in *Jezebel, Dial M for Murder,* and *A Streetcar Named Desire* wear red dresses, and Nathaniel Hawthorne's Hester Prynne was forced to advertise her adulterous past by wearing a scarlet letter A, rather than a letter of green, blue, or black. Meanwhile, a red heart signifies the romance of Valentine's Day, and red-light district workers wear red lipstick and blusher to encourage business. In general, the colour red signifies sexuality and attraction, both for biological reasons and because we've come to associate red with sexuality in literature and popular culture.

Among lower-order male animals, the colour red is a sign of health, vitality, status, and virility. For example, male mandrills display patches of red on their faces and genitalia, and these patches are particularly vivid among alpha males. The same deep red coloration distinguishes alpha amphipods, sticklebacks, finches, gelada baboons, and males of numerous other species from their sexually inferior counterparts. Humans show similar tendencies, with dominant males across time and cultures wearing distinctive red face paint and garments. The most powerful men of ancient Rome were known as *coccinati*, literally "the ones who wear red"; they distinguished themselves from the plebs by wearing bright red clothing. Even today VIPs and luminaries strut down a red carpet, while the masses cheer from the grey concrete sidelines.

Since evolutionary anecdotes suggest that the colour red should appeal to both sexes, two social psychologists decided to test whether irrelevant patches of red enhance the sexual attractiveness of men and women. They asked heterosexual men and women to rate the attractiveness of members of the opposite sex depicted in printed photographs. In one round of experiments, they varied whether the men and women in the photographs wore red shirts and sweaters or shirts and sweaters of another colour. The same photos earned higher attractiveness ratings when their subjects wore red clothing. The results held regardless of whether the student raters were American, English, German, or Chinese, suggesting that the effects weren't merely driven by a pro-red bias that affects people from some cultures but not others. Furthermore, the men and women who wore red weren't rated more positively on all dimensions; for example, they didn't seem more likeable, friendly, or outgoing. Instead, they specifically seemed more sexually attractive and worthy of sexual attention. In another experiment, the researcher showed the men a photo of a woman wearing either a red or blue shirt, and led them into a room where they would ostensibly meet her a few minutes later. In the meantime, they were told to arrange two chairs so that the two of them could have a conversation. As a display of desired intimacy, the men moved the two chairs significantly closer together when the woman wore a red shirt (about five feet apart) than when the woman wore a blue shirt (about six feet apart). The differences disappeared when heterosexual men rated the attractiveness of other men, and when heterosexual women rated the attractiveness of other women; in short, red shirts only made people seem more attractive to potential mates. The message here couldn't be simpler: if you're trying to attract a member of the opposite sex, red dresses and red shirts give you a slight advantage romantically speaking.

Colours at Work and School

When people aren't seeking romantic partners, they spend much of their time at work, and one critical component of professional success is intellectual achievement. Most classical accounts describe academic prowess as the product of good genes, a nurturing environment, and plenty of hard work, but very few if any experts include ambient colour in the list of relevant factors. But here, too, colours play a surprisingly prominent role. For a start, people are far more likely to remember pictures of a place presented in colour rather than in black and white, and memory is a critical component of intellectual performance. According to the psychologists who studied the phenomenon, we're able to bury coloured scenes deeper in our memory, and later to retrieve them more effectively than identical scenes presented in black and white. In a sense, memories are like fish that float through the sea of our minds, and we're more likely to snag an old memory if we plunge many hooks into the sea. Colour is a particularly large hook covered with tasty bait, and black-and-white memories are therefore comparatively elusive.

Coloured memories are better retrieved than black-and-white memories, but not all colours have the same effect on intellectual performance. Students learn to fear the presence of red ink on exams and assignments, and some US and Australian states have even banned teachers from correcting academic work with red ink. Experts who prefer black or blue ink argue that red ink has become inextricably linked with failure and criticism, so students are likely to disengage when they're faced with a page covered in red. Some quarters perceive this policy as needlessly paternalistic, and one conservative politician in the Australian state of Queensland described the policy as "kooky, loopy, loony, and lefty". The policy may indeed be loopy and lefty, but it also has strong support from a number of academic studies.

In one study, researchers asked a group of university undergraduates to correct an essay that was ostensibly written by a student who was learning to speak English. In fact, the experimenters fabricated the essay and inserted a range of errors. The undergraduates were asked to identify any errors in spelling, grammar, word choice, and punctuation. Some of the students were randomly selected to correct the essay using a blue pen, and the others were randomly selected to use a red pen. Although the students read exactly the same essay, those who were given a red pen found an average of twenty-four errors, whereas those who were given a blue pen found an average of only nineteen errors. In a follow-up study, students read an essay advocating the benefits of school field trips, and again they graded the essay using either a red pen or a blue pen. On average, those who used the red pen gave the essays a score of 76/100, whereas those who used the blue pen gave the essays a score of 80/100. The "don't grade in red pen" policy may be eccentric, but students can't be blamed for asking to be graded in blue pen when their grades suffer under the scrutiny of red ink.

Unfortunately, red ink is a double-edged sword, also causing students to perform more poorly in the first place. In a landmark series of studies, students attained lower test scores when they were exposed to the colour red, rather than black, green, grey, or white. In some studies, the students wrote an experiment's ID number in red, green, or black pen before completing fifteen anagram puzzles. The puzzles required the students to unscramble letter strings like NIDRK to form English words (in this case, DRINK). The students who wrote their ID number with a red pen answered an average of 22 percent fewer questions correctly than those who wrote their ID number in black or green pen. In other studies, the first page of the test booklet was coloured red, grey, white, or green. Again, the students achieved lower scores on several different tests when the first page was red rather than grey, white, or green. In one test they solved 18 percent fewer number-string completion puzzles (e.g., which number comes next: 18, 16, 19, 15, 20, 14, 21,__; the answer is 13); in another, they solved 37 percent fewer analogy questions (e.g., expensive is to rarely as cheap is to __; the answer is frequently).

It's worth taking a moment to compare the magnitude of these effects with the subtlety of the colour manipulations. Students study for days on end and parents pay thousands of pounds for professional tutoring, but even diligent students with wealthy parents would be delighted to find that their hard work and hard-earned cash yielded test-score improvements in the neighbourhood of 37 percent. Meanwhile, these studies suggest that replacing your red pen with a black or green pen, or reprinting the red cover page of an exam in a different colour, has similar effects.

The same researchers also wanted to know *why* red hampers academic performance. It turns out that the colour red activates the right hemisphere of the frontal cortex, a pattern of brain activity that typically indicates avoidance motivation. Avoidance motivation is the technical term for a state in which you're more concerned with avoiding failure than you are with achieving success. It's a distracting state of mind that all but guarantees poorer performance when you're trying to solve questions that require insight and mental effort. Psychologists have also shown that people literally recoil from the colour red, leaning slightly further backward in their seats when they're about to begin a test with a red rather than green cover. None of these effects occurs consciously, but when they occur together it becomes clear why the colour red can be so damaging in academic contexts.

Despite these results, there's an important twist to this story. For some intellectual tasks, the tendency for red to prime avoidant mindsets promotes just the right kind of thinking. Avoidance is also associated with vigilance, so tasks that require attention to detail are easier when we're in a more vigilant mindset. In one study, for example, students were far more vigilant when proofreading a text for errors and memorizing a list of words when those tasks were presented against a red background rather than a blue background. Here vigilance and avoidance were precisely the mental states that promoted success. (In other experiments, when the tasks required creativity, the researchers replicated the earlier results, since avoidant states tend to stifle creative thinking.) To conclude, then, the colour red inspires academic underachievement, but only when the task doesn't require vigilance or attention to detail. For those tasks, red enhances rather than impairs performance.

Far from the intellectual world of school and academic performance, colour also has a striking impact in the sporting arena. The margin of error among elite sportspeople is tiny—a few extra pounds of muscle and an extra training session are often enough to decide who wins and who loses. For all the effort that elite athletes put into training, sports experts have traditionally ignored the role of colour in the sporting arena. According to one result, sometimes the difference between Olympic gold and no medal at all comes down to whether an athlete is randomly drawn to wear red or blue.

Colours and Sports

Six athletes from the 2004 Athens Olympic Games—wrestlers Istvan Majoros, Artur Taymazov, and Jung Ji-Hyun, boxers Alexander Povetkin and Odlanier Solis, and tae kwon do competitor Moon Dae-Sung—shared two important features. All six remained undefeated and won gold medals in their respective events, and before each of their quarter-final, semi-final, and final bouts, Olympic officials had randomly assigned them to wear red uniforms rather than the alternative blue uniforms. In the world of competitive sports, where superstitious athletes refuse to wash lucky underwear, it's hard to ignore the coincidence—and two anthropologists set out to show that the relationship between victory and the colour red comes down to more than a random fluke.

The researchers began by collecting the results of all the Greco-Roman wrestling, freestyle wrestling, tae kwon do, and boxing matches at the 2004 Athens Olympic Games. For each of the 457 matches, they recorded whether the competitor wearing red beat the competitor in blue. The results were astonishing. In all four sports, the red competitors won more bouts than the blue competitors, and red competitors won 55 percent of their bouts overall. The effect was especially strong when the competitors were evenly matched—when, theoretically, even trivial factors might tip the balance one way or the other. When the competitors were seeded identically, the red competitor won a staggering 62 percent of all matches. It's hard to escape the irony that the same sporting bodies that seek to eliminate performance-enhancing drugs also require one of the two competitors in each bout to wear a performance-enhancing red uniform.

There's no obvious reason why red should function like a psychological steroid. It's certainly not a physical or tangible aid, because the red uniforms are identical to the blue uniforms in fabric and fit, so the only remaining possibility is that people think and act differently when they see the colour red. One possibility, which overlaps with the mating advantages of wearing red, is that the colour red is biologically and evolutionarily associated with dominance and aggression. When animals fight, their blood vessels dilate and their faces redden with the flush of physical exertion. Competitors who wear red might, therefore, feel more dominant than competitors who wear blue, and competitors who wear blue might perceive their red-clothed opponents as particularly aggressive or dominant. Since the outcomes of pugilistic events such as boxing and wrestling are decided in part by which competitor is more dominant, aggressive, and psychologically commanding, the outcome is subtly biased in favour of the competitor who wears red.

While red-clad competitors might feel more dominant and commanding than their blue-clad counterparts, the referee who decides the outcome of the match might be partly responsible for the effect. Several sports psychologists showed that referees are indeed swayed by the colour of the competitors' clothing. They asked forty-two professional tae kwon do referees to score a series of tae kwon do bouts between a competitor wearing red protective gear and a second competitor wearing blue protective gear. The referees applied official World Taekwondo Federation rules, in which competitors earn two points for striking their opponent in the face, one point for striking their opponent in the body, and a one-point deduction for illegal conduct. The rules are designed to be objective, so two referees should ideally award the same number of points for the same conduct. Half of the pool of referees scored the original video footage of the bouts, with one competitor wearing red and the other wearing blue. Meanwhile, the researchers digitally altered the footage so the remaining referees watched *exactly* the same footage, except this time they switched the colour of the competitors' protective gear. Now the competitor who wore red in the original footage wore blue protective gear, and the competitor who wore blue in the original footage wore red. If the referees were insensitive to colour, the same competitor should have received the same score regardless of whether he wore red or blue clothing—but that's not what the researchers found. The competitors who wore red clothing in the original footage scored, on average, 8 points to their competitors' average score of 7 points. Then, when the colours were reversed, the competitor wearing red (and formerly wearing blue in the original footage) won the bouts by an average score of 8–7. The referees therefore awarded the competitors wearing red more points than they awarded the competitors wearing blue, even when they were judging an identical (but recoloured) performance.

In the world of professional team sports, one colour seems to trump the aggression implied even by red. In the mid-1980s, two social psychologists examined the penalty records of twenty-one National Hockey League and twenty-eight National Football League teams. They paid special attention to the five NHL and five NFL teams with black uniforms—those whose uniforms were more than 50 percent black. Not only did a group of students perceive those uniforms to be particularly malevolent, but the teams wearing those uniforms also attracted many more penalties than their less darkly coloured competitors. Meanwhile, when the Pittsburgh Penguins and the Vancouver Canucks traded in their non-black NHL uniforms for black uniforms in the late 1970s, they almost immediately began conceding more penalties. Pittsburgh, relatively polite in their non-black 1970s incarnation, conceded a fairly tame eight penalty minutes per game. Their new black uniforms ushered in a penalty-rich era, during which they conceded twelve penalty minutes per game—a record trumped only by their black-wearing Pennsylvanian rivals, the Philadelphia Flyers. The researchers considered two possible explanations for these results, and found evidence for both: people behave more aggressively when they wear black clothing; and referees and onlookers see more aggression in the same actions when they're committed by people wearing black rather than grey or white clothing.

These results show how difficult it can be to guarantee fairness in the world of professional sports. Even when two competitors eschew steroids, blood doping, and other illegal performance-enhancing aids, the lucky competitor assigned to wear red is at a distinct advantage. Similarly, teams that wear aggression-inducing black uniforms seem inevitably drawn to the penalty box. These results show not only how insidiously the world around us shapes how we think, feel, and behave, but also how difficult it can be to construct a fair and just world free from bias. Red uniforms create an unfair advantage, black uniforms provoke undue aggression, and blue and white uniforms inspire comparatively meek behaviour.

Colours and Morality

It doesn't take a big leap to connect sporting colours with moral concepts—the dominance of red; the meekness of blue; and, perhaps most damaging in a world obsessed with skin colour, the brutality of black and the purity of white. Given these associations, would sporting contests be fairer if athletes were forced to wear different shades of grey? Unfortunately, even this bland solution addresses only part of the problem, because the labels "light" and "dark" have their own intrusive connotations. If you were forced to decide which of the terms "light" and "dark" represents virtue, morality, and nobility, and which represents vice, immorality, and baseness, which would you choose? If you're anything like most Americans, Germans, Danes, Indians, and even central African Ndembu tribespeople, you probably associate lightness with morality and darkness with immorality. These associations fall naturally from the world that surrounds us. White snow is pristine, but only until dirt and mud sully its purity. One drop of black paint similarly ruins a bucket of white paint, but a bucket of black paint overwhelms a wayward drop of white paint. These natural relationships feed into metaphorical relationships between blackness and contaminating evil on the one hand, and whiteness and frail, virtuous purity on the other.

Lending empirical heft to this claim, two social psychologists have shown that people struggle to reverse the association between white and good, and black and bad. To study the relationship between blackness and morality, the researchers adopted a popular experimental test called the Stroop task. To give you a sense of how the Stroop task works, look at the two words written below. Your task is to state *the colour of the text in which each word is written*:

RED   BLUE

It's not easy to utter correctly the words "black, white" when you're simultaneously reading the words "red, blue". The Stroop task turns one of our strengths—the ability to read effortlessly—into a weakness, by asking us to ignore the words that we're reading and instead to focus on the colour of the text. The experimenters cleverly tweaked the Stroop task to show that we tend to associate whiteness with virtue and morality, and blackness with vice and immorality. As with the classic example, the students who completed their study were asked to decide whether words like these below were written in black or white text:

CHEAT VIRTUE   SIN   BRAVE

The students had no trouble indicating that the word CHEAT was written in black, and the word BRAVE was written in white—after years of associating blackness with immorality and whiteness with morality, they were primed to perceive the "moral" words as white and the "immoral" words as black. They had significantly more trouble stating that the word VIRTUE was written in black and the word SIN was written in white, since these pairings violated the associations they'd formed over many years.

Why should we care if people are slow to state that the word SIN is written in white, while the word VIRTUE is written in black? What could these arcane results mean for the way we live our lives? Imagine now that instead of looking at four abstract words, you're sitting in the jury box looking at a defendant accused of a heinous crime. If you're quicker to associate the black text with cheating than with bravery, you might also more readily associate a black defendant with cheating than bravery. Similarly, if you're quicker to associate white text with virtue than sin, you might struggle to associate the white defendant with the concept of sin rather than virtue. These results are more than mere curiosities; they also suggest one reason why police officers are more likely to stop, detain, and ultimately arrest a black man rather than a white man. Moreover, children aren't born innately prejudiced against black people; until the age of four or five years, perhaps once they've formed associations between whiteness and virtue and blackness and vice, they tend not to show evidence of anti-black prejudice at all. Of course, there are many reasons why people might come to hold damaging stereotypes (some covered earlier in chapter 5), but these results suggest that associations between blackness and immorality might subtly contribute to the ongoing problem of anti-black prejudice.

Colours shape how we think and behave across a diverse array of contexts, and sometimes the same colour has different effects depending on the context. Red fosters romance as it signals the flush of attraction, but it also prompts alertness and vigilance in the face of taxing mental tasks. Blue deters would-be criminals from misbehaving, but it also alleviates the symptoms of exhaustion and seasonal depression. Some of these effects are grounded in human biology: red acts as matchmaker because it signals sexual arousal, and blue light halts the production of

sleep-inducing melatonin by mimicking the properties of natural sunlight. Other effects capitalize on associations, as blue appears to deter
crime by invoking the blue lights on a police car, while red promotes
vigilance by calling to mind the colour of stop signs and flashing lights
on emergency vehicles.

For all their considerable power, colours are but one feature of the
physical environments that we inhabit as we live our lives. These locations differ along countless other dimensions, from the presence or absence of nature and noise to the overcrowding that comes when we insist
on living in already overpopulated cities. Some of these features are good
for us, but others join together to form oppressive environments that dis-
turb our thoughts, dampen our moods, and disrupt our behaviours.

8.

LOCATIONS

Oppressive Environments

When Japanese troops left Hong Kong at the end of World War Two, they left behind a crumbling fort that covered an area the size of six football pitches. Refugees invaded the structure and lived in hundreds of makeshift dwellings until the government built water pipes and tall concrete apartment blocks in the 1960s. The area, known as Kowloon Walled City, became an emblem for the plague of overpopulation. Many of the city's apartments were barely larger than an office desk, its alleyways were rarely more than a few feet wide, and most of the city was shrouded in perpetual darkness. Doctors and dentists established illegal practices, and Triad gangs opened brothels, gambling houses, and opium dens. By 1987, the tiny city's population climbed to more than 33,000 residents, making its population seventy-five times denser than the population of Monaco, the world's most densely populated country. At the same density, the diminutive US state of Delaware could house Earth's entire human population.

In the mid-1960s, not long after Kowloon Walled City's population

skyrocketed, two researchers at a hospital in Oxford subjected young patients to a controversial experiment on overcrowding. The researchers
combed the hospital wards and found fifteen children between the ages
of three and eight years old, whom they categorized as autistic, severely
brain-damaged, or normal. Each day, the children would assemble for
"free play" in a room that was designed to hold small groups. Sometimes
the experimenters ensured that no more than six children played at
once—a comfortable number given the size of the room. At other times
the room held more than a dozen children simultaneously. While the
children played for fifteen-minute periods, nurses and researchers looked
on and recorded their behaviour. As expected, the autistic children rarely
interacted with their playmates—but they also spent far more time nervously hugging the room's periphery when it was overpopulated. When
joined by only three or four playmates, they spent an average of three
minutes on the room's outskirts, but that number jumped to eight minutes when the room held more than a dozen children. The normal and
brain-damaged children didn't fare much better in the densely populated room. They played happily for ten minutes in smaller groups, but
only for five or six minutes when the room was overcrowded. Meanwhile, they spent little more than thirty seconds fighting and snatching
toys when the room was sparsely populated, but up to four minutes bick-
ering when the space was congested. Two of the children even had to be
restrained from biting their playmates. After only minutes in an overcrowded room, the gregarious children became hostile, and the anxious
children were doubly withdrawn.

The Oxford hospital study was groundbreaking, but it left open a
number of important questions. Were the results merely a product of the
study's subjects—a small group of children hampered by temporary or
ongoing psychological trauma? Or would the results also apply to a
larger group of healthy, high-functioning adults? To answer those questions, a large group of psychologists and architects conducted two experiments among eight thousand college students at three institutions in

Massachusetts and Pennsylvania. Some of the students lived in high-density towers, some in medium-density apartment blocks, and others in lower-density halls of residence. The researchers used two subtle techniques to measure whether the students had formed strong social bonds with their neighbours. They began by scattering a series of stamped addressed envelopes inside the buildings, creating the sense that the letters had been lost on the way to the mailbox. They made sure that the letters were dropped in prominent places so the students couldn't miss them. Some of the students saw the letters, assumed they were lost by fellow residents, and kindly posted them—a small gesture suggesting a measure of social kinship. When the researchers returned four hours later, they found that 100 percent of the letters in the low-density housing were posted, 87 percent were posted in the medium-density blocks, and only 63 percent were posted in the high-density towers.

In a different set of apartment blocks that similarly varied in density, the researchers placed boxes asking residents to donate used milk cartons for an art project. Calculating the number of cartons that were used by the residents in the blocks, they found again that high-density dwellers were less helpful. Those in low- and medium-density housing contributed 55 percent of their cartons, whereas the students in high-density housing gave only 37 percent of their cartons. These results suggest that high-density living hampers generosity, and other researchers have shown that overcrowding similarly provokes mental illness, drug addiction, alcoholism, family disorganization, and a generally diminished quality of life.

Extreme overcrowding is also associated with claustrophobia: the fear of closed or very densely populated spaces. In contrast to some other human phobias that people acquire with experience—like triskaidekaphobia (fear of the number 13) and agyrophobia (fear of crossing the street)—claustrophobia appears to be innate. Humans today are just as afraid of small, dark rooms as were their ancestors who stumbled into small, dark caves thousands of years ago. We're driven to preserve a measure of personal space, which is why people respond strongly to brief unintended physical contact. In one study, marketing expert Paco Underhill surreptitiously filmed shoppers as they browsed the aisles of a large department store. Some of the aisles were especially narrow, and the shoppers who stopped to browse in narrower aisles tended to be jostled by other customers who struggled to squeeze past them. Seconds later, the disturbed customers stopped browsing and often left the store altogether. When Underhill later questioned some of the shoppers, they had no idea that they had been persuaded to leave the store because they were jostled—but the results were unambiguous and the prescription clear: customers are more likely to remain in stores if the aisles are wide enough to prevent even light collisions, or butt brushes, as Underhill called them.

Overcrowding also creates noise, and researchers have found that the constant hum of everyday life stifles creativity and learning. In the early 1970s, psychologists visited four 32-story apartment blocks in upper Manhattan. The apartments faced onto Interstate 95, one of the busiest motorways on the East Coast. Among the apartments' residents were seventy-three primary school children who were subjected to the constant rumble of motorway traffic—a sound that reached up to 84 decibels. Some scales define 84 decibels as "very loud", its volume matching the noise from a truck without a silencer, or a loud factory. Prolonged exposure to a noise of that intensity sometimes produces hearing loss, and the noise was formidable even inside the apartments. The children on the towers' lower floors experienced a racket ten times more intense than the relatively muffled sound that reached the children who lived on the top floors. Consequently, when the researchers administered a hearing test, children who had been living on a low floor for at least four years struggled to discriminate between words that sounded similar but had very different meanings. For example, the word pairs *gear* and *beer*, or *cope* and *coke*, are difficult to distinguish when whispered or stifled by background noise. The researchers reasoned that children with poorer hearing are also less likely to engage in conversation and more likely to experience intellectual difficulties. And that's what they found: the children who had lived on the lower floors for many years also struggled to read relative to other children of their age. Most distressing, when the children had lived in the buildings for more than six years, the researchers could predict their reading scores with astonishing accuracy by asking just one question: "On which floor do you live?" Since the effect of the noise grew over time, the researchers were able to rule out the possibility that residents on the higher floors were generally smarter, wealthier, or more dedicated to educating their children. Exposing children to continual noise for an extended period of time—even the background noise that comes with urban living—is enough to hamper their intellectual development.

Overcrowding and noise pollution are relatively recent problems that barely existed a few hundred years ago, before the Industrial Revolution heralded the arrival of generators and engines. Suddenly, large cities replaced scattered towns and hamlets, and the machines that built those cities were themselves noisy. As so often happens, the best solutions to these modern problems recreate the world as it was before they existed. For one researcher, that solution became apparent when he noticed that hospital patients just a few rooms apart were recovering at very different rates.

The Natural Environment as Panacea

Paoli, Pennsylvania, is a small town not too far from Philadelphia, with a local suburban hospital. Patients at Paoli Memorial Hospital recover in a row of rooms facing a small courtyard. In the early 1980s, a researcher visited the hospital and gathered information about patients who had undergone gall-bladder surgery between 1972 and 1981. Gall-bladder surgery is routine and generally uncomplicated, but most patients in the 1970s were kept for a week or two before they returned home. Some took

longer to recover than others, and the researcher wondered whether subtle differences between the hospital rooms might explain this discrep-
ancy. Some of the rooms on one side of the hospital faced onto a brick
wall, whereas others slightly farther down the corridor faced onto a
small stand of deciduous trees. Apart from their differing views, the
rooms were identical.

When the researcher looked at their recovery charts, he was struck by
how much better the patients fared when their rooms looked out onto
the trees rather than the brick wall. On average, those who faced the
brick wall needed an extra day to recover before returning home. They
were also far more depressed and experienced more pain. On average,
their nurses recorded four negative notes per patient—comments like
"needs much encouragement" and "upset and crying"—whereas those
with a view of the trees warranted negative notes only once during their
stay. Meanwhile, very few of the patients who looked out onto the trees
required more than a single dose of strong painkillers during the middle
part of their stay, whereas those facing the wall required two or even
three doses. Apart from their view, the patients had received identical
treatment at the hospital and were otherwise very similar. Each patient
with a view of the trees was matched with a patient whose room looked
out onto the brick wall, so that their age, gender, weight, status as smok-
ers or non-smokers, and attending doctors and nurses were controlled as
tightly as possible. Since those factors were controlled, the only explanation was that patients who looked out at a stand of trees recovered more
quickly because they were lucky enough to occupy rooms with a natural view.

These results are surprising because the effects are so large—much
larger than the effects of many other targeted treatment interventions.
By some measures, patients who gazed out at a natural scene were four
times better off than those who faced a wall. Strong results usually inspire scepticism, but plenty of studies have shown similar effects. In one
of those studies, two environmental psychologists approached 337 sets of

parents who lived with their children in five rural communities in upstate New York. The researcher scored the "naturalness" of each family's home, awarding points for natural views, indoor plants, and grass-covered yards. Some of the children had experienced little stress growing up, rarely fighting or getting punished at school, but others were bullied and struggled to get along with their parents. When the researchers measured the happiness and well-being of the students in their study, they noticed that those who had experienced hardship were distressed and lacking in self-esteem—except when they lived in more natural environments. The presence of nature seemed to buffer them against the stresses that hampered other children who lived in predominantly man-made environments.

In an even more direct test, another group of researchers asked a hundred sets of parents with children who suffered from attention deficit disorder (ADD) how their children responded to different playtime activities. Children who have ADD are often restless and distracted. But the parents reported that green activities—like fishing and soccer—left their children in a far more relaxed, focused state. It wasn't that the children who spent time outside were merely happier, more likely to interact with friends, or more active—in fact, those who sat indoors in a room with natural views were calmer than children who played outside in man-made environments that were devoid of grass and trees.

What is it that sets natural environments apart from others? Why shouldn't a quiet streetscape have the same effect as a quiet natural landscape, for example? Architecture has its own beauty, and some people prefer urban environments to natural environments, so why does nature seem to have such powerful restorative effects? The answer is that natural environments have a unique constellation of features that set them apart from man-made locations. Just before the dawn of the twentieth century, William James, one of the early giants of modern psychology, explained that human attention comes in two different forms. The first is *directed attention*, which enables us to focus on demanding tasks such as driving and writing. Reading a book also requires directed attention, and you'll notice that you start to zone out when you're tired, or you've been reading for hours at a time. The second form is *involuntary attention*, which comes easily and doesn't require any mental effort at all. As James explained, "Strange things, moving things, wild animals, bright things, pretty things, words, blows, blood, etc., etc., etc." all attract our attention involuntarily. Nature restores your mental functioning in the same way that food and water restore your body. The business of everyday life— dodging traffic, slavishly making decisions and judgement calls, interacting with strangers—is depleting, and what man-made environments take away from us, nature gives back. There's something mystical and, you might say, unscientific about this claim, but its heart actually rests in what psychologists call *attention restoration theory*, or ART. According to ART, urban environments are draining because they force us to direct our attention to specific tasks (e.g., avoiding the onslaught of traffic) and grab our attention dynamically, compelling us to "Look here!" before telling us instead to "Look over there!" These demands are draining— and they're also absent in natural environments. Forests, streams, rivers, lakes, and oceans demand very little from us, though they're still engaging, ever-changing, and attention-grabbing. The difference between natural and urban landscapes is *how* they command our attention. While man-made landscapes bombard us with stimulation, their natural counterparts give us the chance to think as much or as little as we'd like, and the opportunity to replenish exhausted mental resources.

In the early 2000s, more than a hundred unlucky Dutch students were subjected to an experiment that revealed nature's capacity for mental restoration. The students entered a lab and sat in front of a screen that began to play scenes from the controversial film *Faces of Death*. First, a woman decapitated a rooster; then sheep and bulls were slaughtered in an abattoir. Two vegetarians, repulsed by the images, left the room and refused to return, while the remaining students stared at the screen transfixed and horrified. As the video ended and the students caught their breath, the researcher began a second video. Mercifully, the second video was less distressing, depicting the scenes a person might view during a seven-minute stroll. For some of the students, the video passed through a Dutch forest, whereas the other students watched a video that progressed down a street in the Dutch city of Utrecht. After watching the video, the students who imagined walking through the forest scene reported feeling happier, more relaxed, and less angry than those who imagined walking through the cityscape. They were also more alert, which enabled them to perform better on a task that required them to search for specific letters of the alphabet among an array dominated by irrelevant characters. Merely asking students to imagine strolling through a natural scene was enough to dampen the distressing and attention-sapping effects of the *Faces of Death* video.

Healers in Japan and Germany have long heralded the benefits of natural therapy, recognizing that humankind has spent 99.99 percent of its history living in natural environments. The Japanese version of natural therapy is *shinrin-yoku*, or forest bathing, which requires that patients walk for extended periods through forested areas while inhaling woodsy scents that complement the sylvan atmosphere. German Kneipp therapy similarly requires that patients perform physical exercises in forest clearings. These alternative therapies aren't just idle cultural quirks, and researchers have found that patients enjoy a wide range of benefits. Among others, compared with people who walked through urban areas, shinrin-yoku patients had lower blood pressure, lower pulse rates, and lower cortisol levels, a marker of reduced stress. People who are exposed to natural scenes aren't just happier or more comfortable; the very building blocks of their physiological well-being also respond positively to natural therapy.

Natural environments promote calmness and well-being in part because they expose people to low levels of stress. These stressful experiences are tame in comparison with the trials and tribulations that most of us associate with stress—workplace drama, traffic jams, and wailing children on international plane journeys. Humans thrive with some stimulation, but we're incapable of coping with extreme stressors, which push us from the comfortable realm of eustress (good stress) to the danger zone of distress (bad stress). Interesting locations, including busy natural environments, are so beneficial that physicians have begun to suggest that they might offer a cheap and effective way to lessen the effects of certain cancers.

One team of researchers showed that women who were recently diagnosed with early-stage breast cancer were far more capable of completing challenging mental tasks when they immersed themselves in natural environments for two hours each week for approximately two months. The interventions began when the women were diagnosed, and continued beyond surgery into the recovery period. Like many distressed patients who begin to battle life-threatening illnesses, the women struggled to complete difficult mental tasks shortly after they were diagnosed. Those who spent time in natural environments improved progressively, regaining their capacity to devote attention to demanding mental puzzles. Meanwhile, the patients who were not exposed to the nature-based intervention tended to struggle with similar tasks throughout the test period. Paying better attention is obviously a long way from recovery, but patients with sharper minds often respond better to treatment, stick to their treatment regimens, and behave more proactively during recovery.

Unfortunately, nature occupies an ever-smaller portion of the earth's surface, and millions of urbanites live miles from forests, lakes, and oceans. Instead, we're faced with urban clutter in the form of billboards, signs, and other written material, and recent estimates suggest that we process thousands of these written messages each day. Children and teens between the ages of eight and eighteen are especially overloaded, spending almost every minute of leisure time attached to TVs, smartphones, and computers. Research shows that in the absence of natural restoration, the human brain copes with this clutter by going into over-drive, briefly scanning the environment more clearly and deeply than it usually does until fatigue forces it to return to a stable state of shallower mental processing. As two game-show contestants demonstrated, this capacity to engage additional mental resources is sometimes triggered by subtle cues in the environment.

Disfluency and the Tendency to Think More Deeply

Who Wants to Be a Millionaire is one of the most successful TV game shows in history. It's also an excellent place to watch people grapple with disfluency—the experience of struggling to make sense of information. The show has more than a hundred international variants, but in each case contestants answer trivia questions that become increasingly difficult as they're worth larger sums of money. Two of the US show's most famous contestants are John Carpenter and Ogi Ogas, who both walked away with impressive winnings. On 19 November 1999, Carpenter became the first contestant to win $1 million on the US show. For the million-dollar question, the show's host Regis Philbin asked Carpenter which one of the following presidents appeared on the television show *Laugh-In*: Lyndon Johnson, Richard Nixon, Jimmy Carter, or Gerald Ford. Carpenter smiled briefly, then asked to phone his parents. In using this "lifeline", Carpenter implied that he was stumped by the question and sought help by "phoning a friend". Usually, when contestants phone a friend, they rush to ask the question as quickly as possible within the thirty-second time limit, and hope their chosen friend will be able to help. In this case, Carpenter used a very different tack. When Philbin told him to ask the question, he said:

Hi, Dad . . . I don't really need your help, I just wanted to let you know that I'm gonna win the million dollars . . . because the US president that appeared on *Laugh-In* is Richard Nixon. That's my final answer.

Carpenter was right, and he'd known the answer from the second he saw the question. The smirk that briefly crossed his face was the hallmark of fluent—smooth and effortless—mental processing. A small space in his long-term memory bank housed the link between Richard Nixon and *Laugh-In*, and the answer appeared to him without demanding much mental effort. For all the ease in Carpenter's response, Philbin might as well have told him that for a million dollars, he'd need to state his own name aloud or calculate the sum of one and one.

Seven years after Carpenter's suave exhibition, cognitive neuroscientist Ogi Ogas faced his own million-dollar question. Meredith Vieira, the show's new host, asked Ogas which one of these ships was *not* one of the three taken over by colonists during the Boston Tea Party: *Eleanor, Dartmouth, Beaver,* or *William*? Ogas agonized, and you could see him frantically searching the long aisles of his memory. Over the course of four agonizing minutes, he narrowed down the options and almost decided to answer "*William*". Just before he answered, a more conservative voice chimed in and told him to take the $500,000 he'd already won, rather than risk the prospect of walking away with a comparatively measly $25,000. An aversion to risk had cost him the chance of winning $1 million. Later, Ogas wrote about the experience:

I immediately had an intuition that one of the ships at the Tea Party was *Dartmouth*. I reflected on *Dartmouth*, using it as a prime. I repeated the ship's name aloud and silently to myself. Gradually, the name of another ship formed in my mind, echoing each repetition of *Dartmouth*: *Beaver* . . . And then, faintly, like the reflection of the moon on a midnight lake, the name of a third ship dimly waxed upon the murk of my mind: *Eleanor* . . .

I blinked. Suddenly, I became aware of the wobble of the chair, the murmurs of the audience . . . Intuition? What are you thinking?! You're risking a *house*! You can't possibly know the answer to this arcane question! *There's no such thing as intuition*! . . .

"I believe I'll walk with the money I've got. That's my final answer."

With the wobble of a chair and the murmurs of the audience—environmental triggers that tempered his confidence—Ogas suddenly realized that $475,000 was too much to risk on a hunch. In the face of environmental disfluency, he paused, reconsidered, and chose to take the more conservative route. The differences between Carpenter's and Ogas's experiences show that disfluency often functions as a useful gauge for determining confidence. Carpenter's response arose fluently, and he was right to be confident, whereas Ogas's response arose haltingly without the same sense of ease that people generally associate with certainty. In a series of experiments I ran with three other psychologists, I tested whether disfluency might be a useful signal that tells people to commit extra mental resources to a problem. We may be cognitive misers most of the time, thinking as little as possible, but that's not true all the time. There must be prompts that tell us to think more deeply when the situation demands more effort.

In the world at large, most of the information we process arrives in the form of letters, words, sentences, and paragraphs arranged to form coherent statements. Most of the time those pieces of information are easy to read, because designers have perfected fonts and typefaces that print clearly and legibly. Sometimes, though, for one reason or another, people choose to print written information in fonts that have the same effect as Ogi Ogas's wobbly chair—they're difficult to read, so they disrupt the mental reverie that accompanies most of our thinking. While most written words are printed in clear fonts, from Times New Roman to Arial, and Courier to Calibri, some are printed in elaborate and condensed alternatives, such as *Vladimir Script* and **Haettenschweiler**, or *Gigi* and ***Kaufmann***. Advertisers rely on these fonts to distinguish their messages from their competitors' messages, often written in simple, clear, overused fonts. One classic example is the widely used and eminently readable **Helvetica**, which is the font of New York City subway signs and dozens of company logos, including those of Nestlé, American Airlines, Lufthansa, American Apparel, and Jeep. But how do people think differently when the environment features words printed in complex fonts that are far more difficult to read?

My colleagues and I tried to answer that question when we asked students to answer a set of three brain-teasers that form a measure of intelligence known as the Cognitive Reflection Test. The questions are devilishly tricky, because they inspire immediate answers that are both wrong and intuitively appealing. Those answers arise fluently, like John Carpenter's response to the million-dollar question. People with patience eventually notice that the answer is wrong, and with extra mental commitment they're able to answer with the correct alternative. Here's one of the questions from the test (the others are printed in this chapter's notes at the end of the book):

A bat and a ball cost $1.10 in total. The bat costs $1 more than the ball. How much does the ball cost?

Most people arrive instinctively at the conclusion that the bat costs $1 and the ball costs 10 cents—which is wrong when you think more carefully. Yes, the two sum to $1.10, but the bat costs only 90 cents more than the ball. The right answer, which anyone with basic arithmetic skills can verify, is that the ball costs 5 cents. Many people answer this question incorrectly precisely because they're cognitive misers, impatient and ready to move on to the next task that demands mental resources.

In the experiment, we wondered whether disfluency might signal to people that the question demanded more mental effort, so half the students answered the questionnaire printed in a fluent font, whereas the other half answered the questionnaire printed in a smaller, grey, italicized text:

A bat and a ball cost $1.10 in total. The bat costs $1 more than the ball. How much does the ball cost?

As expected, people answered the three questions correctly more often when they were difficult to read. On average, they correctly answered 2.45 of the three questions correctly, whereas the students who read the questionnaire printed in a clear font averaged only 1.90 correct answers to the three questions. Later, we showed the same effect with complex logic problems, again showing that people answered them correctly more often when they were printed in a disfluent font.

The complex fonts that populate modern environments function like an alarm, signalling that we need to recruit additional mental resources to overcome that sense of difficulty. Just like other alarms, sometimes it proves faulty. Though we need to know when to think more deeply, the same alarm also makes us more conservative, sending a warning that something in the environment is risky or dangerous.

This link between disfluency and riskiness probably explains why cognitive psychologist Danny Oppenheimer and I found that people began submitting increasingly revealing confessions on the website *Grouphug.us* in August 2008. The website invites people to share anonymous confessions in exchange for hugs from sympathetic readers. Some confessions are very revealing, whereas others are tame and barely warrant anonymity. Before August 2008, the site was formatted quite disfluently, with grey text against a similarly dark black background:

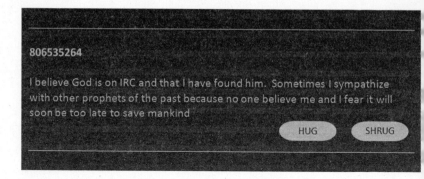

Then in August 2008 the site's creator had a change of heart. He decided to make the text darker and the background lighter—the standard black text on white background format:

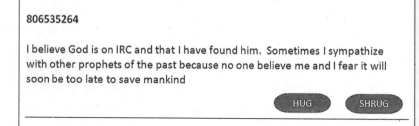

Now the text on the site was far easier to read, and people who considered submitting their own confessions were greeted with a fluent mental experience. When Danny Oppenheimer and I combed the site for confessions, we found that the confessions were more revealing after the site's creator adopted the new, fluent format. In other studies, we found that people were more willing to disclose revealing personal flaws when prompted by a request that was printed in a clear font, rather than a light grey font on a white background.

The same mental alarms that prevent people from revealing personal information also signal the presence of immorality. Imagine, for example, that you're told the following tale about a questionable culinary decision:

A family's dog was killed by a car in front of their house. They had heard that dog meat was delicious, so they cut up the dog's body and cooked it and ate it for dinner.

The family wasn't hurting anyone (or anything—the dog was already dead), but most Westerners would consider eating a dead pet dog morally questionable. If I asked you to rate the family's behaviour on a scale that ranged from zero to ten, where zero indicates not morally wrong at all and ten indicates very morally wrong, what rating would you assign? What about a case where a brother and sister kiss passionately on the lips? How wrong is that behaviour? Again, assuming the kiss is consensual and it doesn't harm anyone, it's difficult to find moral fault with the act except to say that it doesn't feel right, or offends some higher notion of religious or transcendent propriety. When fellow psychologists Simon Laham, Geoff Goodwin, and I asked people to rate the moral wrongness of these acts, we also introduced a fluency manipulation. For some of the raters, the acts were described in writing against a speckled grey background, whereas for others the text was much easier to read. Here's another example in similar formats:

A high school teacher burns the U.S. flag in class.

Moral transgression printed in disfluent format.

A high school teacher burns the U.S. flag in class.

Moral transgression printed in fluent format.

People generally found the violations quite offensive, rating them around 9 out of 10 on the moral wrongness scale—but these ratings dropped to 7.5 when the violations were printed fluently after earlier violations had been printed disfluently. When the later violations were surprisingly easy to read, the raters interpreted that experience to imply that the violations were less morally offensive.

The written words that fill modern urban environments shape how deeply we think, and whether we're more likely to open up to other people or judge them for behaving immorally. Just as disfluent experiences direct us to think more deeply, other cues in the environment tell us how to behave in novel situations. Like chameleons, we blend into the background, unconsciously adopting the behaviours that strike a balance between appropriate and rewarding.

Mental Chameleons

Artificial illumination is a modern miracle, blurring a line that separated night and day for millions of years before mankind found a reliable way to turn darkness into light. Today lighting is taken for granted to such an extent that we barely notice the light fittings as we enter a room for the first time. It takes some effort and attention to direct your gaze towards the ceiling, to determine whether the lightbulb is incandescent, halogen, or fluorescent, and to decide whether you might be more comfortable if the resulting glow were slightly brighter or dimmer. Though we're apt to overlook a room's brightness, US Supreme Court justice Louis Brandeis was onto something when he said, "Sunlight is said to be the best of disinfectants."

In a recent paper, three psychologists tested the truth of Brandeis's statement. Students at the University of North Carolina participated in an experiment that gave them the opportunity to earn up to $10. The students had five minutes to complete as many of twenty maths problems as they could. For each problem, they searched for three numbers from an array of twelve that came to ten. The problems were time-consuming and took plenty of mental effort. The following is a sample question to

1.03	1.96	2.69
1.21	2.44	3.27
4.77	5.98	5.02
3.57	5.74	2.33

Three of these numbers add up to ten. The solution is in this chapter's notes, at the end of the book.

give you a sense of the students' task—and keep in mind that they had only five minutes to complete twenty similar problems.

Each of the students completed the experiment in the same small room, but the room was brightly lit with twelve lightbulbs for some of them, and more dimly lit with only four bulbs for others. The dimly lit room was still bright enough to allow the students to complete the task without difficulty, but it was noticeably darker than most rooms in an average university building. After five minutes had elapsed, the students told the experimenter how many problems they had answered correctly, and collected 50 cents for each completed problem. The students struggled regardless of the room's illumination, completing about seven problems during the five-minute period—but their claims varied greatly depending on the room's brightness. Students in the bright room were reasonably honest, reporting that they completed between seven and eight problems. Meanwhile, those in the dimly lit room inflated their scores by roughly 50 percent, claiming an average of more than eleven completed problems! Somehow, the students in the dimly lit room were liberated from the moral constraints of behaving honestly, a result that the authors attributed to the illusion that the darkness preserved their anonymity.

A room's lighting remains largely unchanged as time passes, but locations change as they come to reflect the people who inhabit them. Some of that social residue inspires good behaviour, but some marks out the location as a hotbed of immorality and crime. For example, the heavily debated *broken windows theory* suggests that would-be offenders are encouraged to commit crimes in neighbourhoods with broken windows, which suggest that the area's residents don't care enough to maintain their property. The theory's authors, James Wilson and George Kelling, gave two examples to illustrate the theory:

> Consider a building with a few broken windows. If the windows are not repaired, the tendency is for vandals to break a few more windows. Eventually, they may even break into the building, and if it's unoccupied, perhaps become squatters or light fires inside. Or consider a street. Some litter accumulates. Soon, more litter accumulates. Eventually, people even start leaving bags of rubbish from takeaway restaurants there or breaking into cars.

Since 1982, when Wilson and Kelling proposed their theory, the second littering example has received plenty of experimental support. In one study, social psychologists placed flyers on 139 cars in a large hospital car park. They were curious about whether the cars' drivers would throw the flyers in the bin, or whether they would instead litter by leaving them in the car park. Before some of the cars' drivers emerged from the car-park lift, the researchers scattered discarded flyers, sweet wrappers, and coffee cups throughout the car park. At other times, they removed every last cigarette butt and piece of rubbish from the car park floor, conveying the idea that littering was both unusual and inappropriate. Nearly half of all drivers littered when the car park was already covered in litter—what's one more piece on top of a layer of rubbish?— but only one in ten drivers littered when the car park was spotless. The researchers added another twist, asking a plant to drop an unwanted flyer conspicuously on the ground just as some of the drivers were exiting the lift. This act drew the drivers' attention to the existing state of the car park, either emphasizing that it was already full of litter, or highlighting how neat it was *before* the plant callously cast aside his discarded flyer. When the plant drew the drivers' attention to the state of the car park, only 6 percent littered in the clean car park, whereas a dramatically higher 54 percent littered in the already untidy car park. The drivers adopted the behaviour that seemed most appropriate given their understanding of the area's prevailing norms.

Even subtler cues that you might expect to fade into the background shape how we think about the world. In a series of studies, social psychologist Virginia Kwan and I asked a researcher to approach people in various parts of New York City. All of them were Caucasian Americans, but some were walking through Chinatown, while others were walking through Manhattan's Financial District and Upper East Side. The researcher asked them to complete a few brief questions, some that asked them to predict how financial stocks would perform in the coming six months, and others that asked them to predict weather conditions following a string of sunny or rainy days. As I mentioned in chapter 6, on culture, American and Chinese people have very different ideas about how the world changes. Americans are often surprised by change, expecting financial stocks that have performed well in the past to continue to do well in the future, and similarly expecting weather conditions to remain relatively consistent. In contrast, many Chinese people subscribe to the Taoist *I Ching* principles, which suggest that change is inevitable; financial stocks and weather conditions that seem favourable today are likely to take a turn for the worse tomorrow, but a downturn in the stock market and rainy weather today are likely to precede a burst of stock appreciation and sunny weather tomorrow.

As you might expect, then, the Americans in the Financial District and Upper East Side completed the questionnaires like typical Americans: they preferred to invest in stocks that appreciated, and expected weather patterns to continue unabated. But the Americans passing through Chinatown, who were otherwise indistinguishable from those in the more typical American neighbourhoods, perceived the world very differently. For that brief moment, they thought more like Chinese people than like Americans. They expected the appreciating stocks to depreciate over the coming six months, and they expected sunny days to be replaced by rain, and rainy days to be replaced by sun. These effects were strongest, as you might expect, among the Americans who were aware of the Chinese belief in change embodied in the *I Ching*. Merely responding in a location filled with Chinese paraphernalia led those people to adopt Chinese cultural norms.

We found the same patterns of results when a research assistant approached people outside a Chinese supermarket in New Jersey. Some of them were entering the market—not yet exposed to the plethora of Chinese sights and sounds—while others were leaving after finishing their shopping, already bombarded by reminders of Chinese culture. Those who were leaving the supermarket adopted a mindset associated with Chinese cultural beliefs, expecting appreciating stocks to depreciate imminently and investing $300 less of a fictional $1,000 sum in those stocks, whereas those who were yet to enter the market tended to think like typical Americans, investing almost the entire sum in appreciating stocks.

These studies tell us something profound and perhaps a bit disturbing about what makes us who we are: there isn't a single version of "you" .When you're surrounded by litter, you're more likely to be a litterbug; when you're walking past buildings with broken windows, you're more likely to disrespect the property that surrounds you. These norms change from minute to minute, as quickly as a New Yorker walks from one part of the city to another. It's comforting to believe that there's an essential version of each of us, that good people are good, bad people are bad, and that those tendencies reside within us rather than in the sights, sounds, and symbols that populate the landscapes that surround us from moment to moment. But social psychology calls that belief into question. In fact, even our memories—the building blocks that construct the evolving story of who we are across time—are tagged with the locations where they were formed. Emotionally jarring memories adhere to this tag with particular determination, which explains why people remember where they were when they learned of JFK's assassination, the death of Princess Diana, and the string of tragedies on 11 September 2001. These memories aren't always perfectly accurate, but as their name suggests, so-called flashbulb memories are vivid snapshots of a moment and place in time when we learn an emotional and personally relevant piece of news. These tags, which bind events to the places where they occurred, explained a strange anomaly forty years ago, when thousands of Vietnam War veterans returned to the United States with a potentially calamitous drug addiction.

Context Reinstatement

During the Vietnam War, a combination of boredom and anxiety pushed many enlisted soldiers to try heroin and opium. In 1970, at the height of the epidemic, 40 percent of all enlisted men had tried at least one of the two drugs. When the US government discovered that soldiers had been using heroin, they feared that the war's end would herald a public health crisis. Heroin relapse rates are as high as 90 percent in the short term, so the government had good reason to worry. The men returned from the war with many problems, but to the surprise of many drug experts, very few of them relapsed. Psychologists and doctors continue to debate the issue today, but most agree that the critical difference between most heroin users and the soldiers who used heroin in Vietnam was that the soldiers were forced to leave the location in which they had used the drug. Unlike most recovering addicts, who find themselves in locations that reinstate the drug-using context, few Vietnam vets found themselves in the tropical jungle setting that coloured their original exposure to the drug.

Part of the reason why context reinstatement—returning to an emotionally charged location—plagues heroin users is that the location forces them to relive old, related memories. Wise teachers turn this fact on its head by telling students to study for exams in a situation that mirrors the exam context as closely as possible. Their advice draws on a classic psychology experiment that showed that locations form a lens through which we perceive newly acquired information. The researchers asked eighteen scuba divers from a university diving club to memorize lists of words. Sometimes the divers memorized the lists underwater, and sometimes they memorized them onshore. Randomly selected words would be just as easy to remember on land as underwater if they weren't somehow associated with the location where they were first encountered. But the scholars found that the divers who memorized the words underwater recalled them much more accurately when they were again immersed in the water, whereas the divers who memorized the words on land recalled them with greater accuracy when they were again back on dry land. The divers who learned the lists underwater perceived them through a watery mental lens, and that location-based tag was activated when they were again immersed in the water, pushing those words to rise more rapidly to the surface of their minds. Similar studies have shown that studying while drunk is beneficial only if you're also drunk during the exam. In a famous example that later inspired the scuba-diving study, seventeenth-century philosopher John Locke told the story of a man who learned to dance in a room containing an old trunk, and couldn't dance thereafter unless he shared the room with the same trunk.

Locations vary along countless dimensions, each playing a distinct role in shaping our thoughts, feelings, and behaviours. At one end of the spectrum, Locke's man was fixated on the narrowest of cues—a particular trunk—but at the other end, some environmental cues are considerable in scope. Perhaps the grandest of all cues in the world around us are the weather conditions that define every moment we spend outdoors. Each time you leave the sheltered indoors, you subject yourself to the whims of the seasons. As the New York Mets discovered during one baseball game in 2009, it's much harder to remain cool-headed when a hot day compounds the heat of competition.

9.

WEATHER AND WARMTH

Summertime War, Wintertime Love

On a warm afternoon in August 2009, as the mercury hovered near 90°F (32°C), the New York Mets hosted the San Francisco Giants at Citi Field baseball stadium in New York City. The game remained tense into the fourth inning as both teams were unable to break the scoreless deadlock. San Francisco pitcher Matt Cain threw a clumsy 93 mph fastball that slipped just as it left his fingers, sailing right into the helmet of Mets all-star and fan favourite David Wright. Wright collapsed to the ground and lay facedown and completely still. Eerily quiet at first, the crowd watched as trainers tended to the injured player; then people began jeering, which built to a crescendo that shook the stadium. Everyone on the field acknowledged that Cain's errant pitch was a mistake; he didn't intend to hit Wright, and based on the state of the game, Wright's injury conferred very little strategic advantage. Still, Wright's teammates were angry, and it fell to Mets pitcher Johan Santana to exact revenge. Three innings later, Santana earned a warning from the umpire when he threw a pitch that came dangerously close to striking the Giants' Pablo Sandoval. Flouting the warning, Santana struck the very next batter, Bengie Molina, in the elbow, and later claimed without apology that he had "to protect" his teammates who were "all in it together".

It's impossible to know whether Santana would have responded differently on a cooler afternoon, but social psychologists have shown that baseball pitchers tend to hit more batters, and to retaliate more often, as the temperature rises. In one study, researchers tallied how many batters were hit during hundreds of Major League Baseball games played during the 1986, 1987, and 1988 seasons, and plotted the number of hit batters alongside the maximum temperature in each city on game day. Batters were much more likely to be struck by errant pitches on hotter days. The researchers also ruled out the possibility that hotter days produced greater inaccuracy because, for example, pitchers were struggling with sweaty hands, by showing that their pitches were just as accurate on warm days as they were on cool days.

A second group of researchers scoured an even larger database of almost sixty thousand MLB games from 1952 to 2009, and found that pitchers were far more likely to retaliate when their teammates were struck by the opposing team as the temperature climbed. After crunching thousands of data points, they concluded that pitchers retaliated 22 percent of the time on days that peaked at 55°F (13°C), whereas their rate of retaliation rose to 27 percent when the temperature reached 95°F (35°C). This 5 percent difference may not seem particularly large, but across the course of one MLB season, 121 additional batters would be hit in retaliation if every day of the season peaked at 35°C rather than 13°C.

Beyond sports, road rage also escalates when the temperature rises. In one experiment, two social psychologists paid a female research assistant to sit in her car at a particular junction in Phoenix, Arizona for fifteen consecutive Saturdays, from 11.00 a.m. to 3.00 p.m. The temperatures during that period, from April to August, ranged between 29°C and 42°C. The research assistant was paid to sit in her car, immobile, as the traffic lights in the single-lane junction turned green and cars piled up behind her. Meanwhile, a second observer sat nearby, just out of sight, timing how long it took the increasingly annoyed drivers to honk their horns. The hidden observer tallied how many times the cars honked, how long those honks lasted, and how long it took them to honk in the first place. As the researchers expected, the honks were more urgent, lasted longer, and were more frequent on warmer days, showing that road rage escalates as the temperature rises.

What is it about the heat that provokes aggression during baseball games and on the road? One popular explanation is that heat makes people physically excited—their hearts beat more quickly and they sweat more—and they later mistake this sense of excitement for anger when confronted with a frustrating situation. The same logic explains why, in another study, male college students were more strongly attracted to a female researcher after crossing a precariously swaying suspension bridge than after crossing a wider, solid bridge. Like the overheated baseball players and drivers who confused physical excitement for anger, the fearful men on the rickety bridge mistook the rush of blood and adrenalin for sexual arousal.

A second possible explanation is that heat causes discomfort, which in turn conjures related thoughts of anger and aggression. According to this explanation, people repeatedly associate relaxation and calm with an absence of threat and aggravation, so that when they experience occasional bouts of discomfort, they vigilantly scan the environment for threats and prompts of frustration. On a cool night, a pitcher who strikes your teammate might be pardoned with a mental warning, but the same behaviour might demand retaliation on an uncomfortably warm night.

Panning back thousands of miles from baseball diamonds to the planet at large, scientists have found that civil conflicts in tropical regions between 1950 and 2004 were driven substantially by changes in climate. The tropics, warm regions north and south of the equator, oscillate between two major climatic states, known as El Niño and La Niña phases—literally Spanish for "The Boy" and "The Girl". El Niño years are characterized by warmer, dryer weather and unsettled stormy conditions, whereas La Niña years tend to be cooler, wetter, and more meteorologically stable. The results showed that civil conflicts in tropical regions are twice as likely to erupt during warmer El Niño years as during cooler La Niña years, and El Niño weather systems appear to contribute to one-fifth of all tropical conflicts. These effects are strongest in the tropics because regions beyond the tropics, towards the poles, are more weakly affected by El Niño and La Niña oscillations.

Warm weather, which tends to occur during El Niño periods, also spawns violence between individuals. Judges and police officers across the United States have learned to be especially vigilant on hot days, as the rate of domestic violence tends to mirror the temperature. Some criminologists even believe that the southern states are particularly prone to violent crime because they endure hotter summers than other parts of the country. The same southern states actually experience lower non-violent crime rates, including theft and motor vehicle robbery, which suggests that they aren't simply more crime-ridden across the spectrum of offences; rather, they experience more aggression-related crime specifically. Of course, this relationship might be driven by other factors, since the south differs from other parts of the country in many ways beyond weather (e.g., the retaliatory culture of honour discussed in chapter 6). Interestingly, though, the same patterns persist in many other countries; assaults occur twice as often in southern France as in the cooler central and northern regions of France, while non-violent property crimes are far more common in northern France; similarly, violent crimes become progressively less common in the cooler, northern Italian and Spanish regions.

These broadly painted results are fascinating, but they aren't entirely convincing in isolation. For example, it's possible that crime rates are higher in southern regions of European countries, like the US south, but not because those regions are warmer per se. One possibility is that southern cultures in the Northern Hemisphere tend to be more passionate than their northern counterparts—fiery cultures that formed centuries ago perhaps partly in response to warmer temperatures. It's possible, then, that cultural differences rather than the warmer weather are responsible for increased aggression, and it's largely irrelevant that those regions happen to be warmer than more northerly regions.

To rule out that possibility, researchers have analysed crime data using numerous clever techniques to show that weather conditions rather than regional cultural differences fuel violent crime when the temperature rises. In some studies, they "control for" all sorts of possible irrelevant factors, which allows researchers to rule out the possibility that these factors are responsible for apparent links between the weather and violent crime. For example, even controlling for the contribution of education levels, wealth, income, religiosity, and many other potential differences between the northern and southern parts of the United States, they find that the south still has higher crime rates. Crime rates also rise during the hotter months of the year within each city, and those escalations are more pronounced during unusually hot summers. These results are true for numerous violent crimes, including homicide, assault, sexual assault, domestic violence, and riots, each of which spikes during June, July, and August and plummets again as the weather cools.

The heat of summer breeds war, but it's the cold of winter that breeds love. In a study conducted during 2004 and 2005, two Polish researchers approached a hundred heterosexual men and asked them to share their opinions about female attractiveness. The men rated their impressions of silhouetted women in swimsuits and female breasts of various sizes. They completed the same questionnaire during different seasons throughout the year, and their ratings rose as the weather cooled. The same images that produced lukewarm responses in the summer inspired more positive responses in the winter, which the researchers attributed to a so-called contrast effect. They explained colourfully that the men were spoiled in the summer because they were exposed to female body shapes "in a swimsuit or partly covered breasts or tight-fitting T-shirts". In contrast to these images, the silhouettes and breasts were only moderately appealing. In the wintertime, as the weather cooled, they were deprived of the same images and the swimsuit silhouettes and breasts were especially alluring.

Ten years earlier and a thousand miles to the north-west in Tromsø, Norway five medical researchers proposed a very different explanation for why men preferred to look at female bodies in the wintertime. They had measured the testosterone levels of 1,500 Norwegian men between 1994 and 1995, and their findings confirmed what many other researchers had claimed: men experience seasonal testosterone peaks in the winter months, and similar troughs in the summer months, producing about 30 percent more testosterone in wintertime. The authors cleverly ensured that the men weren't merely drinking more beer in the summer months—which tends to lower testosterone counts—and the effects persisted even when they excluded seasonal differences in exercise and body fat.

As you might expect, seasonal effects are strongest in hot climates, where testosterone declines most dramatically in the hot summer months. In one study, researchers examined seasonal birth rates among women across the United States and other countries. In warmer US states—southern states such as Louisiana and Georgia—birth rates dipped dramatically in April and May, and rose steeply in August, September, and October. In Louisiana, for example, birth rates were 45 percent higher in the summer months, so that for every two babies born in the winter, three were born in the summer. Of course, counting back nine months, these results suggest that many more babies are conceived in winter than in summer. Researchers haven't agreed on why conception rates rise in winter, though they've identified several possibilities: people spend more time indoors; men are more likely to seek romance because their testosterone levels rise in winter; men are more attracted to the female figure as they're exposed to it less often when the weather cools. There's also one final, fascinating explanation that began with a cloth-covered monkey fifty years ago, and ends with a cup of hot coffee today.

The Literal Chill of Social Isolation

In the late 1950s, psychologist Harry Harlow conducted one of the most famous psychological studies of all time. Two decades earlier, Harlow was studying intelligence in baby rhesus monkeys when he became fixated on something far more interesting. Each time he separated the baby monkeys from their mothers, they would cling to the terry cloth towels lining the floors of their cages. When he tried to remove the cloth from their cages, the monkeys threw violent tantrums, screeching and pounding the floor of the cage until he returned the fabric. He began to wonder whether the monkeys, lonely without their mothers, found some small consolation in the warmth of their tatty towels.

Harlow's observation was a revelation. In the 1950s, most psychologists assumed that baby animals "loved" their mothers because they needed food and water. In fact, the word "love" was anathema because it implied some deeper mental experience that was too woolly for scientific study. They decided instead that baby animals were demonstrating "proximity"—a survival instinct that drove them to latch on to their mothers. But Harlow could see that these young, traumatized monkeys were seeking more than milk. They were looking for warmth and affection.

Harlow's research interests took a dramatic turn. He stopped focusing on animal intelligence and turned his mind to the question of why baby monkeys, like human infants, cling to their mothers for support. Was it because their mothers fed them and kept them alive, just as wild animals try not to stray too far from an isolated lake in the dry season? Or was it because their mothers provided comfort and warmth, particularly when the young monkeys were scared or anxious? Harlow knew that mothers fulfilled both needs—biological and social—but he wondered which one was most directly responsible for mother–infant bonding. To answer his question, he removed newborn monkeys from their mothers and placed each one in a cage with two artificial "mothers". One mother was constructed of an unyielding wire frame, but the researchers attached a bottle to the frame so the infant monkeys were forced to return to her whenever they wanted milk. The other "mother" was covered in soft fabric, but she had no milk. Harlow watched as the traumatized young monkeys met their new mothers for the first time. Almost immediately they clung to their cloth mothers, avoiding the severe wire mother except when they reluctantly approached her for milk. Harlow's monkeys were far more attracted to the cloth mothers' physical warmth than they were to the wire mothers' promise of nourishment. Baby monkeys aren't supposed to be separated from their mothers, and the warmth they experienced when clinging to their cloth mothers was a stand-in for the genuine motherly comfort they should have been receiving from their real mothers.

Fifty years later, social psychologists took Harlow's findings one step further when they began to wonder whether physical warmth actually compensates for the pain of social isolation. In one experiment, students met an experimenter in the university's psychology department lobby. Together they went up in a lift to the experimental lab on the building's fourth floor. During the ride, the experimenter asked the student to hold her cup of coffee just briefly, so she could quickly write down the student's name and experiment time. Half of the students held a cup of hot coffee, while the other half held a cup of iced coffee instead. About fifteen seconds later, when the lift reached the fourth floor, they continued to the psychology lab, and the student completed a brief questionnaire. The questionnaire described an anonymous "Person A" as intelligent, skilful, industrious, determined, practical, and cautious, and the students were asked to rate Person A's personality on a range of scales. For example, did he seem generous or ungenerous, caring or selfish, attractive or unattractive, strong or weak? When the researchers looked at the results, they found that the students rated Person A as significantly warmer and friendlier (but not more attractive or strong) when they had earlier held the cup of hot coffee rather than the cup of iced coffee. The students confused the physical sensation of cradling a warm cup of coffee for the metaphorical sense that Person A was warm and friendly.

In other experiments, students held a therapeutic pack that was either heated in a microwave or cooled in a freezer. Those who held the pack when it was cold reported feeling lonelier, claiming that they were starved for company and had no one to talk to more often than did the students who held the heated pack. Other students who were asked to remember a time when they felt lonely or socially excluded were later more interested in spending time with close friends—unless they held a heated therapeutic pack in the interim. The sensation of physical warmth alleviated the need for social contact, suggesting that the brain interprets physical and social warmth very similarly. One brain region that responds to both cool temperatures and social isolation is known as the *insula*, a small region buried in a fold of the mammalian brain's outer layer. The insula processes all sorts of visceral information, from pain to temperature changes, while also responding to the experience of trusting other people when forming social connections. Some researchers believe that physical coldness activates the insula, which leads people to feel lonely and socially isolated, and to seek social comfort in an attempt to overcome this sense of loneliness.

There's a lesson for film studios buried in this research, which comes down to a question of timing. Building on the relationship between cold and loneliness, two marketing researchers turned their attention to romantic comedies, the cinematic equivalent of Harlow's cloth mother and a cup of warm coffee. The best romantic comedies place their central character in a cold, affectionless wasteland, before redeeming him (or, increasingly often, her) with a warm, new-found love interest. Since romantic comedies are designed to warm a frigid heart, in two experiments people who were handed a cup of iced coffee, or a cold therapeutic pack (rather than a cup of hot coffee or a heated therapeutic pack) were willing to pay an average of 20 percent more to see a romantic comedy film. They weren't willing to pay more for action films, comedies, or thrillers, presumably because those films lacked the heart-warming promise of romantic comedies. The experimenters concluded by looking at the film rental patterns of 2,500 US residents, focusing on the relationship between daily temperatures and genre preferences. Even when they excluded Valentine's Day—a cold mid-February day that heralds a spike in romantic comedy rentals—they found that when the weather was colder, people rented more romantic comedies than films of other genres.

Bad weather brings us together, but protracted rain, snow, and darkness are also responsible for great unhappiness. As he led a group of sailors through dense Arctic ice floes in the late nineteenth century, US explorer Frederick Cook noticed that his men were becoming more and more lethargic. Cook was confused, because he'd never seen a crew descend so quickly into a collective malaise, and he also realized that every last man would perish unless he intervened.

Weather and Well-Being

As Cook's ship laboured through the roiling, icy sea, he began to wonder whether he and the sailors would die in the darkness. After considering a range of far-fetched causes and remedies that were completely ineffective, Cook realized that the men were suffering from an acute lack of sunlight, so he devised several ingenious treatments. His "light cure" required that affected men sit in front of an open fire for several hours each day, bathing in its heat and glow. After each treatment, the men were briefly reinvigorated, returning to their former summery selves. Cook's cure was remarkably prescient, coming a century before blue SAD lamps were invented. Meanwhile, other men were forced to march in circles on the ship's small, icy deck, an area that the men dubbed "the madman's promenade". Exercise, like natural light, undid the ravages of the prolonged Arctic darkness. Later, Cook observed a group of Inuit people who had adapted to the dark winter over generations. Mimicking the behaviour of hibernating animals, the Inuit hunkered down during the winter and welcomed the chance to enjoy prolonged sleep and extended sessions of small talk and gossip. When the sun finally rose, they were seized by a springtime euphoria that included dancing and courting.

Scientists now recognize that SAD is tied to the ebbs and flows of our circadian rhythm—the internal body clock that regulates when we sleep and stir. As I mentioned earlier, in chapter 7, when this internal clock is disrupted—for example, when we traverse time zones and experience jet lag—our bodies and brains struggle to complete even basic mental and biological tasks. In humans, the hormone melatonin is largely responsible for driving the circadian cycle. Melatonin, secreted by the pineal gland, is absent during daylight and begins to flood the body before bedtime. As the days shorten in winter, sufferers of SAD are forced to fight against a soporific tide of melatonin for longer periods, struggling to accomplish during the shortened day what they would otherwise accomplish more easily during the longer days of summer. As we saw earlier, physicians often treat wintertime SAD with blue light that mimics the wavelengths of natural sunshine. These SAD lights are effective because they emit up to 10,000 lux of light, far more than the 300 lux that it takes to halt melatonin production, or the 700 lux emitted by the rising sun.

Across the ages, these summer highs and winter lows have been especially pronounced among artists, writers, and intellectuals. Vincent Van Gogh swung wildly between his famous periods of wintertime melancholy and extreme periods of summertime elation. On the shortest, darkest, coldest night of the year in December 1888, Van Gogh fought viciously with his erstwhile friend and fellow painter Paul Gauguin, first throwing a glass of absinthe at Gauguin's head and then chasing him down a dark street with a cut-throat razor. Later that night, Van Gogh

used the same razor to sever his right earlobe, which he supposedly
mailed to a prostitute named Rachel. Van Gogh's artworks were similarly swayed by the seasons, dominated by ominous clouds and darkness
in the winter months, and optimistic sunshine, light, and stars during
the summer months. His aggressive brushstrokes, loaded with mounds
of paint, became more frenzied in the winter months and lost some of
their intensity when summer arrived. Van Gogh wasn't alone; German
polymath Johann Wolfgang von Goethe complained that "excellent
personalities"—including his own—"suffer most from the adverse effects of the atmosphere". Composers Handel and Mahler also succumbed
to the seasons, producing many of their great works in the autumn and
spring, when they weren't at the mercy of debilitating wintertime lows
and manic summertime highs.

Like SAD, many of the weather's strongest effects are based in animal biology. Although weather events affect humans, certain lower-
order animals are more attuned to changes in the weather, so they
respond more quickly and dramatically than do humans. In the particularly active Atlantic hurricane season of 2004, scientists tracked the
movement of sharks in the bays along Florida's west coast. Long before
the wind and rain from Hurricane Charley chased Floridians from the
coast in August 2004, the sharks fled en masse to the deeper, safer waters
of the Gulf of Mexico. Scientists were baffled, until they discovered that
the sharks had responded to rapid drops in barometric pressure—early-
warning signs of an impending storm. Other researchers have found
similar behaviour among dogs, bees, birds, and elephants, which seek
shelter and higher ground when air pressure falls before hurricanes,
tropical storms, and even earthquakes and tsunamis. Humans aren't
quite as shrewd, but studies have shown that people exhibit a wide range
of surprisingly disordered responses when the weather changes.

As storms and high winds begin to affect an area, they introduce
electrically charged particles, or ions, into the atmosphere. For decades
throughout the twentieth century, observers claimed that the onset of

strong winds—such as the Santa Ana in California, the chinook in the Pacific North-West, the sirocco in Italy, and the sharav in Israel—brought strange changes in human behaviour. In *Red Wind*, his classic 1938 hard-boiled detective story, Raymond Chandler mentions the malevolent Santa Ana twenty-six times. The wind becomes a bona fide character, responsible for drunken parties that end in fights, and wives who contemplate slitting their husbands' throats with carving knives.

Residents of Alpine Europe commonly associate the local foehn winds with a range of maladies from migraines to psychosis, and aspirin bottles in Germany sometimes advertise the medication's ability to treat *Foehnkrankheit*, or foehn sickness. Foehn winds roll down mountainsides, warming the weather by up to 28°C in a matter of hours, and they're largely responsible for central Europe's relatively mild temperatures. Adolf Hitler's friend Heinrich Hoffman claimed that a foehn wind was responsible for Hitler's headache when the two went election campaigning on the evening of 18 September 1931—the same night that Hitler's niece Geli Raubal was found dead having shot herself in the chest.

In the early 1960s, German researchers investigated the relationship between the foehn winds in Alpine Europe and accident and injury rates in German factories. They divided the weather into six phases, three of them relatively calm and three associated with disturbances from foehn winds, storms, and post-storm recovery. During the three disturbed foehn phases, people were slower to react to visual cues at a traffic exhibition in Munich, accident rates at a heavy-machinery plant were especially high, and workers at a second industrial plant were more likely to report to the plant's doctor's office for medical attention. After observing the behaviour of almost thirty thousand German exhibition visitors and industrial workers, the researchers concluded that foehn sickness was a real phenomenon, and that atmospheric changes were responsible for symptoms as varied as slowed reaction times and physical illness.

Twenty years later, two American researchers were puzzled by exactly why seasonal winds affected people so dramatically. Obviously *something* in the winds was causing headaches and other sickness, but the epidemiological data that established the link left many questions unanswered. Since winds and storms change the electrical composition of the atmosphere, the researchers decided to investigate how people in closed labs responded when electrically charged ions were carefully released into the air. They expected these positive ions to interfere with participants' central nervous-system functioning, increasing production of a neurotransmitter known as serotonin 5-HT, which contributes to hyperactivity and aggression. Nearly a hundred people responded to advertisements, each spending ninety minutes in a sealed room fitted with three ion generators. Each person sat in the room twice, once with the generators switched on, mimicking the atmospheric effects of an oncoming gale by slowly increasing the concentration of positive ions in the air, and once with the generators switched off—a control condition that was identical to the storm condition, except that the room wasn't filled with positive ions. Throughout each ninety-minute period, the participants completed a series of scales and tasks designed to measure their emotional and mental functioning. When the researchers analysed the results, they found that the positive ions made the participants more tense and tired, and less sociable and happy. According to the researchers, this constellation of damaging responses explained why winds and weather changes are associated with suicide, depression, irritability, crime, and industrial and road-traffic accidents.

But it isn't just unsettled weather that blunts the mind, as researchers have begun to discover more recently. Every year Mercer, a global human resources company, rates the quality of life in major cities around the world. The ratings combine thirty-nine different measures, from crime to restaurant quality to political stability. Chief among those measures is climate, which elevates sunnier cities with mild temperatures, and hampers cities with long, cold winters and plenty of rain. Paradoxically, though Mercer rates mild, sunny cities more favourably than wintry, rainy cities, one group of researchers has cast a metaphorical cloud over sunny cities.

Sunshine Dulls the Mind to Risk and Thoughtfulness

The same mental haze that sets in after weeks on a summer holiday also muddles the mind from one sunny day to the next. This might seem like an outrageous claim—that sunnier days bring on a mental stupor—but it's a claim that's backed with real evidence. In one study, social psychologists sprang a surprise memory test on shoppers who were leaving a small magazine shop in Sydney, Australia. Before the shoppers entered the shop, the researchers placed ten small ornamental objects on the shop counter—four plastic animals, a toy cannon, a piggy bank, and four Matchbox cars. After leaving the shop, the shoppers were asked to remember as many of the ten items as possible, and also to choose the ten items from a list of twenty that included the ten correct items and ten new items. The researchers conducted the experiment on fourteen different days across a two-month period, between 11.00 a.m. and 4.00 p.m.; some of those days were clear and sunny, whereas others were cloudy and rainy. The shoppers recalled three times as many items on the rainy days as on the sunny days, and they were approximately four times as accurate when identifying the ten objects from the longer list of twenty items.

The researchers explained that gloomy weather hampers our mood, which in turn makes us think more deeply and clearly. Humans are biologically predisposed to avoid sadness, and they respond to sad moods by seeking opportunities for mood repair and vigilantly protecting themselves against whatever might be making them sad. In contrast, happiness sends a signal that everything is fine, the environment doesn't pose an imminent threat, and there's no need to think deeply and care-

fully. These contrasting mental approaches explain why the shoppers remembered the ten trinkets more accurately on rainy days; the rainy days
induced a generally negative mood state, which the shoppers subconsciously tried to overcome by grazing the environment for information
that might have replaced their dampened sad moods with happier alternatives. If you think about it, this approach makes sense. Mood states are
all-purpose measurement devices that tell us whether something in the
environment needs to be fixed. When we're facing major emotional
hurdles—extreme grief, an injury that brings severe pain, blinding
anger—our emotional warning light glows red and compels us to act.
Most of the time we sail smoothly through calm waters, allowing much
of the world—including small trinkets on a shop counter—to pass by
unnoticed.

The same vigilance brought on by poor weather also tempers the enthusiasm of financial experts, who tend to avoid investing on rainy days.
In the early 1990s, an economist managed to gather data on weather
conditions and stock-exchange data in New York City between 1927 and
1989. Noting that stock traders, like all people, tend to be happier and
therefore more optimistic on sunny days, the economist predicted that
the stock markets would appreciate in value on sunny rather than on
cloudy days. Indeed, traders were more bullish on sunny days, driving
prices upward as they invested with relative abandon. Meanwhile, returns on Monday, which usually decline as people lament the close of the
weekend, barely fell at all on sunny days, dropping by only five basis
points (five-hundredths of a percent) rather than the usual eighteen basis
points. Taking this analysis one step further, two finance professors
showed that twenty-six financial markets across the globe experienced
larger gains on sunny than on cloudy days. The result held in markets as
diverse as Helsinki, Kuala Lumpur, Sydney, and Vienna, each of them
receiving a small upward nudge on sunny days.

There's not much we can do about adverse weather conditions, but some researchers argue that government policymakers exacerbate sunshine-related problems by insisting on daylight saving policies. Daylight saving time mandates that clocks advance an hour in the spring, increasing the number of waking hours we spend in daylight during the spring and summer months. The policy is popular largely because it allows people to enjoy the warmth of long summer evenings. Accordingly, much of the world, including most of the fifty US states, recognizes daylight saving time, which gained a strong foothold between 1942 and 1945 during Franklin Roosevelt's wartime presidency. Roosevelt appealed to patriotic ideals, claiming that valuable fuel resources would be conserved if Americans spent more waking hours in daylight, and less time relying on electric lighting. In fact, decades of research have shown that the policy contributes to overconsumption, as people spend more of the day using power-hungry air conditioners and cooling devices that demand fewer resources during night-time hours.

More recently, researchers have shown that altering people's body clock twice a year has its own significant costs, especially when they lose an hour of sleep in the spring. The day after daylight saving time begins, thousands of drivers labour under a regional case of jet lag, and accident rates rise by 7 percent on that day. Even more damaging, one anti–daylight saving researcher has claimed that students in daylight saving regions spend seven months of the year out of phase with their natural biorhythms. Consequently, when the researcher compared the SAT scores of students in Indiana counties that observe daylight saving time, he found that they scored sixteen fewer points than their fellow students in counties that chose to observe standard time all year round. Indiana is one of a few states where students who attend schools separated by county lines no more than a few miles apart, spend seven months a year living in different time zones. Education policymakers devote millions of dollars each year to closing small SAT performance gaps that unfairly disadvantage one group of students relative to another, and these results suggest that eliminating daylight saving time might offer one relatively inexpensive solution.

Humans have harnessed nuclear energy, and have sent a spacecraft more than 12 billion miles from the earth, but we still haven't found a way to control the weather. Some of the world drowns in floods while other parts wither in drought, and tornadoes and hurricanes are more and more powerful and unpredictable in the wake of global warming. In contrast to the other mental forces in the world around us—colours and locations—weather conditions are difficult to tame. But the volatility of weather patterns also has an unexpected upside, because it tells us something fascinating about the human mind. The story of their overlap begins more than fifty years ago, as an American scientist grappled with the Sisyphean task of forecasting the weather.

EPILOGUE

Lorenz's Butterfly

On a winter's day in 1961, celebrated American meteorologist Edward Lorenz tinkered with a weather prediction model he'd created a year earlier. Each time he punched in a string of numerical values, the model spat out a meteorological forecast. Those numbers were very precise, accurate to the nearest millionth, and he grew tired of entering them one after another: 79.325532, 68.698787, 57.056473 . . .

Late in the day, the model delivered an interesting result, and like any careful scientist, Lorenz decided to replicate the effect before continuing. Wearied by a full day of typing, he took a shortcut and entered the numbers to the nearest thousandth instead of the nearest millionth. The loss of precision seemed immaterial, and it saved him plenty of time. Now instead of typing 65.506127, for example, he typed 65.506. Lorenz left his primitive computer to crunch the data, and returned to inspect the output an hour later.

Much to his frustration, the new forecast looked nothing like its predecessor. He checked the sluggish computer's vacuum tubes, but everything was functioning perfectly. Changing the temperature from 87.123432°F to 87.123°F seemed trivial, but the model saw radically different weather conditions when it peered into the future. A few millionths of a degree appeared to turn sunshine into rain. Some years later Lorenz described the epiphany in a talk that he famously titled "Does the Flap of a Butterfly's Wings in Brazil Set Off a Tornado in Texas?" With one part laziness and one part serendipity, Lorenz had stumbled on the butterfly effect.

At its heart, this book is designed to show that your mind is the collective end point of a billion tiny butterfly effects. Your thoughts, feelings, and actions are the products of chaotic chain reactions, fuelled in no small part by the nine forces described in this book. Human behaviour is hard to predict, then, in part because it's so sensitive to each wingbeat of Lorenz's proverbial butterfly. With a few early tweaks, you might have turned out to be a very different person, as this hypothetical case study illustrates.

A Tale of Two Tims

Imagine that Jane Davis and John MacEochagan marry and decide to take on Jane's simpler surname. Their son, Tim Davis, becomes a mediocre lawyer, strong enough to garner a couple of borderline promotions but far from the firm's rising star. In a parallel world, Jane and John adopt John's surname instead, and their son—the same person at birth apart from his name—lives his life as Tim MacEochagan. He also becomes a mediocre lawyer, but as we saw in chapter 1, his name ever so slightly hampers his quest for partnership. Where Tim Davis gets the benefit of the doubt, the partners pass over "that Tim guy with the long surname".

As luck would have it, the two Tims have a rebellious streak. In their late thirties, they decide to present their wives with a gift of cosmetics.

Tim Davis walks into a department store and pilfers a tube of mascara and a bottle of nail polish. A security guard happens to catch him as he leaves the store, the manager decides to press charges, and Tim's legal career hangs in the balance. Meanwhile, when Tim MacEochagan picks up the same items, he sees that the mascara packaging features a pair of long-lashed eyes. With the sudden sense that someone's watching, he feels compelled to behave honestly and leaves both items in the store.

Later in life, each Tim has a son. With their wives and little Timmy they look for a new apartment. They fall in love with a small but modern apartment in a thirty-storey building, not too far from a noisy motorway. The building has two available apartments: one on the third floor and another on the thirtieth floor. Tim Davis decides to pay an extra £100 each month for the higher floor's view, but Tim MacEochagan chooses the third-floor apartment instead. The noise is terrible on the third floor, and little Timmy struggles to hear when his parents are talking. He learns to read slightly more slowly than his little Timmy counterpart who lives in an alternate universe on the thirtieth floor, and his parents choose to hold him back from school for an extra year. Because he's older, he's also slightly bigger and more mature than the other children when he reaches high school, so he gets plenty of attention from the school's football coach. With that extra attention, he becomes Timmy MacEochagan, star centre forward. Timmy Davis follows in his dad's footsteps and becomes a mediocre lawyer.

And so on. This is just an invented story, but the tale it tells isn't particularly far-fetched. The features that distinguish their lives—different names, the opportune presence or absence of a pair of eyes, and a poorly or well-chosen home—have magnified effects further down the line. And those differences begin at the level of our nine cues: the forces within us, between us, and around us.

The forces in *Drunk Tank Pink* affect us every day: at work, at play, when we're alone, when we're interacting with other people, and when we're making decisions that range from the trivial to the life-changing.

And once we know that they exist, we're better placed to capitalize on them when they help and resist them when they hurt. Request a hospital room with a view; pay more for a flat in town on the top floor—not just because of the view, but because you'll be farther from the noise below; and keep in mind that your decisions are likely to change as you move from Brixton to Kensington, from summer to winter, and from rooms painted blue to rooms painted red. No matter where you go, Drunk Tank Pink and other cues will follow—and, having read this book, you'll be in a much better place to identify them, recognize how they'll affect you, and harness or overcome them to maximize your health, wisdom, wealth, and well-being.

ACKNOWLEDGEMENTS

To borrow from Edward Lorenz, this book is the tornado that arrived some time after a butterfly flapped its wings in Brazil. The wingbeat that put this chaotic process in motion was an article on some of my research in the *Boston Globe*, written beautifully by Drake Bennett. My agent, Katinka Matson, read the article and suggested I write a book proposal, without which there would be no *Drunk Tank Pink*. Katinka coaxed a far stronger proposal from me than I could have managed alone, and she's remained a constant source of insight and support since the book found a home. A huge thank-you to my first editor, Eamon Dolan, who saw promise in the proposal and taught me to turn mildly interesting nuggets into narrative bars of gold. Laura Stickney stepped in ably as my second editor, and Colin Dickerman has done a wonderful job of steadily and patiently turning the rough manuscript into a polished book. Thanks also to Kaitlyn Flynn, Mally Anderson, Samantha Choy, and the entire team at Penguin Press.

Thanks to my parents, Ian and Jenny, for always encouraging me despite how far my journey has carried me from home, and to my brother, Dean, for his constant support. To Sara, my biggest supporter and sharpest editor: I couldn't imagine the journey of the past couple of years without your sweetness, intelligence, and love.

I was lucky to have the support and advice of an army of family and friends, near and far. In particular, for reading earlier drafts and offering advice, thanks (alphabetically) to: Corinne Alter, Dean Alter, Ian Alter, Jenny Alter, Jessica Alter, Peter Alter, Chloe Angyal, Amitav Chakravarti, Adrian de Froment, Greg Detre, Louise Frenkel, Svetlana German, Nicole Golembo, Geoff Goodwin, Dena Gromet, Hal Hershfield, Tom Meyvis, Sara Ricklen, Dave Schneider, Romy Schneider, Anuj Shah, Eesha Sharma, Hana Shepherd, Joe Simmons, Abby Sussman, Alison Swartz, Les Swartz, and Rebecca Swartz. For research assistance, and facilitating my quest for anecdotes, thanks to: Bill Bokoff, Gabriella Chiriños, Casey Greulich, Sarah Jones, Karen Olsoy, Anna Paley, Eva Sharma, and Evelyn Wang.

Thanks to Michael Olesker, a fearless and talented writer, for advice about the writing process, to Suzy Olesker for moral support and nourishment in the form of Berger Cookies, and to both Mike and Suzy for an endless tide of care and encouragement. To Alex Schauss, the godfather of the colour Drunk Tank Pink, thanks for agreeing to be interviewed, and for telling the story of the colour's origin so vividly.

Thanks also to my four academic advisers: Joe Forgas and Bill von Hippel at the University of New South Wales, and John Darley and Danny Oppenheimer at Princeton—four intellectual giants who graciously allowed me to stand on their shoulders.

NOTES

Prologue

1   **Paper in *Orthomolecular Psychiatry:*** Schauss, A. G. (1979). Tranquilizing effect of color reduces aggressive behavior and potential violence. *Orthomolecular Psychiatry*, 8, 218–221.

2   **Anecdotes on miraculous tranquilizing power:** much of the anecdotal information comes from a telephone interview with Alex Schauss, 30 May 2012. See also Schauss (1979), above, and Schauss, A. G. (1985). The physiological effect of colour on the suppression of human aggression: Research on Baker-Miller Pink. *International Journal of Biosocial Research*, 2, 55–64; and Walker, M. (1991). *The power of color*. New York: Avery.

3   **Frenzy of academic interest; some found weaker effects:** Schauss, ever the scholar, continued to test the effect, sometimes but not always finding support for the colour's tranquillizing effect. Today he remains convinced that there's something to the effect, and he's lent his name to *Schauss*, a company that sells sheets of Baker-Miller Pink for personal use. A partial list of publications that found partial or full support: Pellegrini, R. J., Schauss, A. G., Kerr, T. J., and Ah You, B. K. (1981). Grip strength and exposure to hue differences in visual stimuli: Is postural status a factor? *Bulletin of the Psychonomic Society*, 17, 27–28; Pelligrini, R. J., and Schauss, A. G. (1980). Muscle strength as a function of exposure to hue differences in visual stimuli: An experimental test of the kinesoid hypothesis. *Orthomolecular Psychiatry*, 9, 148–150; Profusek, P. A., and

Rainey, D. W. (1987). Effects of Baker-Miller Pink and red on state anxiety, grip strength, and motor precision. *Perceptual and Motor Skills*, 65, 941–942. A partial list of publications that found little or no support: Gilliam, J. E., and Unruh, D. (1988). The effects of Baker-Miller Pink on biological, physical, and cognitive behavior. *Journal of Orthomolecular Medicine*, 3, 202–206; Smith, J. M., Bell, P. A., and Fusco, M. E. (1986). The influence of color and demand characteristics on muscle strength and affective ratings of the environment. *Journal of General Psychology*, 113, 289–297; Dunwoody, L. (1998). Color or brightness effects on grip strength? *Perceptual and Motor Skills*, 87, 275–278; Keller, L. M., and Vautin, R. G. (1998). Effect of viewed color on hand-grip strength. *Perceptual and Motor Skills*, 87, 763–768; Pellegrini, R. J., Schauss, A. G., and Miller, M. E. (1981). Room color and aggression in a criminal detention holding cell: A test of the "tranquilizing pink" hypothesis. *Orthomolecular Psychiatry*, 10, 174–181.

Chapter 1: Names

7   **Jung and nominative determinism:** Many of the examples are from a Wikipedia catalogue of aptronyms, available at http://en.wikipedia.org/wiki/Aptronym. The discussion about *nominative determinism* took place in the Feedback column in two issues of the *New Scientist* magazine: 5 November 1994, and 17 December 1994. Some of the information here is based on an email exchange with the Feedback column's editors at the time (and still today), John Hoyland and Mike Holderness. The term is attributed to a contributor, C. R. Cavonius.

7   **Splatt and Weedon:** Splatt, A. J., and Weedon, D. (1977). The urethral syndrome: experience with the Richardson urethroplasty. *British Journal of Urology*, 49, 173–176.

8   **Nigerian naming practices:** Lapidos, J. (9 September 2010). Is Goodluck Jonathan lucky? Naming practices in Nigeria. Available at http://www.slate.com/articles/news _and_politics/explainer/2010/09/is_goodluck_jonathan_lucky.html.

9   **Story of Boch (BOHdVF260602):** *Russian Times* news video and interviews, available at http://rt.com/news/digit-named-boy-ignored-by-authorities/.

9   **Decline of names Adolf, Donald, and Ebenezer:** Lieberson, S. (2000). *A matter of taste: How names, fashions, and culture change.* New Haven, CT: Yale University Press.

10   **Demographic baggage of names like Dorothy and Ava:** Namipedia website: http:// www.babynamewizard.com/namipedia. See also Levitt, S. D., and Dubner, S. J. (2005). *Freakonomics: A rogue economist explores the hidden side of everything.* New York: Morrow.

12   **Sending out job applications with black and white names:** Bertrand, M., and Mullainathan, S. (2004). Are Emily and Greg more employable than Lakisha and Jamal? A field experiment on labor market discrimination. *American Economic Review*, 94, 991–1013.

13 **Some pundits describe society as "post-racial":** Kaplan, H. R. (2011). *The myth of post-racial America: Searching for equality in the age of materialism.* Lanham, MD: Rowman and Littlefield; Parks, G., and Hughey, M. (2011). *The Obamas and a (post) racial America?* Series in Political Psychology. New York: Oxford University Press; Tesler, M., and Sears, D. O. (2010). *Obama's race: The 2008 election and the dream of a post-racial America.* Chicago: University of Chicago Press.

13 **Name-letter effect:** Nuttin, J. M., Jr. (1985). Narcissism beyond Gestalt and awareness: The name-letter effect. *European Journal of Social Psychology*, 15, 353–361; Nuttin, J. M., Jr. (1987). Affective consequences of mere ownership: The name-letter effect in twelve European languages. *European Journal of Social Psychology*, 17, 381–402. A recent paper has cast doubt on a number of prominent name-letter effects, so I chose to omit them from the book. See Simonsohn, U. (2011). Spurious? Name similarity effects (implicit egotism) in marriage, job, and moving decisions. *Journal of Personality and Social Psychology*, 101, 1–24.

14 **Hurricane donations:** Chandler, J., Griffin, T. M., and Sorenson, N. (2008). In the "I" of the storm: Shared initials increase disaster donations. *Judgment and Decision Making*, 3, 404–410.

13 **Surname effect:** Carlson, K. A., and Conard, J. M. (2011). The last name effect: How last name influences acquisition timing. *Journal of Consumer Research*, 38, 300–307.

17 **Name fluency:** For a comprehensive review of fluency, see Alter, A. L., and Oppenheimer, D. M. (2009). Uniting the tribes of fluency to form a metacognitive nation. *Personality and Social Psychology Review*, 13, 219–235.

17 **Political candidates with good and bad names:** O'Sullivan, C. S., Chen, A., Mohapatra, S., Sigelman, L., and Lewis, E. (1988). Voting in ignorance: The politics of smooth-sounding names. *Journal of Applied Social Psychology*, 18, 1094–1106. See also Yardley, W. (10 November 2010). Nurkowski? Makowski? Murckoski? Counting the write-in votes in Alaska. *New York Times.* Available at http://thecaucus.blogs.nytimes.com/2010/11/10/nurkowski-makowski-murckoski-counting-the-write-in-votes-in-alaska/.

19 **Name fluency and success at law firms:** Laham, S., Koval, P., and Alter, A. L. (2012). The name-pronunciation effect: Why people like Mr Smith more than Mr Colquhoun. *Journal of Experimental Social Psychology*, 48, 752–756.

21 **Stock-market performance and names:** Alter, A. L., and Oppenheimer, D. M. (2006). Predicting short-term stock fluctuations by using processing fluency. *Proceedings of the National Academy of Sciences*, 103, 9369–9372.

23 **Cuddly and powerful names:** Köhler, W. (1929). *Gestalt psychology.* New York: Liveright; Maurer, D., Pathman, T., and Mondloch, C. J. (2006). The shape of boubas: Sound-shape correspondences in toddlers and adults. *Developmental Science*, 9, 316–322.

Chapter 2: Labels

27 **Russian blues experiments:** Winawer, J., Witthoft, N., Frank, M. C., Wu, L., Wade, A. R., and Boroditsky, L. (2007). Russian blues reveal effects of language on color discrimination. *Proceedings of the National Academy of Sciences*, 104, 7780–7785. On brain regions: Tan, L. H., Chan, A. H. D., Kay, P., Khong, P. L., Yip, L. K. C., and Luke, K. K. (2008). Language affects patterns of brain activation associated with perceptual decision. *Proceedings of the National Academy of Sciences*, 105, 4004–4009.

29 **Whorfian linguistic relativity:** Much of Whorf's work is collected here: Whorf, B. (1956). *Language, thought, and reality: Selected writings of Benjamin Lee Whorf.* John B. Carroll (ed.). Cambridge, MA: MIT Press.

31 **Seeing a face according to its race:** Eberhardt, J. L., Dasgupta, N., and Banaszynski, T. L. (2003). Believing is seeing: The effects of racial labels and implicit beliefs on face perception. *Personality and Social Psychology Bulletin*, 29, 360–370.

31 **Seeing darkness of face according to its race:** Levin, D. T., and Banaji, M. R. (2006). Distortions in the perceived lightness of faces: The role of race categories. *Journal of Experimental Psychology: General*, 135, 501–512.

31 **Image of three faces:** appears courtesy of American Psychological Association, publisher of Levin and Banaji (2006). Distortions in the perceived lightness of faces: The role of race categories.

32 **Claims about working-class aptitude:** Beckford, M. (June 4, 2008). Working classes "lack intelligence to be doctors", claims academic. *Telegraph*. Available at http://www.telegraph.co.uk/news/uknews/2074651/Working-classes-lack-intelligence-to-be-doctors-claims-academic.html.

32 **Hannah experiment:** Darley, J. M., and Gross, P. H. (1983). A hypothesis-confirming bias in labeling effects. *Journal of Personality and Social Psychology*, 44, 20–33.

34 **Ptolemy's decision to place north above south:** Boorstin, D. (1983). *The discoverers.* New York: Random House.

35 **People believe north to be above south:** Nelson, L. D., and Simmons, J. P. (2009). On southbound ease and northbound fees: Literal consequences of the metaphoric link between vertical position and cardinal direction. *Journal of Marketing Research*, 46, 715–724; Meier, B. P., Moller, A. C., Chen, J., and Riemer-Peltz, M. (2011). Spatial metaphor and real estate: North-south location biases housing preference. *Social Psychological and Personality Science*, 2, 547–553.

36 **The QWERTY effect:** Jasmin, K., and Casasanto, D. (2012). The QWERTY effect: How typing shapes the meanings of words. *Psychonomic Bulletin and Review*. The effect has received plenty of attention from bloggers, and Casasanto's response is available at http://www.casasanto.com/QWERTY.html.

38 **Jane Elliott's classroom demonstration:** Bloom, S. G. (2005). Lesson of a lifetime. *Smithsonian*, 36, 82–87.

40 **Bloomers in the classroom:** Rosenthal, R., and Jacobson, L. (1992). *Pygmalion in the classroom.* New York: Irvington.

42 **Different languages paint different worlds:** Levinson, S. C. (2003). *Space in language and cognition: Explorations in cognitive diversity.* Cambridge: Cambridge University Press; Boroditsky, L., Schmidt, L., and Phillips, W. (2003). Sex, syntax, and semantics. In *Language in mind: Advances in the study of language and thought.* D. Gentner and S. Goldin-Meadow (eds.), 61–68. London: MIT Press.

42 **John Haviland and the Guugu Yimithirr:** Deutscher, G. (2010). *Through the language glass: Why the world looks different in other languages.* New York: Picador.

44 **Loftus's memory studies:** Loftus, E. F., and Palmer, J. C. (1974). Reconstruction of automobile destruction: An example of the interaction between language and memory. *Journal of Verbal Learning and Verbal Behavior*, 13, 585–589.

46 **Phantom scar experiment:** Kleck, R. E., and Strenta, A. (1980). Perceptions of the impact of negatively valued physical characteristics on social interaction. *Journal of Personality and Social Psychology*, 39, 861–873.

48 **Hysteria, borderline personality disorder, ADHD:** Briggs, L. (2000). The race of hysteria: "Overcivilization" and the "savage" woman in late nineteenth-century obstetrics and gynecology. *American Quarterly*, 52, 246–273; Aviram, R. B., Brodsky, B. S., and Stanley, B. (2006). Borderline personality disorder, stigma, and treatment implications. *Harvard Review of Psychiatry*, 14, 249–256; Beard, G. (1880). *A practical treatise on nervous exhaustion.* New York: William Wood; Elder, T. E. (2010). The importance of relative standards in ADHD diagnoses: evidence based on exact birth dates. *Journal of Health Economics*, 29, 641–656.

Chapter 3: Symbols

51 **John Mock's swastika building:** *Sydney Morning Herald*, available at http://www.smh .com.au/news/technology/complex-mistake/2007/09/27/1190486482564.html; *Jewish Sightseeing* blog, available at http://www.jewishsightseeing.com/dhh_weblog/2006 -blog/2006-12/2006-12-13-coronado-swastika.htm. Another building, a retirement home in Decatur, Alabama has the same profile from the air, available at http://www .msnbc.msn.com/id/23633404/ns/us_news-life/. Note that the Nazi swastika was right-facing, with the four L-shapes rotating clockwise. Some religious swastikas (sometimes called *sauwastikas*) are left-facing, with the L-shapes rotating counterclockwise.

54 **Swastika experiment:** Alter, A. L., and Kwan, V. S. Y. (2012). How symbols shape thinking. (Unpublished manuscript.) New York University.

56 **Apple logo experiment:** Fitzsimons, G. M., Chartrand, T. L., and Fitzsimons, G. J. (2008). Automatic effects of brand exposure on motivated behavior: How Apple makes you "think different." *Journal of Consumer Research*, 35, 21–35.

58 **Lightbulb experiment:** Slepian, M. L., Weisbuch, M., Rutchick, A. M., Newman, L. S., and Ambady, N. (2010). Shedding light on insight: Priming bright ideas. *Journal of Experimental Social Psychology*, 46, 696–700.

60 **Burning money and the K Foundation:** Reid, J. (1994). Money to burn. *Observer.* Available at http://www.libraryofmu.org/display-resource.php?id=387. A YouTube video captures the burning money at http://www.youtube.com/watch?v=XOMsJBinU_o.

61 **Scanning people's brains as they watch money destroyed:** Becchio, C., Skewes, J., Lund, T. E., Frith, U., Frith, C., and Roepstorff, A. (2011). How the brain responds to the destruction of money. *Journal of Neuroscience, Psychology, and Economics*, 4, 1–10.

62 **Experiments on money and independence, helping, and pain:** Vohs, K. D., Mead, N., and Goode, M. R. (2006). The psychological consequences of money. *Science, 314,* 1154–1156; Vohs, K. D., Mead, N. L., Goode, M. R. (2008). Merely activating the concept of money changes personal and interpersonal behavior. *Current Directions in Psychological Science*, 17, 208–212; Zhou, X., Vohs, K. D., and Baumeister, R. F. (2009). The symbolic power of money: Reminders of money alter social distress and physical pain. *Psychological Science*, 20, 700–706.

65 **Chávez and flag protests:** Government video criticizing the flag protest, available at http://www.youtube.com/watch?v=31QJEFvYmMI.

65 **Barbara Frietchie flag quote:** Whittier, John Greenleaf (1864). "Barbara Frietchie". Available at http://www.poemhunter.com/poem/barbara-frietchie/.

66 **American flag primes liberty:** Butz, D., Plant, E. A., and Doerr, C. E. (2007). Liberty and justice for all? Implications of exposure to the U.S. flag for intergroup relations. *Personality and Social Psychology Bulletin*, 33, 396–408.

67 **Israeli flag primes centrism:** Hassin, R. R., Ferguson, M. J., Shidlovski, D., and Gross, T. (2007). Subliminal exposure to national flags affects political thought and behavior. *Proceedings of the National Academy of Sciences*, 104, 19757–19761.

68 **For news watchers, American flag primes aggression:** Ferguson, M. J., and Hassin, R. R. (2007). On the automatic association between America and aggression for news watchers. *Personality and Social Psychology Bulletin*, 33, 1632–1647.

69 **Cross primes honesty in Christians:** Alter, A. L., and Kwan, V. S. Y. (2012). How symbols shape thinking. (Unpublished manuscript.) New York University.

70 **Pope primes poorer self-conception:** Baldwin, M. W., Carrell, S. E., and Lopez, D. F. (1990). Priming relationship schemas: My advisor and the Pope are watching me from the back of my mind. *Journal of Experimental Social Psychology*, 26, 435–454.

72 **Purchasing with real and altered currency:** Alter, A. L., and Oppenheimer, D. M. (2008). Easy on the mind, easy on the wallet: The effects of familiarity and fluency on currency valuation. *Psychonomic Bulletin and Review*, 15, 985–990.

Chapter 4: The Mere Presence of Other People

79 **Eyes as surveillance in Newcastle University psychology department coffee room:** Bateson, M., Nettle, D., and Roberts, G. (2006). Cues of being watched enhance cooperation in a real-world setting. *Biology Letters*, 2, 412–414.

80 **Genie's enforced isolation:** documentary discussing Genie and her partial recovery, available at http://www.youtube.com/watch?v=dEnkY2iaKis. The Wild Boy of Aveyron is another classic case. Some experts believe he may have been autistic, making it difficult to determine how he responded to social deprivation. See, for example, the case study on BBC Radio 4 (30 November 2008): The Wild Boy of Aveyron: Claudia Hammond presents. 23:40 UTC. Available at http://www.bbc.co.uk/programmes /b00b7lrb.

80 **Schachter's isolation experiment:** Schachter, S. (1959). *The psychology of affiliation*. Stanford, CA: Stanford University Press.

81 **Cave experiments by Michel Siffre:** interview with Michel Siffre: Foer, J., and Siffre, M. (2008). Caveman: An interview with Michel Siffre. *Cabinet*. Available at http:// www.cabinetmagazine.org/issues/30/foer.php.

81 **Grassian's inmates:** Grassian, S. (1983). Psychopathological effects of solitary confinement. *American Journal of Psychiatry*, 140, 1450–1454.

82 **Haney's studies at Pelican Bay:** Haney, C. W. (2003). Mental health issues in long-term solitary confinement and "supermax" confinement. *Crime and Delinquency*, 49, 124–156. See also Atul Gawande's article on the same topic: Gawande, A. (30 March 2009). Hellhole. *New Yorker*. Available at http://www.newyorker.com/reporting/2009/03/30 /090330fa_fact_gawande; and Vasiliades, E. (2005). Solitary confinement and international human rights: Why the U.S. prison system fails global standards. *American University International Law Review*, 21, 71–99.

83 **Some questions can only be answered with a comparison standard:** Hsee, C. K., and Zhang, J. (2010). General evaluability theory. *Perspectives on Psychological Science*, 5, 343–355. Energy use statistics available at http://www.eia.gov/consumption/residen tial/index.cfm.

84 **Opower:** Information on the Opower website: www.opower.com.

85 ***Noor* and Brazilian soap opera:** Rohde, D. (8 March 2012). Inside Islam's culture war. Reuters. Available at http://blogs.reuters.com/david-rohde/2012/03/08/inside -islams-culture-war/; Gubash, C. (31 July 2008). Soap opera upends traditional Arab gender roles. *NBC News World Blog*. Available at http://worldblog.msnbc.msn .com/_news/2008/07/31/4376465-soap-opera-upends-traditional-arab-gender -roles; Associated Press (July 27, 2008). Soap opera shakes customs of Arab married life. Available at http://abclocal.go.com/wpvi/story?section=news/entertainment& id=6290501; *Emirates 24/7* (April 4, 2012). Turkish soap opera blamed for UAE divorces. Available at http://www.emirates247.com/news/emirates/turkish-soap-opera

-blamed-for-uae-divorces-2012-04-04-1.452235; *Infoniac.com* (April 6, 2009). More divorces and less children in Brazil due to racy soap operas. Available at http://www.infoniac.com/offbeat-news/more-divorces-and-less-children-in-brazil-due-to-racy-soap-operas.html.

86 **Maier's hints in the cord task:** Maier, N. R. F. (1931). Reasoning in humans: II. The solution of a problem and its appearance in consciousness. *Journal of Comparative Psychology*, 12, 181–194.

88 **Steve McClaren:** Two illustrations of McClaren's staccato pseudo-Dutch available at http://www.youtube.com/watch?v=2ZnoP4sUV90; and http://www.youtube.com/watch?v=xhtq1ObGHy8.

88 **Gaits synchronize when we talk on cell phones:** Murray-Smith, R., Ramsay, A., Garrod, S., Jackson, M., and Musizza, B. (2007). Gait alignment in mobile phone conversations. *Proceedings of the Ninth International Conference on Human Computer Interaction with Mobile Devices and Services,* 214–221.

88 **Chameleon effect studies:** Chartrand, T. L., and Bargh, J. A. (1999). The chameleon effect: The perception-behavior link and social interaction. *Journal of Personality and Social Psychology*, 76, 893–910; Tanner, R. J., Ferraro, R., Chartrand, T. L., Bettman, J. R., and van Baaren, R. (2008). Of chameleons and consumption: The impact of mimicry on choice and preferences. *Journal of Consumer Research*, 35, 754–766; Lakin, J. L., Jefferis, V. E., Cheng, C. M., and Chartrand, T. L. (2003). The chameleon effect as social glue: Evidence for the evolutionary significance of nonconscious mimicry. *Journal of Nonverbal Behavior*, 27, 145–162. Note that mimicry has to go unnoticed by onlookers, otherwise it reflects poorly on the mimicker: Kavanagh, L. C., Suhler, C. L., Churchland, P. S., and Winkielman, P. (2011). When it's an error to mirror: The surprising reputational costs of mimicry. *Psychological Science*, 22, 1274–1276.

90 **Triplett's studies:** Triplett, N. (1898). The dynamogenic factors in pacemaking and competition. *American Journal of Psychology*, 9, 507–533.

91 **Social inhibition study:** Pessin, J., and Husband, R. W. (1933). Effects of social stimulation on human maze learning. *Journal of Abnormal and Social Psychology*, 28, 148–154.

92 **Zajonc's cockroaches:** Zajonc, R. B. (1965). Social facilitation. *Science, 149,* 269–274; Zajonc, R. B. (1966). Social facilitation of dominant and subordinate responses. *Journal of Experimental Social Psychology*, 2, 160–168.

92 **Novice and expert pool players:** Michaels, J. W., Blommel, J. M., Brocato, R. M., Linkous, R. A., and Rowe, J. S. (1982). Social facilitation and inhibition in a natural setting. *Replications in Social Psychology*, 2, 21–24.

93 **People do better against fewer competitors:** Garcia, S. M., and Tor, A. (2009). The N-Effect: More competitors, less competition. *Psychological Science*, 20, 871–877.

95 **Tragic story of Hugo Tale-Yax:** Sulzberger, A. G., and Meenan, M. (26 April 2010).

Questions surround a delay in help for a dying man. Available at http://www.nytimes.com/2010/04/26/nyregion/26homeless.html.

95 **Kitty Genovese's death:** The *New York Times* has a fascinating collection of articles on the case, available at http://www.nytimes.com/keyword/kitty-genovese.

96 **Darley and Latané's bystander intervention studies:** seizing student: Darley, J. M., and Latané, B. (1968). Bystander intervention in emergencies: Diffusion of responsibility. *Journal of Personality and Social Psychology*, 8, 377–383; smoke-filled room: Latané, B., and Darley, J. M. (1968). Group inhibition of bystander intervention in emergencies. *Journal of Personality and Social Psychology*, 10, 215–221.

Chapter 5: The Characteristics of Other People

101 **Maslow's childhood:** the entire fall 2008 issue of the *Journal of Humanistic Psychology* was devoted to recounting Maslow's life and intellectual legacy. See especially Hoffman, E. (2008). Abraham Maslow: A biographer's reflections. *Journal of Humanistic Psychology*, 48, 439–443. See also Hoffman, E. (1988). *The right to be human: A biography of Abraham Maslow*. New York: St Martin's.

102 **Maslow's hierarchy:** Maslow, A. H. (1943). A theory of human motivation. *Psychological Review*, 50, 370–396. Some psychologists are particularly critical of Maslow's suggestion that people pursue the motives in order, beginning with the lower-order motives and moving on to the higher-order motives. See, for example, Wahba, M. A., and Bridwell, L. G. (1974). Maslow reconsidered: A review of research on the need hierarchy theory. *Organizational Behavior and Human Performance, 15,* 212–240. Others question whether the hierarchy applies to people who live outside Western culture: Hofstede, G. (1984). The cultural relativity of the quality of life concept. *Academy of Management Review*, 9, 389–398.

104 **Beautiful chess players:** Dreber, A., Gerdes, C., and Gränsmark, P. (2012). Beauty queens and battling knights: Risk taking and attractiveness in chess. (Unpublished manuscript.) Available at http://ftp.iza.org/dp5314.pdf.

105 **Skateboarders and beautiful women:** Ronay, R., and von Hippel, W. (2010). Power, testosterone and risk-taking: The moderating influence of testosterone and executive functions. *Journal of Behavioral Decision Making*, 23, 439–526; Ronay, R., and von Hippel, W. (2010). The presence of an attractive woman elevates testosterone and risk-taking in young men. *Social Psychological and Personality Science*, 1, 57–64.

107 **Lap dancers and menstrual cycles:** Miller, G., Tybur, J. M., and Jordan, B. D. (2007). Ovulatory cycle effects on tip earnings by lap dancers: Economic evidence for human estrus? *Evolution and Human Behavior*, 28, 375–381.

108 **Martin Luther King sees a black president in twenty-five years:** interview available at http://www.youtube.com/watch?v=aUbcKCRraGs.

109 **Black faces prime weapons:** Eberhardt, J. L., Goff, P. A., Purdie, V. J., and Davies, P. G. (2004). Seeing Black: race, crime, and visual processing. *Journal of Personality and Social Psychology*, 87, 876–893.

110 **Three-frame image of gun becoming progressively clearer:** appears courtesy of the American Psychological Association, publisher of Eberhardt, Goff, Purdie, and Davies (2004). Seeing Black: race, crime, and visual processing.

110 **"Looking deathworthy" paper:** Eberhardt, J. L., Davies, P. G., Purdie-Vaughns, V. J., and Johnson, S. L. (2006). Looking deathworthy: Perceived stereotypicality of Black defendants predicts capital-sentencing outcomes. *Psychological Science*, 17, 383–386.

111 **Race and the ape metaphor:** Goff, P. A., Eberhardt, J. L., Williams, M. J., and Jackson, M. C. (2008). Not yet human: Implicit knowledge, historical dehumanization, and contemporary consequences. *Journal of Personality and Social Psychology*, 94, 292–306.

113 **Detecting shooters by race:** Correll, J., Park, B., Judd, C. M., and Wittenbrink, B. (2002). The police officer's dilemma: Using ethnicity to disambiguate potentially threatening individuals. *Journal of Personality and Social Psychology*, 83, 1314–1329.

114 **Muslim headgear and detecting shooters:** Unkelbach, C., Forgas, J. P., and Denson, T. (2007). The turban effect: The influence of Muslim headgear and induced affect on aggressive responses in the shooter bias paradigm. *Journal of Experimental Social Psychology*, 43, 513–528.

114 **Two-frame image of shooter-detection task:** appears courtesy of the American Psychological Association, publisher of Correll, Park, Judd, and Wittenbrink (2002). The police officer's dilemma: Using ethnicity to disambiguate potentially threatening individuals.

115 **Vero Labs and Liquid Trust:** information from websites: http://oxytocinnasalspray.org/; http://www.verolabs.com/how.asp.

116 **Oxytocin induces trust:** Kosfeld, M., Heinrichs, M., Zak, P. J., Fischbacher U., and Fehr, E. (2005). Oxytocin increases trust in humans. *Nature, 435,* 673–676; Uvnas-Moberg, K. (1998). Oxytocin may mediate the benefits of positive social interaction and emotions. *Psychoneuroendocrinology*, 23, 819–835; Bartels, A., and Zeki, S. (2004). The neural correlates of maternal and romantic love. *Neuroimage*, 21, 1155–1166.

117 **Oxytocin makes people more aggressive towards out-groups:** De Dreu, C. K. W., Greer, L. L., Van Kleef, G. A., Shalvi, S., and Handgraaf, M. J. J. (2011). Oxytocin promotes human ethnocentrism. *Proceedings of the National Academy of Sciences USA*, 108, 1262–1266. A number of other studies have similarly contradicted oxytocin's oversimplified billing as the "cuddle chemical" or the "love hormone". For a summary, see Yong, E. (11 February 2012). Dark side of love. *NewScientist,* 39–42. See also: Declerck, C. H., Boone, C., and Kiyonari, T. (2010). Oxytocin and cooperation under conditions of uncertainty: the modulating role of incentives and social information. *Hormones & Behavior*, 57, 368–374; Bartz, J., Simeon, D., Hamilton, H., Kim, S., Crystal, S., Braun

A., Hollander, E (2011). Oxytocin can hinder trust and cooperation in borderline personality disorder. *Social Cognitive and Affective Neuroscience*, 6, 556–563; Bartz, J. A., Zaki, J., Ochsner, K. N., Bolger, N., Kolevzon, A., Ludwig, N., and Lydon, J. E. (2010). Effects of oxytocin on recollections of maternal care and closeness. *Proceedings of the National Academy of Sciences, U. S. A.*, 107, 21371–21375; Shamay-Tsoory, S. G., Fischer, M., Dvash, J., Harari, H., Pelach-Bloom, N., and Levkovitz, Y. (2009). Intranasal administration of oxytocin increases envy and schadenfreude (gloating). *Biological Psychiatry*, 66, 864–870.

118 **Looking at partner's photo reduces physical pain:** Eisenberger, N. I., Master, S. L., Inagaki, T. I., Taylor, S. E., Shirinyan, D., Lieberman, M. D., and Naliboff, B. (2011). Attachment figures activate a safety signal-related neural region and reduce pain experience. *Proceedings of the National Academy of Sciences*, 108, 11721–11726; Master, S. L., Eisenberger, N. I., Taylor, S. E., Naliboff, B. D., Shirinyan, D., and Lieberman, M. D. (2009). A picture's worth: Partner photographs reduce experimentally induced pain. *Psychological Science*, 20, 1316–1318; Younger, J., Aron, A., Parke, S., Chatterjee, N., and Mackey, S. (2010). Viewing pictures of a romantic partner reduces experimental pain: Involvement of neural reward systems. *PLoS ONE*, 5, e13309.

120 **Childhood memories promote moral behaviour:** Gino, F., and Desai, S. D. (2012). Memory lane and morality: How childhood memories promote prosocial behavior. *Journal of Personality and Social Psychology*, 102, 743–758.

121 **Looking in the mirror prompts honesty:** Diener, E., and Wallbom, M. (1976). Effects of self-awareness on antinormative behavior. *Journal of Research in Personality, 10,* 107–111; Batson, C. D, Thompson, E. R., Seuferling, G., Whitney, H., and Strongman, J. A. (1999). Moral hypocrisy: Appearing moral to oneself without being so. *Journal of Personality and Social Psychology*, 77, 525–537.

Chapter 6: Culture

125 **The Müller-Lyer illusion:** the illusion was originally published in Müller-Lyer, F. C. (1889). Optische Urteilstäuschungen. *Archiv für Physiologie Suppl.,* 263–270.

126 **WEIRD people:** Henrich, J., Heine, S. J., and Norenzayan, A. (2010). The weirdest people in the world. *Behavioral and Brain Sciences*, 33, 61–83.

126 **Cultural differences in the Müller-Lyer illusion:** Segall, M. H., Campbell, D. T., and Herskovits, M. J. (1963). Cultural differences in the perception of geometric illusions. *Science*, 193, 769–771; for more on why these differences emerge, see Howe, C. Q., and Purves, D. (2005). The Müller-Lyer illusion explained by the statistics of image-source relationships. *Proceedings of the National Academy of Sciences*, 102, 1234–1239.

128 **Chinese and American students remember photos differently:** Masuda, T., Gonzalez, R., Kwan, L., and Nisbett, R. E. (2008). Culture and aesthetic preference: Comparing

the attention to context of East Asians and European Americans. *Personality and Social Psychology Bulletin*, 34, 1260–1275; Chua, H. F., Boland, J. E., and Nisbett, R. E. (2005). Cultural variation in eye movements during scene perception. *Proceedings of the National Academy of Sciences*, 102, 12629–12633; Ji, L., Peng, K., and Nisbett, R. E. (2000). Culture, control, and perception of relationships in the environment. *Journal of Personality and Social Psychology*, 78, 943–955; Kitayama, S., Duffy, S., Kawamura, T., and Larsen, J. T. (2003). A cultural look at New Look: Perceiving an object and its context in two cultures. *Psychological Science*, 14, 201–206. Other relevant papers: Miyamoto, Y., Nisbett, R. E., and Masuda, T. (2006). Culture and physical environment: Holistic versus analytic perceptual affordance. *Psychological Science*, 17, 113–119; Masuda, T., and Nisbett, R. E. (2001). Attending holistically vs. analytically: Comparing the context sensitivity of Japanese and Americans. *Journal of Personality and Social Psychology*, 81, 922–934; Nisbett, R. E., and Masuda, T. (2003). Culture and point of view. *Proceedings of the National Academy of Sciences*, 100, 11163–11175.

130 **Context in emotion perception for American and Japanese students:** Masuda, T., Ellsworth, P. C., Mesquita, B., Leu, J., Tanida, S., and van de Veerdonk, E. (2008). Placing the face in context: Cultural differences in the perception of facial emotion. *Journal of Personality and Social Psychology*, 94, 365–381.

130 **Image of cartoon figures with happy and sad expressions:** appears courtesy of the American Psychological Association, publisher of Masuda, Ellsworth, Mesquita, Leu, Tanida, and van de Veerdonk (2008). Placing the face in context: Cultural differences in the perception of facial emotion.

131 **Importance of harmony to East Asians:** Kim, H. S., and Markus, H. R. (1999). Deviance or uniqueness, harmony or conformity? A cultural analysis. *Journal of Personality and Social Psychology*, 77, 785–800. For a more general discussion of individualism and collectivism, see Markus, H. R., and Kitayama, S. (1991). Culture and the self: Implications for cognition, emotion, and motivation. *Psychological Review*, 98, 224–253.

131 **Asch's conformity experiment:** Asch, S. E. (1956). Studies of independence and conformity: A minority of one against a unanimous majority. *Psychological Monographs*, 70, Whole No. 416.

133 **Cross-cultural differences in Asch's conformity result:** Bond, R., and Smith, P. B. (1996). Culture and conformity: A meta-analysis of studies using Asch's (1952b, 1956) line judgment task. *Psychological Bulletin*, 119, 111–137.

133 **Microbe levels and individualism and collectivism:** Fincher, C. L., Thornhill, R., Murray, D. R., and Schaller, M. (2008). Pathogen prevalence predicts human cross-cultural variability in individualism/collectivism. *Proceedings of the Royal Society B: Biological Sciences*, 275, 1279–1285.

135 **Mathematics and children in Brazil:** Saxe, G. B. (1988). The mathematics of child street vendors. *Child Development*, 59, 1415–1425.

137 **What makes art appealing in different countries:** Masuda, T., Gonzalez, R., Kwan, L., and Nisbett, R. E. (2008). Culture and aesthetic preference: Comparing the attention to context of East Asians and European Americans. *Personality and Social Psychology Bulletin*, 34, 1260–1275.

139 **Culture of honor in the American south:** Cohen, D., Nisbett, R. E., Bowdle, B., and Schwarz, N. (1996). Insult, aggression, and the southern culture of honor. *Journal of Personality and Social Psychology*, 70, 945–960; Cohen, D., and Nisbett, R. E. (1997). Field experiments examining the culture of honour: The role of institutions in perpetuating norms about violence. *Personality and Social Psychology Bulletin*, 23, 1188–1199.

143 **Accidents, violence, and the culture of honor:** Barnes, C. D., Brown, R. P., and Tamborski, M. (2012). Living dangerously: Culture of honor, risk-taking, and the nonrandomness of "accidental" deaths. *Social Psychological and Personality Science*, 3, 100–107; Cohen, D. (1998). Culture, social organization, and patterns of violence. *Journal of Personality and Social Psychology, 75,* 408–419.

143 **Cultural maladies:** Dzokoto, V. A., and Adams, G. (2005). Understanding genital-shrinking epidemics in West Africa: Koro, juju, or mass psychogenic illness? *Culture, Medicine and Psychiatry*, 29, 53–78; Iwata, Y., Suzuki, K., Takei, N., Toulopoulou, T., Tsuchiya, K. J., Matsumoto, K., Mori, N. (2011). Jiko-shisen-kyofu (fear of one's own glance), but not taijin-kyofusho (fear of interpersonal relations), is an East Asian culture-related specific syndrome. *Australian and New Zealand Journal of Psychiatry*, 45, 148–152. A compendium of similar ailments: Bering, J. (11 July 2011). A bad case of the brain fags. *Slate.* Available at http://www.slate.com/id/2298453. Note that *koro* affects South-east Asians as well. In particular, epidemiologists have reported several prominent "outbreaks" in Malaysia and China.

146 **Andrew Lam and growing up bicultural:** PBS interview with Andrew Lam, available at http://www.pbs.org/wgbh/amex/daughter/sfeature/sf_cultures.html.

147 **Frame switching and biculturalism:** Benet-Martinez, V., Leu, J., Lee, F., and Morris, M. W. (2002). Cultural frame-switching in biculturals with oppositional versus compatible cultural identities. *Journal of Cross-Cultural Psychology*, 33, 492–516; Hong, Y., Morris, M. W., Chiu, C., and Benet-Martinez, V. (2000). Multicultural minds: A dynamic constructivist approach to culture and cognition. *American Psychologist*, 55, 709–720. Frame-switching is mentally taxing: Hamilton, R., Vohs, K. D., Sellier, A., and Meyvis, T. (2011). Being of two minds: Switching mindsets exhausts self-regulatory resources. *Organizational Behavior and Decision Processes*, 115, 13–24.

147 **Necker Cube as biculturalism metaphor:** Necker, L. A. (1832). Observations on some remarkable optical phenomena seen in Switzerland; and on an optical phenomenon which occurs on viewing a figure of a crystal or geometrical solid. *London and Edinburgh Philosophical Magazine and Journal of Science*, 1, 329–337.

149 ***Beverly Hills, 90210* and changing names in France:** Disdier, A.-C., Head, K., and

Mayer, T. (2010). Exposure to foreign media and changes in cultural traits: Evidence from naming patterns in France. *Journal of International Economics*, 80, 226–238.

150 **Multiculturalism, weather, and stock prediction:** Alter, A. L., and Kwan, V. S. Y. (2009). Cultural sharing in a global village: Extracultural cognition in European Americans. *Journal of Personality and Social Psychology*, 96, 742–760.

Chapter 7: Colours

157 **Blue streetlights prevent crime and discourage suicide:** *Yomiuri Shimbun* (11 December 2008). Blue streetlights believed to prevent suicides, street crime. *Seattle Times* available at http://seattletimes.nwsource.com/html/nationworld/2008494010_bluelight11.html.

158 **Blue lights help sawmill workers:** Sasseville, A., and Hebert, M. (2010). Using blue-green light at night and blue-blockers during the day to improve adaptation to night work: A pilot study. *Progress in Neuro-Psychopharmacology & Biological Psychiatry*, 34, 1236–1242.

160 **Kurt Goldstein's early work in colour science:** Goldstein, K. (1942). Some experimental observations concerning the influence of colors on the function of the organism. *Occupational Therapy and Rehabilitation*, 21, 147–151; Birren, F. (1978). *Color psychology and color therapy.* New York: Citadel.

160 **Auroratone therapy:** Rubin, H. E., and Katz, E. (1946). Auroratone films for the treatment of psychotic depressions in an army general hospital. *Journal of Clinical Psychology*, 2, 333–340. Restored snippet from an Auroratone film available at http://www.youtube.com/watch?v=uFXku4MntpY.

161 **Felix Deutsch's tachycardiac patient:** Deutsch, F. (1937). Psycho-physical reactions of the vascular system to influence of light and to impression gained through light. *Folia Clinica Orientalia*, Vol. I, No. 3–4.

162 **The Hawthorne effect as an alternative explanation:** Roethlisberger, F. J., and Dickson, W. J. (1939). *Management and the worker.* Cambridge, MA: Harvard University Press.

163 **Red and colour shock:** James, W. T., and Domingos, W. R. (1953). The effect of color shock on motor performance and tremor. *Journal of General Psychology*, 48, 187–193; Gerard, R. M. (1958). Color and emotional arousal. *American Psychologist*, 13, 340.

164 **Cerebellar disease:** Goldstein, K. (1942). Some experimental observations concerning the influence of colors on the function of the organism. *Occupational Therapy and Rehabilitation*, 21, 147–51; Birren, F. (1978). *Color psychology and color therapy.* New York: Citadel.

166 **How Japanese students use crayons:** Imada, M. (1926). Color preferences of school children. *Japanese Journal of Psychology*, 1, 1–21.

166 **Colour preferences across countries:** Madden, T. J., Hewett, K., and Roth, M. S. (2000). Managing images in different cultures: A cross-national study of color meanings and preferences. *Journal of International Marketing*, 8, 90–107; Palmer, S. E., and Schloss, K. B. (2010). An ecological valence theory of human color preference. *Proceedings of the National Academy of Sciences*, 107, 8877–8882; Miller, E. G., and Kahn, B. E. (2005). Shades of meaning: The effect of color and flavor names on consumer choice. *Journal of Consumer Research*, 32, 86–92.

167 **OkCupid data:** available from *OkCupid* blog at http://blog.okcupid.com/index.php /online-dating-advice-exactly-what-to-say-in-a-first-message/.

167 **Female hitchhikers appeal to male drivers when they wear red:** Guéguen, N. (2010). Color and women hitchhikers' attractiveness: Gentlemen drivers prefer red. *Color: Research and Application*, 37, 76–78.

168 **French women and T-shirt colour on dating profiles:** Guéguen, N., and Jacob, C. (2012). Color and cyber-attractiveness: Red enhances men's attraction to women's internet personal ads. *Color: Research and Application,* to be published.

168 **Biology behind the appeal of red, and studies showing red appeals:** Kayser, D. N., Elliot, A. J., and Feltman, R. (2010). Red and romantic behavior in men viewing women. *European Journal of Social Psychology*, 40, 901–908; Elliot, A. J., and Niesta, D. (2008). Romantic red: Red enhances men's attraction to women. *Journal of Personality and Social Psychology*, 95, 1150–1164; Elliot, A. J., Kayser, D. N., Greitmeyer, T., Lichtenfeld, S., Gramzow, R. H., Maier, M. A., and Liu, H. (2008). Red, rank, and romance in women viewing men. *Journal of Personality and Social Psychology*, 139, 399–417. Another explanation for this effect, proposed by Adam Pazda and his colleagues, is that men perceive red-clad women as more sexually receptive: Pazda, A. D., Elliot, A. J., and Greitmeyer, T. (2012). Sexy red: Perceived sexual receptivity mediates the red-attraction relation in men viewing women. *Journal of Experimental Social Psychology*, 48, 787–790; Elliot, A. J., and Pazda, A. D. (2012). Dressed for sex: Red as a female sexual signal in humans. *PLoS ONE*, 7, e34607.

170 **Colour scenes are more memorable:** Spence, I., Wong, P., Rusan, M., and Rastegar, N. (2006). How color enhances visual memory for natural scenes. *Psychological Science*, 17, 1–6.

171 **Red pen banned in Queensland:** ABC News article, available at http://www.abc.net .au/news/2008-12-03/qld-govt-slams-tasteless-red-pen-debate/228210.

171 **More mistakes found when examiners use red pen:** Rutchick, A. M., Slepian, M. L., and Ferris, B. D. (2010). The pen is mightier than the word: Object priming of evaluative standards. *European Journal of Social Psychology*, 40, 704–708.

172 **Red pen hampers intellectual performance:** Elliot, A. J., Maier, M. A., Moller, A. C., Friedman, R., and Meinhardt, J. (2007). Color and psychological functioning: The effect of red on performance attainment. *Journal of Experimental Psychology: General,*

136, 154–168; Elliot, A. J., and Maier, M. A. (2007). Color and psychological functioning. *Current Directions in Psychological Science*, 16, 250–254; Elliot, A. J., Maier, M. A., Binser, M. J., Friedman, R., and Pekrun, R. (2009). The effect of red on avoidance behavior. *Personality and Social Psychology Bulletin*, 35, 365–375.

173 **Red is better for vigilance; blue for creativity:** Mehta, R., and Zhu, R. J. (2009). Blue or red? Exploring the effect of color on cognitive task performances. *Science*, 323, 1226–1229.

174 **Olympians do better in red than in blue:** Hill, R. A., and Barton, R. A. (2005). Red enhances human performance in contests. *Nature*, 435, 293.

175 **Referees award more points to red-clad competitors:** Hagemann, N., Strauss, B., and Leissing, J. (2008). When the referee sees red. *Psychological Science*, 19, 769–771.

176 **Teams with black uniforms are more aggressive:** Frank, M. G., and Gilovich, T. (1988). The dark side of self- and social perception: Black uniforms and aggression in professional sports. *Journal of Personality and Social Psychology*, 1988, 54, 74–85.

177 **Black is associated with immorality; white with morality:** Sherman, G. D., and Clore, G. L. (2009). The color of sin: White and black are perceptual symbols of moral purity and pollution. *Psychological Science*, 20, 1019–1025.

Chapter 8: Locations

181 **Kowloon Walled City:** Lambot, I., and Girard, G. (1999). *City of darkness: Life in Kowloon Walled City.* Chiddingfold, UK: Watermark.

182 **Autistic, brain-damaged, and normal children in hospital:** Hutt, C., and Vaizey, M. J. (1966). Differential effects of group density on social behavior. *Nature*, 209, 1371–1372.

183 **College students donating milk cartons:** Bickman, L., Teger, A., Gabriele, T., McLaughlin, C., Berger, M., and Sunaday, E. (1973). Dormitory density and helping behavior. *Environmental Behavior*, 5, 465–490.

183 **Problems with overcrowding:** Zlutnick, S., and Altman, I. (1971). Crowding and human behaviour, in J. Wohlwill and D. Carson (eds.), *Environment and the social sciences: Perspectives and applications.* Washington, DC: American Psychological Association.

184 **"Butt-brush effect" in the supermarket:** Underhill, P. (1999). *Why we buy: The science of shopping.* New York: Simon & Schuster.

184 **Home noise and reading skills in children:** Cohen, S., Glass, D. C., and Singer, J. E. (1973). Apartment noise, auditory discrimination and reading ability. *Journal of Experimental Social Psychology*, 9, 407–433.

186 **Nature improves recovery after surgery:** Ulrich, R. S. (1984). View through a window may influence recovery from surgery. *Science*, 224, 420–421.

187 **Nature dampens the effects of stress:** Wells, N. M., and Evans, G. W. (2003). Nearby nature: A buffer of life stress among rural children. *Environment and Behavior*, 35, 311–330; Louv, R. (2008). *Last child in the woods: Saving our children from nature-deficit disorder.* New York: Algonquin.

187 **Nature calms children with ADD:** Taylor, A. F., Kuo, F. E., and Sullivan, W. C. (2001). Coping with ADD: The surprising connection to green play settings. *Environment and Behavior*, 33, 54–77.

187 **William James on two types of attention:** James, W. (1962). *Psychology: The briefer course.* New York: Collier. (Original work published 1892.)

188 **Attention restoration therapy:** Kaplan, S. (1995). The restorative benefits of nature: Toward an integrative framework. *Journal of Environmental Psychology, 15,* 169–182; Berman, M. G., Jonides, J., and Kaplan, S. (2008). The cognitive benefits of interacting with nature. *Psychological Science*, 19, 1207–1212; Raghubir, P., Chakravarti, A., and Meyvis, T. (2012). The water conjecture: Does the presence of water increase the blue vote? Working paper, New York University; White, M., Smith, A., Humphryes, K., Pahl, S., Snelling, D., and Depledge, M. (2010). Blue space: The importance of water for preference, affect, and restorativeness ratings of natural and built scenes. *Journal of Environmental Psychology*, 30, 482–493.

188 **Nature helped Dutch students who watched horrific video:** Van den Berg, A. E., Koole, S. L., and Van der Wulp, N. Y. (2003). Environmental preference and restoration: (How) are they related? *Journal of Environmental Psychology*, 23, 135–146.

189 **Forest walks reduce stress:** Tsunetsugu, Y., Park, B.-J., and Miyazaki, Y. (2010). Trends in research related to "Shinrin-yoku" (taking in the forest atmosphere or forest bathing) in Japan. *Environmental Health and Preventive Medicine*, 15, 27–37; Ulrich, R. S., Simons, R. F., Losito, B. D., Fiorito, E., Miles, M. A., and Zelson, M. (1991). Stress recovery during exposure to natural and urban environments. *Journal of Environmental Psychology*, 11, 201–230.

190 **Women with breast cancer think more clearly around nature:** Cimprich, B., and Ronis, D. L. (2003). An environmental intervention to restore attention in women with newly diagnosed breast cancer. *Cancer Nursing*, 26, 284–292.

190 **Teens and leisure time:** Lewin, T. (20 January 2010). If your kids are awake, they're probably online. *New York Times*. Available at http://www.nytimes.com/2010/01/20/education/20wired.html.

191 **John Carpenter's million-dollar win:** Vigoda, A. (22 November 1999). Million-dollar winner untaxed by celebrity. *USA Today*, 1D.

192 **Ogi Ogas struggles with the million-dollar question:** Ogas, O. (9 November 2006). A researcher uses his understanding of the human brain to advance on a popular quiz show. *Seedmagazine.com*, available at http://seedmagazine.com/content/article/who_wants_to_be_a_cognitive_neuroscientist_millionaire/.

193 **Fonts in the environment:** much of the information on fonts and their uses is from Garfield, S. (2012). *Just my type.* New York: Gotham.

194 **Cognitive Reflection Test:** Frederick, S. (2005). Cognitive reflection and decision making. *Journal of Economic Perspectives*, 19, 25–42.

The full test:

(1) A bat and a ball cost $1.10 in total. The bat costs $1.00 more than the ball. How much does the ball cost? _____ cents

Correct response: 5 cents. Intuitive and incorrect response: 10 cents.

(2) If it takes 5 machines 5 minutes to make 5 widgets, how long would it take 100 machines to make 100 widgets? _____ minutes

Correct response: 5 minutes. Intuitive and incorrect response: 100 minutes.

(3) In a lake, there is a patch of lily pads. Every day, the patch doubles in size. If it takes 48 days for the patch to cover the entire lake, how long would it take for the patch to cover half of the lake? _____ days

Correct response: 47 days. Intuitive and incorrect response: 24 days.

195 **Disfluent font makes people think more deeply:** Alter, A. L., Oppenheimer, D. M., Epley, N., and Eyre, R. N. (2007). Overcoming intuition: Metacognitive difficulty activates analytic reasoning. *Journal of Experimental Psychology: General*, 136, 569–576; see also Simmons, J. P., and Nelson, L. D. (2006). Intuitive confidence: Choosing between intuitive and nonintuitive alternatives. *Journal of Experimental Psychology: General*, 135, 409–428.

195 **Fluency prompts deeper confessions on Grouphug.us:** Alter, A. L., and Oppenheimer, D. M. (2009). Suppressing secrecy through metacognitive ease: Cognitive fluency encourages self-disclosure. *Psychological Science*, 20, 1414–1420.

197 **Fluent violations seemed more moral:** Laham, S., Alter, A. L., and Goodwin, G. P. (2009). Easy on the mind, easy on the wrongdoer: Unexpectedly fluent violations are deemed less morally wrong. *Cognition*, 112, 462–466.

198 **Lighting in modern life:** Gallagher, W. (1993). *The power of place.* New York: Harper-Collins.

199 **Darker rooms prompted dishonesty:** Zhong, C. B., Lake, V. B., and Gino, F. (2010). A good lamp is the best police: Darkness increases dishonesty and self-interested behavior. *Psychological Science*, 21, 311–314; digit adding task from Mazar, N., Amir, O., and Ariely, D. (2008). The dishonesty of honest people: A theory of self-concept maintenance. *Journal of Marketing Research*, 45, 633–644. The three numbers that add up to 10 are 1.96, 3.27, and 4.77.

199 **Broken windows theory:** Wilson, J. Q., and Kelling, G. L. (1982). Broken windows. *Atlantic Monthly.* Available online at http://www.theatlantic.com/magazine/archive/1982/03/broken-windows/4465/.

200 **Cars, flyers, and littering:** Cialdini, R. B., Reno, R. R., and Kallgren, C. A. (1990). A

focus theory of normative conduct: Recycling the concept of norms to reduce littering in public places. *Journal of Personality and Social Psychology*, 58, 1015–1026; Cialdini, R. B. (2003). Crafting normative messages to protect the environment. *Current Directions in Psychological Science*, 12, 105–109.

201 **Study on Americans in Chinatown and Chinese supermarkets:** Alter, A., and Kwan, V. S. Y. (2009). Cultural sharing in a global village: Evidence for extracultural cognition in white Americans. *Journal of Personality and Social Psychology*, 96, 742–760.

203 **Flashbulb memories:** Brown, R. and Kulik, J. (1977). Flashbulb memories. *Cognition*, 5, 73–99.

203 **Vietnam veterans recovered surprisingly well from drug addiction:** Robins, L. N. (1993). Vietnam veterans' rapid recovery from heroin addiction: A fluke or normal expectation? *Addiction*, 88, 1041–1054; Robins, L. N., Davis, D. H., and Nurco, D. N. (1974). How permanent was Vietnam drug addiction? *American Journal of Public Health Supplement*, 64, 38–43.

204 **Classic psychology experiment on scuba divers and context-dependent memory:** Godden, D. R., and Baddeley, A. D. (1975). Context-dependent memory in two natural environments: On land and underwater. *British Journal of Psychology*, 66, 325–331.

Chapter 9: Weather and Warmth

206 **Heat leads to retaliation in baseball pitching:** Reifman, A. S., Larrick, R. P., and Fein, S. (1991). Temper and temperature on the diamond: The heat-aggression relationship in major league baseball. *Personality and Social Psychology Bulletin*, 17, 580–585; Larrick, R. P., Timmerman, T. A., Carton, A. M., and Abrevaya, J. (2011). Temper, temperature, and temptation: Heat-related retaliation in baseball. *Psychological Science, 22,* 423–428.

206 **Heat leads to road rage:** Kenrick, D. T., and MacFarlane, S. W. (1984). Ambient temperature and horn-honking: A field study of the heat/aggression relationship. *Environment & Behavior*, 18, 179–191. See also Baron, R. A. (1976). The reduction of human aggression: A field study of the influence of incompatible reactions. *Journal of Applied Social Psychology*, 6, 260–274. For a more general review, see Anderson, C. A. (1987). Temperature and aggression: Effects on quarterly, yearly, and city rates of violent and nonviolent crime. *Journal of Personality and Social Psychology*, 52, 1161–1173.

207 **Men confused anxiety for sexual attraction on a swaying bridge:** Dutton, D. G., and Aron, A. P. (1972). Some evidence for heightened sexual attraction under conditions of high anxiety. *Journal of Personality and Social Psychology*, 30, 510–517.

209 **Winter breeds love:** Lam, D. A., and Miron, J. A. (1994). Global patterns of seasonal variation in human fertility. *Annals of the New York Academy of Sciences*, 709, 9–28.

209 **Polish researchers showed that winter brings love:** Pawlowski, B., and Sorokowski,

P. (2008). Men's attraction to women's bodies changes seasonally. *Perception*, 37, 1079–1085.

210 **Why men prefer looking at women in winter:** Svartberg, J., Jorde, R., Sundsfjord, J., Bonaa, K. H., and Barrett-Connor, E. (2003). Seasonal variation of testosterone and waist to hip ratio in men: The Tromsø study. *Journal of Clinical Endocrinology & Metabolism*, 88, 3099–3104.

211 **Harry Harlow and his baby rhesus monkeys:** Harlow, H. F. (1958). The nature of love. *American Psychologist*, 13, 673–685; background in Slater, L. (21 March 2004). Monkey love. *Boston Globe*. Available at http://www.boston.com/news/globe/ideas/articles /2004/03/21/monkey_love/.

212 **Warmth compensates for social isolation:** Williams, L. E., and Bargh, J. A. (2008). Experiencing physical warmth promotes interpersonal warmth. *Science*, 322, 606–607; Bargh, J. A., and Shalev, I. (2012). The substitutability of physical and social warmth in daily life. *Emotion*, 12, 154–162.

213 **The role of the insula in trust and the sensation of warmth:** Kang, Y., Williams, L. E., Clark, M. S., Gray, J. R., and Bargh, J. A. (2011). Physical temperature effects on trust behavior: The role of insula. *Social Cognitive and Affective Neuroscience*, 6, 507–515.

213 **Romantic films are more popular when it's cold:** Hong, J., and Sun, Y. (2012). Warm it up with love: The effect of physical coldness on liking of romance movies. *Journal of Consumer Research* (forthcoming). For an insightful take on the romantic-comedy genre and why it appeals to people, see Angyal, C. S. (14 February 2012). I spent a year watching rom-coms and this is the crap I learned. *Jezebel.com*. Available at http://jeze bel.com/5884946/the-crappy-lessons-of-romantic-comedies.

214 **Frederick Cook and seasonal affective disorder:** Gallagher, W. (1993). *The power of place*. New York: HarperCollins.

215 **Mood disorders affect artists and writers:** Kay, J. (1989). Mood disorders and patterns of creativity in British writers and artists. *Psychiatry*, 52, 125–132.

216 **Sharks respond to hurricanes:** Vatalaro, M. (May 2005). Sharks' sixth sense. *BoatU.S. magazine*. Available online at http://findarticles.com/p/articles/mi_m0BQK/is_3_10 /ai_n13778822/.

217 **Foehn winds and Hitler's headache:** Hoffman, H. (1955). *Hitler was my friend*. London: Burke.

217 **Germans investigate effects of foehn winds on accident rates:** Muecher, H., and Ungeheuer, H. (1961). Meteorological influence on reaction time, flicker fusion frequency, job accidents, and the use of medical treatment. *Perceptual and Motor Skills*, 12, 163–168.

218 **American researchers investigate the role of ions in seasonal wind effects:** Charry, J. M., and Hawkinshire, F. B. W. (1981). Effects of atmospheric electricity on some sub-

strates of disordered behavior. *Journal of Personality and Social Psychology*, 41, 185–197; see also Giannini, A. J., Jones, B. T., and Loiselle, R. H. (1986). Reversibility of serotonin irritation syndrome with atmospheric anions. *Journal of Clinical Psychiatry*, 47, 141–143.

218 **Mercer's quality-of-life ratings:** Mercer's 2011 report is available at http://www.mercer.com/press-releases/quality-of-living-report-2011.

219 **Bad weather improves memory:** Forgas, J. P., Goldenberg, L., and Unkelbach, C. (2009). Can bad weather improve your memory? An unobtrusive field study of natural mood effects on real-life memory. *Journal of Experimental Social Psychology*, 45, 254–257.

220 **Financial stocks appreciate when the weather's good:** Hirshleifer, D., and Shumway, T. (2003). Good day sunshine: Stock returns and the weather. *Journal of Finance*, 58, 1009–1032; Saunders, E. M., Jr (1993). Stock prices and Wall Street weather. *American Economic Review*, 83, 1337–1445.

221 **Daylight saving time hampers intellectual performance:** Gaski, J. F., and Sagarin, J. (2011). Detrimental effects of daylight saving time on SAT scores. *Journal of Neuroeconomics, Psychology, and Economics*, 4, 44–53.

Epilogue

224 **Edward Lorenz's butterfly effect:** Lorenz's original paper is Lorenz, E. N. (1963). Deterministic nonperiodic flow. *Journal of the Atmospheric Sciences*, 20, 130–141; background information from Mathis, N. (2007). *Storm warning: The story of a killer tornado*. New York: Touchstone; Palmer, T. N. (2008). Edward Norton Lorenz. *Physics Today*, 61, 81–82; Palmer, T. N. (2009). Edward Norton Lorenz, 23 May 1917–16 April 2008. *Biographical Memoirs of Fellows of the Royal Society*, 55, 139–155.

INDEX

ABOUT THE AUTHOR

Adam Alter is an associate professor of marketing at New York University's Stern School of Business, with an affiliated appointment in the psychology department. His research focuses on decision-making and social psychology, and he has been published in leading psychology journals. He has written for *The New Yorker*, *The Atlantic*, and *Slate*, among other publications and his work has been featured in a variety of media, from the *Sun* to the *Economist*.